MACHISMA:
WOMEN AND DARING

By Grace Lichtenstein

A LONG WAY, BABY

DESPERADO

MACHISMA: WOMEN AND DARING

MACHISMA:

WOMEN AND DARING

Grace Lichtenstein

Doubleday & Co., Inc., Garden City, New York   1981

ISBN: 0-385-15109-8
Library of Congress Catalog Card Number: 79-7114
Copyright © 1981 by Grace Lichtenstein

This is for my sister,

Laura Rosenthal Dankner

CONTENTS

I'm the breathless woman
I'm the hurried woman
I'm the girl with the unquenchable thirst

                    flowers that clean as I go
                    water that cleans
                    flowers that clean as I go

hey you there
hey you there, boss
I'm talking

                    from "Fast Speaking Woman" by Anne Waldman

ACKNOWLEDGMENTS

I owe the spark that ignited the idea of *Machisma* to the magical macha mystery tour through Canyonlands National Park in Utah, in 1977, and my intrepid companions on it. I owe the time to put the initial idea into words to another event, the New York newspaper strike of 1978.

Many friends and acquaintances were wonderfully imaginative in offering suggestions on people, reference books, comics and clippings, plus their own views. Among them were Bill Comstock, Linda Amster, Lorraine Rorke, Lindsey Miller, Lesley Oelsner, Susan Brownmiller, John Rockwell, Steve Lichtenstein, Freyda Rothstein, Norman Pearlstine, Elaine Freeman, Kathrin Seitz, Sharon Johnson, Herbert Meyer, Esther Kartiganer, Jeannie Ramseier, Deborah Boldt, Hilary Maddux, Judy Klemesrud and Larry Van Gelder.

Several editors provided story assignments that coincided with my theme and I am grateful to them, too: Martin Arnold, Barbara Dubivsky, Judith Daniels, Harriet Lyons, Joan Downs, the staff of *Ms.*, Michael Sterne, Dick Schaap, Kate Reading and Wenda Wardell Morrone.

Valuable research material was made available to me by, among others, Major Julie Kelly of the U. S. Air Force, Lieutenant Colonel Patrick F. Cannan of the U. S. Army, Dr. Marvin Zuckerman, Professor Lois DeFleur, Ray Robinson and Bruce

Gershfield (the *Seventeen* poll), Jon Hennessey (the Roper/Virginia Slims poll), China Galland and Warren Hoge.

My thanks also go to Jean Kidd for her conscientious tape transcriptions, to Janet West for additional typing, to William Wilkinson for indexing, to Blanche Lark for coping with the myriad details of production, to Pat Connolly for thoughtful copy editing, to Kay Ellen Consolver for race training, to the gang at Manhattan Plaza Racquet Club for physical therapy and to Paul Goldberger and Steve Robinson for a curved room of one's own.

This book would not have been possible had it not been for the calm reassurances of Wendy Weil, my agent, as well as the abiding faith and wise counsel of Betty Prashker, my editor. Catherine Breslin's invaluable thoughts on the manuscript were equaled only by her spirited pep talks.

For additional inspiration, I am indebted to Virginia Woolf, Donna Summer, Ari Kiev, Judith Rossner, Dr. Pepper, Talking Heads and Neil Young.

Finally, a special thanks goes to Jamie Dupont, whose beer, hugs and hand-holding again proved to me that true friendship is a gift to be cherished.

MACHISMA:
WOMEN AND DARING

ADVENTURING

Part One

1

THE GIRL WITH THE UNQUENCHABLE THIRST

The incident is as vivid in my father's mind today as it was when it happened, more than two decades ago. I was sixteen years old. We were in front of the Grand Canyon, peering into its depths from a comfortable distance. Without thinking, I hopped over the safety barrier and marched closer, closer, closer to the rim. My father's heart was in his mouth. Why did his oldest daughter always do this?

Every chance I've had, I've loved to go as far as I can to the edge . . . any edge.

Since childhood, I have been fascinated by women who go not just *to* the edge, but beyond—women who break barriers, who take risks, who are adventurous. *Machisma* began as an account of the boldest physical women I could find: athletes, mountaineers, daredevils, thrill-seekers. Since I never had any desire to become a female George Plimpton, my plan was to remain strictly the journalist/observer, not a participant in the book.

Almost immediately both the idea of limiting my subjects to "physical" adventurers, and of leaving myself out of the action, fell by the wayside. As soon as I got the opportunity to study race-car drivers and jet pilots, my research schedule impelled me to take a major risk in my *own* life; I quit one of the most prestigious jobs in journalism, that of staff reporter for the New York *Times*. It was not a physical risk, but resigning was as bold as any step I had ever taken on the edge of a cliff.

The act of quitting my job made me realize that "daring" extends to feats of mental, intellectual and emotional risk, which could be as profound as flinging one's body into space on the wings of a hang-glider. Women I admired, legends such as Mata Hari, Mae West, Katharine Hepburn and Bessie Smith, had taken risks throughout their lives. They were adventurers. So are contemporary women like Bella Abzug and Barbara Jordan in politics, Bonnie Raitt and Patti Smith in music, Jane Fonda and Faye Dunaway in films, Bettina Parker and Jane Cahill Pfeiffer in business, Barbara Hetzel in prostitution. Surely these women had put themselves on the line, every inch as much as had Suzy Chaffee, the skier, or Beverly Johnson, the solo rock climber. Their examples had to be included.

And as for myself? After reporting on adventure and risk, how could I not become an occasional participant?

What is the definition of a "macha" woman and how do you recognize her? Let's start by saying she makes things tough for herself, and then deliberately makes them tougher. She jumps at the chance to climb Annapurna. . . . She picks up the check at lunch with a male companion in an expensive restaurant and flashes a gold American Express card to pay for it. . . . She dreams of becoming an astronaut and tells of her exploits as a tomboy. . . . She flies first class to Hawaii for a weekend on a whim. . . . She subscribes to *Field and Stream* and hides *Vogue* in the bathroom. . . . She lets male campers know that her back-

pack is five pounds heavier than theirs. . . . She prefers Clint
Eastwood movies to Dustin Hoffman ones. . . . She'd rather be
superintendent of a tiny national park in Alaska than a higher-
ranked bureaucrat in Washington. . . . Her favorite sister in *Little Women* is Jo. . . . She manages to let slip how many men
she's dated in the past week. The macha woman "goes for it."

Instead of trying to swim the "tame" English Channel again,
Diana Nyad dives into a shark cage off Cuba to attempt the
longest, most dangerous marathon swim ever. In the awesome
canyons of southern Utah, a usually deskbound businesswoman
angrily refuses male help as she struggles down a thousand-foot
rock staircase with fifty pounds of camping equipment slung
over her shoulders. On a mist-shrouded Maine island, a boat
from Outward Bound deposits a fifty-seven-year-old homemaker
who is to spend three days alone there with a water jug and a
sleeping bag. Two female mountaineers slog to the summit of
Annapurna, becoming the first Americans to scale it, while two
of their companions plunge to their deaths below.

In an office facing the United Nations headquarters, Bettina
Parker, an international marketing dynamo, plans an audacious
campaign to sell American baby food to Soviet mothers. In the
corporate suites of the National Broadcasting Company, the first
female chairman of the board, Jane Pfeiffer, publicly battles
tooth and nail to keep her job instead of stuffing her attaché case
and losing herself in the Rockefeller Center crowds.

Gael Greene, her appetite already famous as a food columnist,
creates a fictional heroine who would not blush at achieving
more orgasms per minute than any living creature. Suzy Chaffee,
her skills secure as a skier, channels the same energy into get-
togethers with high government officials and into sexual relationships. National political leaders Bella Abzug and Phyllis
Schlafly fight fiercely over equal rights for women, while millions
of partisans from both sexes eagerly take sides.

Katharine Hepburn, instrumental forty years ago in making
pants acceptable for women, dons them again to have a Western
film fling with her macho opposite, John Wayne. Jane Fonda

casts aside her Barbarella image to promote radical politics and to revise everyone's idea of the female film star. Patti Smith and Bonnie Raitt lead a generation of female rock musicians who proclaim themselves love's conquerors, not its victims. Anne Waldman turns poetry into a hard-driving theatrical experience about active women.

And little girls, whose mothers were raised on "Daisy Mae" as well as *Wonder Woman* comics, now flock to newsstands for the latest exploits of the "Savage She-Hulk."

Some of this may sound familiar; some of it is contradictory. A few traits may seem vulgar, silly, quixotic. But something is in the air, something that these disparate women, real and fictional, have in common. It shows that women need to prove themselves. It has the scent of power, of female potency, catered to by advertisements for perfumes with names like "Charlie" and "Babe." It is the reason for the television commercial that shows a young woman leaping in triumph after a racquetball victory over a man. "When it comes to the battle of the sexes, I don't like pushovers," says the winner, "maybe that's why all my men wear English Leather . . . or nothing."

It is the quality of "machisma."

The word "machisma" cannot be found in a dictionary. In Spanish grammar, it would be the female version of "machismo," but of all the terms that describe human behavior, this one is exclusively male. In both Spanish and English usage, it connotes conduct never associated with women. Moreover, among liberated Americans, "machismo" is frequently pejorative, often conflicted, occasionally complimentary. If ever there was a loaded word, it is machismo.

Why, then, compound the problem by coining "machisma?" Because the times call for a blanket term to cover "exaggerated female pride," in the words of Clare Boothe Luce. William Safire, discussing the Luce suggestion in his New York *Times Magazine* column "On Language," asked readers to come up with alternatives to Luce's choice, "facho." "Macha" was a leading contender. Safire preferred "hembra" and "hembrismo," the technical Spanish counterparts ("macho y hembra" means "hook and eye"). But hembrismo is incomprehensible to monolingual Americans, nor does it have the resonance of "machisma," the column's actual headline. "Machisma" is a term that conveys a spirit that I see as a by-product of the sexual, fitness and feminist revolutions of the past two decades. As women have begun taking over male domains in the arts and politics, in careers and in clothing, they have expropriated a range of behavior patterns once reserved for men only. Now that women's liberation has arrived, its macha side cannot be far behind. In fact, it was always there; we simply didn't label it.

And no wonder. We have a hard enough time identifying the components of its male precursor. "Macho" and "machismo" do not lend themselves to easy definitions. One Spanish-English dictionary defines "machismo" as "male chauvinism; exaltation of masculinity, de-manship." For "macho" it offers numerous choices, of which these are only a few:

1. (bot. zool.) male. 2. Manly, virile, strong; robust. 3. Stupid, foolish. 4. Male flower. 5. Hook (of hook and eye); (mec.) male part of coupling. 6. (geol.) Dike. 7. (min.) Unproductive vein. 8. (Cuba) Unshelled rice grain. 9. (C. Rica) Foreigner, Anglo-Saxon; blond . . .

The 1975 *Dictionary of American Slang* hardly clarifies things. Its definition of "machismo" is "male pride; strong and aggressive masculinity; virility," while noting that in Spain and Latin America, "'machismo' is the traditional belief in male superiority and dominance." For "macho," the slang dictionary includes "a virile and aggressive man. Full of masculine pride; virile; manly." In another Spanish dictionary, "machismo" means, first, "the quality of being male," and second, "proven daring." And in still another American English dictionary, it means "a strong or exaggerated quality or sense of being masculine."

The qualities I arbitrarily include under the umbrella term

"machisma" are neither as wide-ranging, nor as derogatory, nor as exalted. Most of all, "machisma" should *not* be presumed to refer to a masculine woman. Since the terms don't exist anyway, I should like to stretch "macha" and "machisma," broadening them in order to discuss women who have stepped out of their sexual stereotype by imitating elements—positive as well as negative—associated with men proving their maleness. For the moment, let us assume "machisma" is a neutral, probably hazy phrase, useful in describing traits in a woman that, even to this day, are at the masculine end of every psychological masculine/feminine scale.

Often, machismo shows up in sports, adventure or games. But the slang adjective "macho" is applied to a much wider set of activities, from militarism to sex, from cowboy boots to convivial bragging. And so it is with "macha." Machisma—the made-up female word—applies to character as much as performance, to attitude as much as occupation. The premise is that machisma is neither good nor bad; it just is. Machisma is a phenomenon, a measure of how divergent "liberation" can get.

Machisma, therefore, is about today's assertive, risk-taking, adventurous, ballsy, gutsy, brave, foolhardy, daredevil, voracious, vivacious, fierce women . . . and those striving to join them. "The girl with the unquenchable thirst" is macha. So is this thirteen-year-old San Franciscan, telling writer Karen Folger Jacobs what happened when she ran her first ten-thousand-meter road race:

> When we ran by, people hollered, "look at that little boy chew up the course! Wow! Look at him go!" It made me mad! Every time somebody called me a boy I yanked off my hat so my long hair would fly around, and I yelled back, "I'm not a boy! I'm a girl! I'm a girl!"

This teenager is a sister in spirit, surely, to the masquerading Rosalind in *As You Like It*. Indeed, as far back as Shakespeare's England and fifteenth century Orleans, maids like Rosalind and

Joan of Arc exhibited styles perfectly consistent with the idea of machisma. Even earlier, Greek and Norse mythology abounded with Amazons and Valkyries. The adventure-seeking girl who dresses in boys' clothing to pursue the kind of life that would otherwise be denied her runs through Western history and literature from Saint Joan to George Sand to Amelia Bloomer. Intrepid, dashing pioneers like Amelia Earhart and Alexandra David-Neel made names for themselves long before the Soviets sent the first female cosmonaut into orbit. Bloodthirsty females, whether they were monarchs or outlaws, have ruled with a demonic hand in stories ranging from that of Hallgerd in the medieval Icelandic *Njal's Saga* to our own Ma Barker and Calamity Jane.

Certainly, there is a distinction between the merely eccentric, masculine, rebellious or nonconformist woman and the one who is macha. Not every female outlaw possessed this quality, although it was an important part of many an outlaw's personality. For every Calamity Jane, there have been dozens of unsung, ordinary female bank robbers who became thieves in order to survive, not because robbery was adventurous. They might have been poorly educated women who took the fling at someone else's suggestion, girl friends of professional bandits who were asked to assist their men, desperate women who joined a robbery scheme for a shot at quick money, or simple-minded women enlisted as decoys who never considered the risk.

Not every female athlete displays machisma, any more than every male athlete displays machismo, although a higher percentage of macha athletes might turn up in a comparison with a nonathlete control group. Success is a kindred trait in athletics, but not an essential one. Billie Jean King was a successful athlete with machisma; Chris Evert Lloyd was just as successful without it. Athletes in high-risk sports show the trait more than those in a sport like tennis, but risk does not guarantee that a woman athlete in such a sport will be macha. Suzy Chaffee is a macha skier; Cindy Nelson is not. Conversely, because a woman plays a nonrisk sport does not mean she automatically lacks machisma.

Nancy Lopez, the golfer, is not macha; JoAnne Carner is. Nancy Lieberman is a macha basketball player; her former Olympic teammate, Anne Meyers, is not. Yet all these players are among the very best in their sport.

Machisma implies not just wanting to win or to be successful, but to beat someone or something, to show off, to strut one's stuff. Charisma—the ability to generate excitement in others, the personal magic in a religious or secular leader that induces others to follow—is a quality likely to be found in those with machisma. But this "star quality" is not an integral part of the macha woman. Ruth Carter Stapleton is charismatic but not macha; Gloria Carter Spann (the other sister of former President Carter, the one who rides motorcycles) has little charisma but plenty of machisma.

A single spark can touch off fireworks of machisma that might have otherwise lain dormant. Jane Pfeiffer, as IBM vice-president, was once offered a cabinet post as Secretary of Commerce. She declined, citing an age-old obstacle: the job would keep her away from her husband too much. How her tune and temperament changed once she was caught in the corporate wringer at NBC!

Returning to one American definition of machismo, there is a controversial adjective closely allied with it: the *exaggerated* side of exhibiting masculinity. Nick Nolte, a movie star who had had his share of macho screen roles, took great pains in a New York *Times* interview to deny that machismo was a side of his off-screen self. "When the critics talk about macho, there's a kind of satire implied," he said. "I think they're talking about a guy who's so caught up in the male side of his personality that he's brutish, bullish, inconsiderate, narcissistic and totally physical."

There comes a point at which the show-offy exhibitionism of machisma crosses over into a parody of female daring, an unattractive side-effect of adventurism. But for now, let us investigate how women approach adventure, why it is a product of the postindustrial revolutions, how women who lean toward adventure are more able to take advantage of their impulses thanks to later or freer marriages, more leisure time, more discretionary income and fewer socially imposed psychological barriers.

2

A WOMAN'S PLACE IS ON TOP

There has been no more thrilling introduction to adventure and the diverse women who seek it, in recent years, than the story of those who achieved a first for both Americans and for their sex: the conquest of Annapurna, tenth highest mountain in the world. It is a story of machisma in excelsus, yet its participants were, in some respects, not far removed from "the girls next door." They were college students and grandmothers, tough women and soft, novice athletes and famous mountaineers, businesswomen and scientists, women married, single, divorced.

Their victory was stupendous, but the price they paid in human lives was staggering. By any standard of adventure, the Annapurna expedition of 1978 was the ultimate.

Even if you never had heard of Annapurna, nor cared anything about mountain climbing, the slogan would have caught your attention: "A Woman's Place Is On Top."

Suddenly, in the summer of 1978, T-shirts with that motto

were cropping up in outdoor circles from San Francisco to the Shawangunks. They were the brainchild of Arlene Blum and nine other climbers who were selling them to raise money for a courageous enterprise: their own expedition to a remote perch of Eastern Nepal. Annapurna I, a 26,504-foot peak, successfully scaled in the past by only four parties, is regarded among mountaineers as an awesome goal. Annapurna was the first peak of 8,000 meters or more to be climbed. But its initial conquerors, the Frenchmen Maurice Herzog and Louis Lachenal, became frostbitten on their way down in 1950, losing fingers and toes and nearly losing their lives. The mountain is notorious for its avalanches, which rumble along the sickle-shaped glaciers on the north side, the easier climbing route.

While Everest stands out as a single spire, Annapurna is an arresting *massif*, an immense tiered crown with not one but a trinity of peaks. From below, it humbles the most experienced climber. "It was a world both dazzling and menacing; the eye was lost in its immensities," wrote Herzog after his expedition.

Annapurna was a worthy goal for any Himalayan expedition, which was a principal reason Arlene Blum had chosen it. Also, both Herzog and the British climber Chris Bonington, among the most macho mountaineers of the post-World War II age, had made their Annapurna conquests legendary.

The women's bold sloganeering, their choice of a mountain with its own charisma, and their individual celebrity were reasons enough for generating high expectations. Still, the fact that success would make theirs the first all-woman American team to surpass 8,000 meters was the overriding issue.

The seed had been planted in a casual trailside conversation six years before, in Afghanistan.

Arlene Blum, a tall, powerfully built woman with an incongruously gentle voice and sweet smile, was ascending a major mountain. Vonda Rutkiewicz, the first European woman to climb Everest, met her on the same route, heading down. The two women warmly embraced. As they chatted, Vonda burst out, "Arlene, we must climb an 8,000-meter peak—just us women!"

Blum, knowing that few women had ever had the chance to try such an adventure, heartily endorsed the idea. They parted, but Arlene, then in her late twenties, kept the idea in the back of her head. As she made new strides into the climbers' world, she had serious bouts with its pervasive male chauvinism. The Everest Bicentennial Expedition of 1976, in which she participated, left a sour taste in her mouth because of the wrangling with men. It also spurred in her a new determination.

Like so many of her sister climbers, Arlene had gotten hooked on mountains while a student. In Oregon at Reed College, Mount Hood was her initiation; from then on, there wasn't a continent whose roof she did not want to explore. Peru, Mexico, Ethiopia, Uganda, Kenya, Kashmir, Russia, India—by 1976, she had climbed all over the world. She treasured the opportunity to travel, to learn foreign customs, to see strange scenery and to meet new people as much as she loved to test her mettle against the rock. Among climbers, she was regarded as slow but steady, resourceful without being reckless. Technical climbing—ropes, pitons, ice picks—was necessary but not vital to Blum's involvement. Her personal test was how enjoyable she could make her climb, rather than how difficult. A feminist, she jumped at the chance to help lead an all-woman ascent of Mount McKinley in Alaska. But she did not shun male climbers. In 1975, she and a Dutch boyfriend, Hans Bruyntjes, were among the lucky ones to escape tragedy on Mount Trisul in India, where one man was accidentally killed as he stepped off a summit ledge during a white-out.

Blum was pleased when she was invited on the 1976 Everest trip. According to Rick Ridgeway, the official scribe, Arlene believed that by climbing Everest she "would once and for all lay to rest what she considered the myth of women's inferiority in high-altitude mountaineering. Arlene believed the opposite to be true—that physiologically women are better suited for high altitude work than men." Arlene did not reach even the South Col of Everest (itself 8,000 meters) because of an attack of dysentery. But more than an intestinal disorder led to her unhap-

piness. Once the Everest climb got going, Arlene felt she was
pushed out of the inner circle. The leaders decided not to put
her on either of the first two climbing teams. "It's because I'm a
woman, damn it, I know it!" she complained. She was on the
verge of leaving, but decided to stick it out.

Later, when the men divided into groups for rope climbing, no
one wanted Arlene; she had a reputation for being slow. Yet she
repeatedly demonstrated her fortitude, at one point scrambling
all the way to Camp 2 despite stomach cramps that forced her to
upchuck a bellyful of bright red Kool-Aid. In his journal, Ridgeway noted Arlene's tendency to point out "people's faults and
weaknesses." But she was almost convinced that the real reason
for the group's fissures was sexism. "Maybe I was being unusually obnoxious," she told the farewell banquet, but "maybe it
was because as a woman trying for the summit, I was being
more closely scrutinized." Hans Bruyntjes would later agree with
her. "Lead climbers were too busy gaining merit for themselves
to let a woman interfere," he said. The men had made Arlene
their victim.

As the American Women's Himalayan Expedition shifted into
high gear two years later, Blum left little doubt that Annapurna
would be different. It would be cooperative, not competitive. A
leading biochemical researcher on carcinogens at the University
of California, Blum lined up a deputy leader, Irene Beardsley
Miller, known for her pioneering ascents in the Peruvian Andes.
Irene, a physicist at the IBM San Jose Research Center, was a
quiet person with burning mountaineering ambitions. The two
set out to find the best climbing women available for their venture—and also those most resistant to thin air.

Rutkiewicz was not available, but Liz Klobusicky-Mailaender,
a thirty-three-year-old lecturer on English Literature in Germany, was. So was Alison Chadwick-Onyszkiewicz, a thirty-six-
year-old British climber who had been on the first team to scale
Gasherbrum III, another of the world's highest peaks. So was
Vera Watson, a radiant forty-four-year-old computer program-
mer for IBM in San Jose. (She was the first woman to make

a solo climb of Aconcagua, highest mountain in the western
hemisphere.) Piro Kramar, a forty-year-old ophthalmologist from
Seattle, was recruited to be the expedition's physician. Joan
Firey, a forty-nine-year-old Seattle resident, part-time painter
and physical therapist, also joined. Vera Komarkova, a tundra
plant ecologist, and two college students, Margi Rusmore,
twenty, of the University of California at Santa Cruz, and her
buddy Annie Whitehouse, twenty-one, of the University of Wyoming, completed the team.

Blum was not content, however, to make it solely a climbers'
adventure. A California psychologist, Karin Carrington, helped
the group prepare for the problems of fear and dissension that
always arose in mountaineering. Dr. Barbara Drinkwater, a research physiologist, gave the climbers physical checkups and advised them on exercise programs. Finally, Blum signed up two
filmmakers in their twenties, Dyanna Taylor and Marie Ashton,
for the documentary shooting; neither had climbed previously.

Physically, Drinkwater found, the climbers were in wonderful
shape; a few were near-Amazons. Some months before they left
for Nepal, she tested eight out of ten. All were above average in
cardiovascular fitness, which was to be expected of mountaineers. (Blum and Miller were also marathon runners.) But
Drinkwater herself was surprised by the women's strikingly superior pulmonary functions—the ability to move air in and out of
their lungs. They could each draw between 40 and 49 milliliters
of oxygen per kilo of body weight per minute, more than women
much younger. Also, most of the climbers carried up to 26 percent less body fat than their peers. Drinkwater thought they
might have a "genetic predisposition" to climbing or any hard-
breathing activity. The older women did as well as or better than
the younger ones, indicating that women dedicated to physical
fitness were not destined to "go downhill after 30." The climbers
themselves were tickled that Irene Miller, then forty-two,
showed greater endurance than all but one other male subject
whom Drinkwater had ever tested.

The physiologist recommended even more physical preparation. Miller kept at her regular soccer games, stepped up her running schedule and began pumping iron, as did Watson. Vera also took to sprinting up a thousand-foot hill not far from her home. Worried initially about the physical strain, the climbers next turned to a far more vexing problem: the psychological strain.

Vera Watson, who showed emotions more openly than some, brought in Karin Carrington. A therapist in the Bay area, Carrington is the kind one would think of as "Marin mellow." She uses words such as "process" a lot, but she can also be down-to-earth. The first time she and the climbers discussed their mental outlook, Carrington's reaction was that they were "narrow-visioned" women with "their kishkas all in a mess." They were at each other's throats over the question of leadership. Blum was so determined to avoid the tyranny she had seen among male climbers that she hovered between forcefulness and indecision. At the opposite pole was Joan Firey, the eldest and the most aggressive. The two quarreled constantly about everything from food to fund-raising.

For hours one spring morning, Carrington and eight climbers grappled with their feelings. Arlene admitted she badly wanted to be boss, but, in what the psychologist saw as typically female fashion, she hated making the actual choices. (Blum and Carrington later jogged together while hashing out decisions facing Arlene.) The others, who tended to be introverts as did many male climbers, gradually voiced their inner thoughts.

The universal feeling they shared was fear, secret, gut-level fear. Of failing? To be sure. But on a more fundamental level, they were afraid of dying. Carrington saw it as "fear of death once removed," since each woman would only express it in terms of how "the others" or "my children" (four were mothers) would handle themselves should the worst occur. Death was the hidden fear they were most reluctant to bring to the surface. It was a case, Carrington thought, of women with "feminine" feelings trying to "squeeze" themselves into a masculine mode. Individually, each displayed a definite assertiveness, but it was a more disciplined, lower-key drive than would have been the norm for men. Theirs was a uniquely female assertiveness developing side by side with a group cohesiveness. Blum's "let's-not-make-men's-mistakes" attitude pulled them one way, while Firey's tough "go-for-it" traditionalism tugged at the other end.

When the session was over, Carrington recorded the group's collective persona: optimistic, positive, highly disciplined. More linear than diffuse thinkers; all committed, tenacious, somewhat introverted loner types. Risk-takers. Assertive, but in a gentle way.

It was as apt a description as any of a mountain-climbing group that happened to be all-female. Herzog, in his account of the first ascent of Annapurna, dwelled on the excitement, the gung-ho mentality, the near-military manners of his all-male expedition. Before the climb in 1950, Herzog solemnly made his men swear an oath of allegiance to obey him. He was the leader, no matter what transpired on the mountain. The very notion of such an oath was unthinkable to Arlene Blum.

In place of an oath, the women had therapy. When they set off in August for Nepal and the arduous monsoon-season trek to the Annapurna base camp, they each carried a letter prepared by Carrington. It talked about the need for continuous verbal communication, about facing fear, about the importance of "switching focus" when an argument was leading nowhere. Mountaineering expeditions never run smoothly, especially on the emotional level. Fearful fights—verbal and physical—are the rule rather than the exception. Individualistic climbers, bound together day after day, in the dizzying atmosphere of high altitude, far from home and safety, are prone to confronting their demons by squaring off against one another. Annapurna 1978, despite the tampons in the medical kit and the long hair tucked under the ski caps and the lectures by the psychologist, was about to unfold in some ways like every expedition that had preceded it.

A mountaineering expedition is high drama, complete with stars, supporting players and extras.

Joan Firey was The Sufferer.

She knew as soon as she enlisted that she would end up disagreeing with Arlene. It had even been suggested by friends, when the pretrip battles got angrier, that Joan drop out. But Joan Firey's life was in such flux during the year before the climb that she believed getting on board the Annapurna Express had been the right option. Her son had recently been confined to a mental institution. (She also had two grown daughters.) After a quarter-century of marriage, she had left her husband, a paternal, older man who had introduced her to climbing. Nearing fifty, her cropped hair a peppery gray, Joan knew that her life in Seattle had been terribly stressful prior to the Annapurna preparations. She also found Arlene Blum an annoying waffler. But Joan was too stubborn to back out. "I don't think you and Arlene should be on the same expedition," Carrington told Joan frankly. The rest of the group was more or less happy with Arlene's leadership. "It's a power struggle," Joan told friends before departing for Nepal. The truth was, she was not sure she could have faith in decisions by anyone except herself on a mountain. Joan, practically old enough to be Arlene's mother, believed that her experience posed a tremendous threat to the younger woman. As they got together in Kathmandu Valley for the twenty-day trek to their base camp, Joan Firey was determined to take a back seat.

The conflict burst out anyway. The Sirdar (head Sherpa) knew Joan best since she had hired him. He kept coming to her with his questions, and Arlene felt this intruded on her authority. What made things worse was that with each passing day, the trek got harder. The monsoons rained on them; leeches crawled up their legs; their skin and clothes were always damp. Kathmandu sits at an altitude of a moderate 4,500 feet, a bit lower than Denver, Colorado; base camp was at 14,500 feet, about the same as Mount Whitney, highest peak in the "lower 48" United States. By the tenth day, Joan, like the others, was exhausted.

Perhaps her condition was worse because she alone was a heavy smoker, and she also had been knocking back tequila every night. ("I'm a hard liver," she would say afterward, without regret.)

On the tenth day, Arlene fell in step with Joan for a momentous talk. She quietly but firmly relieved the older woman of her prime responsibilities on the expedition—food and provisions. It was an agonizing time for both of them. "This is such a blow to my ego!" thought Joan, suddenly feeling her buried insecurities surge to her throat, the insecurities she normally kept tucked under layers of toughness.

Arlene, who was not outwardly tough, tried to explain her decision. She was afraid Joan could throw the entire expedition out of kilter. She said she had to balance Joan's feelings against the well-being of eight other climbers.

For Joan, it was as if Arlene had physically slugged her. She trekked in a daze the rest of the day, tears rolling down her cheeks.

The next morning, Joan awoke with pneumonia.

She was ill for the next several weeks, barely able to make it to base camp, too weak to help with the "carries"—the transporting of tents, food and climbing hardware from base camp to the new camps established like way stations higher and higher up Annapurna itself. The pneumonia turned into pleurisy. Some days, Joan simply lay in her sleeping bag. Months later, she would speculate that her body "had made a choice—to pull out." The illness, she came to believe, was "positive" in that it alleviated the severe tension between herself and Arlene. But she also wondered whether getting sick had been "self-preservative," for who knew what would have happened to her if she *had* been given a shot at the summit?

She probably would not have made a summit assault had she been well. Her forte was exploration. Joan Firey had been a wanderer throughout her life. As a college student, she had given serious thought to medical school, but she "copped out" (her own phrase) by becoming a physical therapist instead, marrying at a young age and having children quickly. Like so many women of her generation, she sublimated her own dominant personality to that of a more dominant male's, her husband. Because he loved climbing, she had taken it up too, finding her niche as an exploratory mountaineer—the one who stakes out new ascent routes. Summitry interested her less than the adventure of probing trackless sections of the northern Cascades, not far from Seattle. Firey became an expert on the region, although later on, she grew restless on mixed-gender climbs; men normally were first on the rope on difficult pitches.

A turning point in Joan's life came in 1974. Her husband led an expedition in the Coast Range of British Columbia. From base camp, Joan announced she wanted to rove around the icefalls and glaciers. Just one other person, a woman, was willing to join her. Her name was Piro Kramar.

The two of them had well-matched skills. Piro excelled at rock and technical climbing, while Joan was the orienteer. As the terrain got tougher, the women got more and more pleasure outwitting it. They wound up on their own for five days. Joan was exhilarated. It confirmed a budding confidence in her own ability and it showed her that women did not have to play a secondary role. Actually, she realized, she was a more aggressive mountain person than her husband. Back home, she began painting more, producing vividly realistic canvases of mountains and seascapes.

The Annapurna plans spurred her on. She was excited by Arlene's expedition for the challenge, of course, but also for the social interaction with other female climbers that was still new to her.

Now, in Annapurna base camp, the most important climb of her life was being reduced to a trauma. The rest of the women had mixed reactions. One viewed Firey's fights with Blum as "obnoxious, hot-dog stuff." Another saw Firey as a brave woman who had burned herself out. The way Joan saw it, her aggressive "yang" side was being demolished, first by Arlene's decision, then by the illness. Joan, a woman who had been climbing longer than she had been driving a car, was being rendered impotent on the eve of what should have been her most exalted achievement, and she was bitter. From the point of her illness on, she consciously withdrew, although she did improve enough to do late "carries." As she summed up her feelings afterward, "I didn't give a shit."

The trek was no summer romp in the woods for anyone, particularly those in the supporting cast like Dyanna Taylor, the camerawoman. Her role was The Novice.

Never having climbed very high anywhere, Dyanna felt making it to base camp in one piece was a major accomplishment. There were moments of exhaustion so intense in the August heat that her body yearned to collapse into the high grass by the side of the trail, regardless of the leeches. One morning, she woke up crying for no reason and kept it up the entire day. She laughed about it later. "I arrived in camp a neurotic crazy," she recalled. "Some of us don't know we're going to 'hit the wall' someday. It's good to know you have limits. My body was saying, 'I don't want to move another inch!' "

Taylor had accepted the opportunity to test her limits because she was a born risk-taker. The idea of filming the expedition totally terrified her; that was exactly her reason for doing it. More experienced camerawomen had turned down the assignment, and Arlene herself had lectured Dyanna about how difficult both the filming and the hiking would be. A voice inside Taylor told her to go anyhow. No expedition had taken an all-women film crew before. Dyanna, the granddaughter of the great documentary photographer Dorothea Lange, felt it was time to live up to her family heritage.

She and Marie Ashton, the film's producer, had tried their best to get in shape. Dyanna wore a backpack around her house. She locked her camera gear in the freezer of a Berkeley ice-cream parlor to make sure it could withstand the Himalayan cold. Nevertheless, by the time she settled in base camp in late August with Christy Tews, the base camp manager, Dyanna was grateful for a rest.

The climbers were eager to start immediately up the face of Annapurna to establish Camp 1. As autumn set in, the skies cleared, revealing the stern visage of the mountain, thrilling and frightening the climbers at the same time. Local wise men advised them that September would be "inauspicious" until the twelfth, so the women held back. Taylor, tired, unused to trekking food (tea, gruel and peanut butter, among other things), and scared by the crackling avalanches above, read the joke-books and the climbers' autobiographies in the base camp "library." She also crawled into her own shell a bit. A serious student of aikido, she believed her strength would lie in her "center." Now she had to poke around and find it.

Meanwhile, the actual climbers started pitching the higher camps. Up, down, up. The nine healthy ones toted regular loads along with porters to Camp 1, at 16,500 feet, on August 28. By September 3, they chopped through ice to a place for Camp 2 at 18,500 feet. On September 12, they finally held the official prayer flag ceremony at base camp, surrounding it with tall, narrow, vertical white cloth banners. Two days later, Arlene started reading *The Thorn Birds* in her tent to relieve the tedium of the daily carries; she finished the thick tome in one night.

Next, the climbers occupied Camp 2 and began to etch a precarious route to an area at 21,500 feet for Camp 3. The path took them along a narrow rib pitched at a steep 55 degrees with a sheer drop-off on one side—"a tightrope of ice," Arlene called it. The women were trying a route more circuitous than Herzog's, but supposedly safer. Once on it, often led by nimble Alison or stalwart Liz, they nevertheless questioned whether it would have been better just to storm straight up the north face as Herzog had done. One day, a blizzard whipped out of the sky like a white dervish, lashing at their jackets and collapsing their tents. Soon, the climbers had to retreat first to Camp 2, then further down to Camp 1 to escape the heavy snows.

At a rest stop ahead of the filmmakers, Joan, Christy and two porters glanced up. A mighty cloud of whiteness was plummeting toward them at what seemed like 150 miles an hour. Falling to their knees, they watched, helpless, as the snow thundered into the filmmakers below.

Dyanna, obsessed with avalanches, unhesitatingly kept the camera recording as the mound of snow approached. "It's so visual!" her professional voice told her. Her survival voice countered, "This is what it feels like when you're about to be in a car crash." As the camera ran out of film, Dyanna and Marie dropped to their knees. The blast of snow barreled into both of them, flinging them like twigs caught in a waterfall, then burying them in a huge puff of white smoke.

Dyanna tried in vain to keep a grip on her $20,000 camera; it was torn from her hands. She was tossed into a crevasse, battered. As the noise stopped, she screamed "Marie! Marie!" Miraculously, Marie, not too far away, shouted back. Joan and Christy, too, were unhurt. They dug Dyanna out of the snow, and everyone punched their arms into the drifts until they located the camera. The single vision that stayed with Dyanna that night was the sight of Marie, climbing over the crevasse, dressed in a coat of snow, looking like a madwoman.

A woman whose pink cheeks and bob of blond hair make her seem younger than her twenty-six years, Dyanna understood now how much she had underestimated the hardships of the trip. To hold back the terror, she played mental games with herself. "You'll never be able to come back," she would tell herself, tiptoeing along the route to Camp 2. "You'll kick yourself if you're lazy and you didn't get that shot. You won't want to live with yourself thinking you didn't push yourself as hard as you could." At night she wished on a star. She conjured up pictures of the strong, dignified photos by her grandmother that lined her study at home. And she thought how wonderful it would be to brag about the expedition to her own grandchildren some day.

Arlene had darker thoughts. Should she abort the climb, considering the unexpected rash of avalanches? She almost did. Then the weather cleared, and a series of hard carries in deep snow brought climbers back to Camp 2. From there, they pushed on again across the tightrope to Camp 3. September drew to a close. Several women were nauseous from the altitude and could not hold down any food (mostly starch, candy bars and freeze-dried protein) even though they needed it to boost their stamina. Then there was the matter of the bathroom. Camp 3's itty-bitty tents were perched on a narrow ledge. The occupants had to grab a rope outside and squat over the edge of the ice. Irene figured that going to the latrine was almost as dangerous as getting caught in an avalanche.

By October 8, Vera Komarkova radioed the news that Camp 4 had been established at 23,200 feet. Two days later, Arlene made another major decision, this one involving her earliest recruit and deputy leader.

Irene Miller, with her iron will and her superb conditioning, was about to play one of the most sublime roles in the drama. Arlene had chosen her to be a Summiteer.

It was not merely that she had trained so single-mindedly. Irene had a laserlike scientist's focus, a self-contained resoluteness that transcended the collective will of the group, powerful as it was. Irene always carried more than her share of loads from one camp to another, always volunteered to plow through the deepest snow. Physically, she was not imposing—about five feet six inches, with a slim, firm body hardened by soccer and weight training. Yet there were other sides of Irene Miller beyond that one-dimensional jock image.

Her disciplined exterior masked a well of self-doubt and need for approval that rose to the surface during one of the group's arguments. With tears running down her cheeks, Irene insisted that she was "bummed out." She felt everything she had done was wrong. She wanted to resign. It took a dramatic embrace from Christy Tews and the coaxing of the rest before she changed her mind.

As a youngster, moving from town to town as a Navy brat, her favorite outdoor activity had been bird-watching. She had spent most of her adolescence in Washington, D.C. and suburban Pennsylvania, which made it possible for her to take a Federal Interior Department course in nature orientation. Music was her indoor love. She was a good enough pianist to have performed recitals in college. She gave up the piano after marrying her first husband, by whom she had two children. A few years later, her daughter began violin lessons, and Irene again got so caught up in music that she learned the cello, and eventually played in chamber ensembles.

In some inexplicable way, climbing satisfied Irene's scientific mind, her esthetic sensibility, her love of the outdoors and her perfectionist's bent, all at once. During her undergraduate years at Stanford, she had gone with the Alpine Club on a practice climb and she was terrible, falling over and over while trying to scramble up a short "chimney" (a narrow opening between two hunks of rock). But Irene's middle name could have been "stubborn." The very next weekend, she joined a trip to Tuolumne Meadows and climbed Cathedral Peak, an admirable achievement for a beginner. By the time she got down, she knew instinctively that she had found a lifelong hobby. She followed her husband, an avid climber, up every imaginable route among the Teton mountains of Wyoming. Had he not been so enthusiastic, she reasoned later, she probably never would have kept at it. But their eventual divorce did not stop Irene from looking for her next summit. By the time the Annapurna expedition came about, she had scaled numerous peaks in the Andes as well as North America.

A woman of candid but not overly florid speech, she once tried to explain why Annapurna would have meant so much to her even if she had not reached the summit. "You concentrate on doing a 'carry,' and then you sit down and rest. You look around, and there is this incredible panorama," she said. "It's indescribable, the peace you get, up that high. It sort of simplifies things for you." Behind her calm demeanor, Irene Beardsley Miller harbored a host of complexities that climbing helped her solve.

It was almost by a process of elimination that Irene became a Summiteer. Various teams were leapfrogging one another, establishing higher and higher camps. But Joan was too ill, Arlene too busy directing traffic, Margi and Annie too young and inexperienced for a summit try. So it happened that Irene and Piro Kramar, the surgeon, started moving up from Camp 3, only to be snowed in by a storm. They were forced to retreat and were trapped inside their tiny Japanese tent for three days with Milky Ways for dinner before they could descend to catch their breath and sleep. (Mountaineers usually take sleeping pills at higher altitudes, but they don't always produce more than a few hours of restless sleep that saps the climber's strength.)

With the weather clearing steadily, Vera Komarkova and Annie Whitehouse finished work at Camp 4 that Irene and Piro had begun. One week later, Irene, Vera K. and Piro, the most rested and the most acclimated in the group, plodded to their summit staging area, Camp 5, at 24,500 feet. They were breathing through oxygen masks intermittently, for the air was so thin that a few minutes of unassisted breathing turned them into slow-motion zombies. Just 2,000 more feet of hard snow climbing, and the top of Annapurna would be theirs.

The morning of October 5, at 7:30, the three women and two Sherpas awoke for the final assault. Piro, a native of Hungary, was as mentally prepared as she would ever be. For fifteen years, first in Iowa, then in medical school and internship in Nebraska, she had been confined to the flatlands. She moved to Portland, then to Seattle, specifically to be closer to mountains. Climbing, for her, was a "gut reaction." She went to "conquer" a mountain, but also to conquer herself—"to test my limits just this side of recklessness," as she put it. High altitudes were fine, but the amount of risk on a lower peak was important, too. A tough battle on an Alpine slope with a 3,000-foot drop-off where one slip could spell death—that was Piro's idea of ecstasy. This morning, she hoped for another ecstatic moment.

Reaching for her camera inside the cramped tent, Piro felt the instrument's metal against bare skin—and she knew at once this ecstatic moment was not to be.

The nylon glove she was wearing had a small hole in the right forefinger. The finger was already turning blue. She dived back into the tent, crampons still strapped to her boots. Eye surgeons, no matter what summit may be awaiting them, need every bit of their operating hands. Rather than risk losing the finger to frostbite, Piro quit the summit team and headed down right away. The finger did not suffer permanent damage. Piro swore she never had any regrets about the summit.

Irene, Vera K. and the two Sherpas slowly set off, carrying, but not wearing, the oxygen cylinders. They soon were pausing almost at every step for breath. Three and a half hours into the climb, the indomitable Vera muttered, "I can feel my brains going!" The two women donned the oxygen masks just after noon. Hearing nothing but the hiss of the oxygen and the crunch of her crampons, Irene could now take one step for every four breaths. The snow became knee-deep, and the Sherpas worried about their pace, when the pitch gradually leveled out. At 3:30 P.M., there were no more steps to climb.

Two women had found their place On Top.

The view north toward Tibet was remarkable, Irene thought to herself, and even more remarkable was the fact that only a handful of humans had ever shared it. There she was, like a refugee from a World War I movie in her "gas" mask, while Vera fumbled with the camera to record the moment. The Sherpas were struggling to hold aloft an ice ax. From it fluttered the flags of Nepal, the United States and the American Women's Himalayan Expedition.

The summit, in that late afternoon light, was isolated by puffs of clouds below and freezing breaths of wind above. Irene registered the colors in her mind: all muted browns, reddish browns, toward Tibet. Turning to Annapurna's renowned South Face, she noticed it was so steep she could look straight down it. Exhausted, Irene Beardsley Miller felt more than anything else "a sense of completion."

It was short-lived. With little daylight or oxygen left, the party began its descent. It was dark as they stumbled safely into Camp 5. The women slept huddled together for warmth in a single tent. Below, word of their success was radioed like an electric charge from camp to camp. Thousands of feet below, Arlene, who had descended that day with Bach's Fourth Brandenburg Concerto playing on the cassette machine in her backpack, cried with joy.

She had already planned the second assault. Alison Chadwick and Vera Watson were the logical second team. Alison had vast experience, while Vera, though not as seasoned, glowed with a near-spiritual delight in climbing. "She actually became transformed as she scampered over rock," Irene Miller was to recall, thinking back to their practice sessions in California. "And she calmly accepted danger for herself." Vera had told friends that a summit like Annapurna's was "every climber's dream." On October 17, 1978, she had a chance at it.

Her dream was cruelly shattered.

As soon as the first climbers had been reported on the summit, the second team trudged up to Camp 4. Two days after Irene and Vera K. descended, Alison and Vera Watson made their move toward Camp 5. Through binoculars, the groups below could see them at dusk, still en route. Because several Sherpas were ill with altitude sickness, the women were climbing alone. That night, radio contact with them was lost.

The next day, everyone anxiously scanned the massive white ridges for a glimpse of movement. There was none. Two Sherpas were finally persuaded to climb beyond Camp 4 to search for the women. A short way from Camp 5, across a deep crevasse, a blotch of red, like a bloodstain, caught one Sherpa's eye. It was Alison's parka.

The two women, still roped together, lay dead some 2,000 feet below a steep ice pitch between Camps 4 and 5. They apparently had lost their footing or missed a belay point (where one climber could anchor herself while the second, on the other end of the rope, could hoist herself up) in the dark. Both were cautious climbers; theirs was the kind of accident that could have killed any of the world's best mountaineers.

No one could risk crossing the crevasse to retrieve the bodies. Heartsick, Arlene called the expedition to a halt and the members descended as quickly as possible to base camp. Christy

Tews flew by helicopter to Kathmandu to telephone Vera Watson's husband, John McCarthy, a Stanford professor. Alison's husband could not immediately be reached; he, too, had been on an expedition, elsewhere in the Himalayas.

At the base of Annapurna, the women chiseled the names of their dead beside seven others who had lost their lives on the same peak. A few prayers, Eastern as well as Western, were said, and the group sang a Quaker song, "'Tis a Gift to be Simple." When it was over, Arlene Blum broke down and wept.

The following month, in the Stanford University Chapel, about one hundred people gathered for a service in memory of Vera Watson. Born in Manchuria of Russian parents, she had lived an eventful life, first in Brazil, where her parents emigrated in 1953, then in the New York region, where she was hired by IBM and where she learned to climb, finally in California. A New York friend, Frances Allen, eulogized her as "a romantic spirit, a determined woman," and Irene Miller, gripping the podium as if she were on a dangerous outcropping of granite, called Vera the expedition member for whom reaching the summit meant perhaps the most. Vera Watson had told friends that if she could not be buried next to her mother, she wanted to be buried on a big mountain. And so she was. Among the mourners, Karin Carrington kept remembering an ironic talk about death she had had with Vera before the trip. The forty-six-year-old climber had confided to Karin, "I don't know how I'll handle it if Margi or Annie dies; they're so young!"

The battle of ten women against the tenth highest mountain was over. The deaths had cast a pall over their success in putting a team on the summit. Yet they *had* succeeded, in that respect. Silently, one or two yielded to the temptation of blaming the tragedy on Arlene, because she was the leader.

Whatever emotions coursed through their minds, the women communicated little of them to one another on the trip back. Instead, a few turned to the men nearest at hand for comfort. One younger woman married her Sherpa in a ceremony on the route back and stayed behind with him for a time in Nepal. One older woman had a tender, passionate affair with a Sherpa half her age, traveling with him for a few weeks after the group dispersed in Kathmandu. She herself was surprised at her own boldness. "I never did anything like that before," the woman told me much later, "it was really incredible. But it was the right thing for me at that time." The Sherpas, so gentle, warm and friendly, so in tune with nature in their Oriental habitat, yet so physically strong, were not men intimidated by smart, self-reliant Western women.

In their twelve-week struggle to conquer Annapurna, the expedition women were able to talk about their fears and feelings either haltingly, or in sudden angry outbursts. Karin Carrington concluded they were not quite able to care for one another on more than a superficial level under conditions of serious stress.

On the other hand, there was little of the intense competitiveness, and none of the fear of being attacked as a sissy, that afflicted so many male expeditions. Arlene, regardless of her troubles with leadership, conveyed a sincere sense of group victory, a joy in the women's ability to work cooperatively. By contrast, Peter Habeler, a companion of the famous climber Rheinhold Messner, was harshly criticized when he almost made his Everest ascent with the help of oxygen. Out of "blind anger" and "just to prove myself to the others," Habeler put his lungs on the line and left the oxygen behind. The Annapurna women showed great daring and exhibited hard-won female pride. But they were neither selfish nor arrogant.

The expedition nevertheless changed their lives. Arlene spent months writing a *National Geographic* article and preparing a book. Irene, who felt herself to be "80 percent still in Nepal" for most of the winter, divorced her young husband well before the first anniversary of her summit assault. She also resumed her maiden name. And, month after month, her dreams were haunted by images of the Himalayas.

Joan Firey, the toughest of the tough, the woman who saw her initial illness as a continuum of her difficulties with Arlene, learned not long after returning to Seattle that she was indeed suffering—from cancer. Somehow, though, a new peace was enveloping her. She accepted the news of the illness, vowing to fight it to the last moment. For Joan Firey, perhaps the most aggressive person in the Annapurna party, the lesson of the mountain had been to come to terms, at age fifty-one, with the softer "ying" side of her character, the side she had neglected until it was almost too late. She died sixteen months after the expedition ended.

3

THE FIRST STEPS
TOWARD ADVENTURE

The number of women with the guts or the inclination of the
Annapurna climbers does not run in the millions. But all of us—
housewives and careerists, fitness freaks and fatties, teenagers
and elderly women—have a streak of adventure lurking inside,
whether or not we ever exhibit it. The same impulse that goads
men into risk-taking to counteract the numbing comfort of everyday life also pulses through "ordinary" modern women.

At the most elementary level, risk-taking manifests itself these
days in a sedentary woman's decision to enter the ranks of
joggers. "Jogging as an adventure?" you protest, "you must be
kidding!" But consider how low an opinion about their bodies so
many adult women have had for so long. Think about a friend
who regarded herself as the antithesis of a jock, and how brave it
was for her to venture outdoors one day in sneakers and running
shorts. (A friend of mine was so self-conscious about her body
that she jogged for the first month in a long-sleeved, long-legged
warmup suit, even though it was eighty degrees outside.) How

many women have you watched as their motivation in jogging
changes from vanity or marital togetherness to challenge and
competitiveness? Who has not heard women boast about how
jogging has given them a newfound, nearly orgasmic pleasure?
Why do thousands of women go past the mere "fun" stage of
running and sign up for road races?

Jogging—not to mention the general fitness craze—is an em-
bryonic concept implicit in machisma. The recognition of one's
body as an active machine rather than a passive receptor is central to a new vision women have of their capabilities. Jogging is
the easiest way to start up the machine. And once it's revved up,
there's no telling where it might go.

Most women do not begin with competition in mind. Quite the
opposite. Joan Ullyot, marathoner and physician, goes so far as
to attribute the initial jogging impulse to rebellion. "Traditionally women have been told from the age of about ten that
they should stop running around and start acting like young ladies. They have been restrained, and now they're throwing off
those chains," Ullyot said in an interview in her San Francisco
home. Women over forty who start jogging were brought up to
believe they should not call attention to themselves. Thus, Ullyot
continued, jogging is their first break from a basic female stereotype. From puberty on, a girl is taught to pay attention to her
body and its cycles, to respect it and even pamper it. Boys learn
to exercise their bodies. In jogging, the lessons are reversed:
women learn to exercise, men to respect their bodies.

As Nancy Friday among others has pointed out, boys also
learn via the rules of sports that "the latent hostility in competitiveness" can be "brought into the open and given expression as
play . . . feeling competitive, acting competitively, *winning* is
not betrayal. It's natural." Until recently, girls lacked boys' experience of team competition. As women, they have developed a
more diffuse perception of competition on the run. Top female
runners such as Martha Cooksey and Micki Gorman are more
encouraging to other women than the top men, Ullyot noted.

Indeed, she might have included herself in that observation.

Ullyot took up jogging after her thirtieth birthday to lose her "middle aged spread." She was certain she was unathletic. Her medical practice and her two children took so much of her energy that she had difficulty keeping up with her husband on a long hike. Her original motive for jogging was 90 percent vanity. The remaining 10 percent? Coping with stress in her work and her marriage. "I was very angry with a person I worked with," she remembered, "and I used to picture his face down on the pavement. I would trample on it for the first half-mile or so."

She eventually dissolved both the marriage and the medical practice, substituting running friends and a new career in sports medicine. The Saturday we met, she was ten years older than when she began running, looked ten years younger, and had just run a "fun" race with her children and a male companion. Ullyot felt "reborn." Still, she felt strongly that competitiveness would never grip women runners as it did men. That view, however, is disputed by more than one member of the younger generation.

Jane Killion is a case in point. She is a twenty-nine-year-old commercial loan officer for a New York bank. But running, not banking, dominates her life. Her acceptance in local running circles was secured when she finished third in a Boston marathon.

Killion was never content to be a noncompetitive jogger. Her first ten-kilometer race told her, "I can do it!" Competition was fun; so was winning. "Being first is great," she said simply. "And it's fun to beat men, although the real competition is against other women." In contrast to Ullyot, Killion agreed that the machisma factor had become ingrained in her. For some runners, tenth or one-thousandth place in a big race is fine—not for Killion. When she dropped back in the pack early in a New York City marathon, she refused to finish the race rather than suffer the ignominy of a "slow" time. "The most horrible thing was living with myself afterward," she said with a rueful grin. Her "failure" upset her so much that two weeks later, without telling anyone, she sneaked into the Washington, D.C. marathon and finished the race in a "respectable" time of under three hours.

Better runners make her feel threatened until she can match their times.

Competitive, not cooperative, behavior comes naturally to Jane Killion. Before a big race, she and other "name" entrants deliberately prance like haughty thoroughbreds behind the starting line. "It's called 'running cocky,'" she laughed. "You run fast and hard in front of everybody. You're like a peacock. You strut."

In other words, any woman, from your physician to your bank loan officer, might be secretly bursting with machisma. Jogging is one realm of everyday life where the secret reveals itself. Opportunities also crop up frequently on vacations, when women are out of their normal environment or are accidentally pushed into trying untested physical skills. I witnessed a vivid illustration on what began as a simple camping trip.

The locale was Canyonlands National Park, a stark jumble of canyons, plateaus and rock formations in southern Utah. Gary, a former park ranger, had assembled twelve people from all over the United States, including myself, to wander with him through his favorite wilderness. Five were women, of whom four were in our thirties. The fifth, Freyda, a New York television producer, was in her mid-forties, the oldest person in the entire group. Freyda had gone canoeing and camping with her husband and children, but that had been years earlier, before her divorce, before her job had usurped the free time she might have spent keeping fit. When the group came together in a remote Utah town in May, Freyda thought she was about to float lazily down some river for a week. Hiking? Climbing? She only heard about those stages of her "vacation" after everyone had piled into jeeps, bound for a world largely inhabited by lizards and coyotes.

Freyda had not prepared for the trip by jogging or anything else. Kathrin, a friend who was also on board, jogged and played tennis, but she had not gone out of her way to get in shape either. For Kathrin, it was an adventure. She was thirty-four, but the prospect of a camping trip made her feel sixteen again. A third woman, Patty, was the youngest at thirty. But her exercising had been confined to getting on and off a bus each day on the way to her desk job. Only Barbara, an environmental activist from New Mexico, and myself, then based in Colorado, had an idea of the physical hardships we would endure.

Loading provisions into the jeeps, the camping party eyed one another with interest, since most were strangers. Freyda was deeply apprehensive. The outfitters, a leathery pair of Westerners, looked like they had stepped out of central casting for a Clint Eastwood movie. They wore pointy tooled boots and sweat-stained cowboy hats and chewed methodically on toothpicks as they maneuvered the jeeps deep into a rocky desert unlike any Freyda had ever seen. Kathrin, also a media executive, was pleased with the hearty men in the group, but she had doubts about little Patty.

The first stop, after a long, bouncy journey over rutted dirt roads, was a dry riverbed called Horse Canyon, whose clay walls were adorned with fascinating early Indian petroglyphs, centuries-old etchings of warriors and basket-carriers. By afternoon, the canyon had heated up to a good ninety degrees. Suddenly, we found ourselves at the canyon's far end, facing a sharply inclined hill with a serpentine footpath winding to its apex.

It was the only way out, and a continent away from the elevators, escalators and limousines the city folk were accustomed to as transportation. The jeeps were waiting just beyond the summit, beer coolers at the ready, Gary assured us. So, he said, just truck those unlimbered bodies right on up the hill!

The strongest of the men were huffing halfway up, and some of us were out of breath, our lungs filled with Utah dust. Not Kathrin, though. With her well-scrubbed face showing almost no sign of strain, her fashionably knotted bandana soaking up the sweat on her brow, she strode directly behind Gary's shadow. *The first big challenge,* she thought to herself . . . *and it's easy.* Once at the jeeps, she gulped her beer with gusto, adrenalin pumping through every capillary. *I'm a Capricorn mountain goat!* She did not bother to watch the others.

Freyda had long before lost sight of Kathrin cruising toward the top. *I'm going to die, right here on the first day.* Her blood pressure, too high under normal conditions, was surely shooting straight off the gauge. Her first tentative steps up the path had made Freyda realize with conflicting emotions that not only was she the senior camper, but the weakest. Before she had gone a hundred yards, her heart was pounding, her face a bright red. Slowly, everyone else drew even with her and then passed by. Alone. Abandoned. In agony. For Freyda, the test had begun and she had never cracked a book. She was two thousand miles from home and faint. Wait. . . . Someone was coming back down toward her, now the solitary figure left on the footpath. Rich—that sweet young man from Idaho—was asking if she was all right! Freyda had no breath left to answer. She nodded dumbly, grateful for his gesture, as she trudged, step by aching step toward the jeeps.

We made camp that night atop a 6,000-foot mesa overlooking a curve of the muddy Colorado River hundreds of feet below. When the sun dipped below the canyon rim, the temperature dropped precipitously, as if someone had switched a thermostat all the way to the "cool" position. Wriggling into their skimpy sleeping bags with shivers, Kathrin and Freyda carried on contrasting interior monologues. *I'm pissed off it's so cold and they didn't bring us warmer equipment,* Kathrin told herself. Yet the kick she got out of the afternoon hike soothed her. As for Freyda, she was cold, all right, but that bothered her less than the climb earlier and its portents. *When I was married, my husband would part the bushes in front of me on hikes,* her inner voice reminded her. Well, she had traded that kind of protection for self-reliance. This was her new life, and, by God, the voice shouted inside her, *you're not going to louse up this trip no matter what!* It was unpardonable, in Freyda's scheme of things, to be a party-pooper. No matter that she had not thrown the party nor knew what it would be like. Freyda's upbringing had taught her that to slow others down in a case like this would be sinful. She made up her mind, tossing in the chilled Utah night, to "pull her weight," regardless.

Patty pulled the sleeping bag over her head and slept.

There were no outrageously hard hikes the next day, nor the three after that. The group hiked, jeeped, cooked out, camped, sang under the moonlight. Freyda found a special niche, leading the group sing-along each night around the campfire. Now, we reached the surreal pasture called "The Doll House," a set of gnarled, outsized rock sculptures on a high, grassy knoll. Test number two was about to get underway.

In order to meet a flotilla of rafts on the river, we would have to hike down a tricky stone "staircase" to the riverbank. The pebbly path was just as steep as the first day's hill. Worse, we had to carry our own gear. By midafternoon, we looked like a band of drunken sailors; each of us staggered under a pair of ungainly duffle bags that hung around our shoulders by means of a rope or belt. The duffles were heavy and tended to pitch their bearer forward unless the hiker was careful with each step. The muscles in my knees and thighs were strained by the time I reached the quarter-way mark.

As usual, Gary led, with Kathrin not far behind. The strongest of the men, a lanky airline pilot from Texas named E.J., was also in front. Freyda was having a difficult time with both legs and luggage. Patty, too, began to drift to the rear, unable to take more than a few dozen steps without rest.

About halfway down, E.J., southern gentleman that he was, fell in with Freyda, offering to relieve her of her duffles. Her personal moment of decision was at hand. She could accept . . . and forever see herself as a laggard. "No!" she yelled at E.J., a hint of anger in her voice. "I can make it by myself!" And she plodded on, a swaying study in determination.

E.J. shrugged off her suggestion and waited for Patty. He made the same offer, realizing she, too, was tiring fast.

Patty didn't hesitate. With a big smile of thanks, she eased the twin duffles off her shoulder. She strolled down the rest of the route unburdened, as E.J. hoisted both his and her duffles on his back.

Seeing what Patty had done, Freyda got inwardly furious. Kathrin felt a wave of scorn, and so did I. *How could she?* Freyda thought, fighting fatigue with every step until at last she collapsed on the soft ledge of the riverbank. *How could she not pull her own weight?* Then a more forceful thought hit Freyda. *I'm old enough to be her mother and I did it myself, alone! Isn't it amazing to really pull your weight, to push yourself farther than you ever imagined possible?* A dab of bliss, of brand new superiority, worked its way through Freyda's sore shoulders as the group spontaneously massaged one another, tired but happy, under a flaming sky of sunset.

For the next few days, we floated with splashy abandon, through the rapids and into the calm of Lake Powell. But the group had changed. Patty, the weak one, was ostracized by the four women.

Contempt. We never talked about it until months later. But each woman felt contemptuous toward Patty the minute she lapsed into dependency on a male companion. Kathrin, whose feelings of machisma had been joyfully reinforced on the trip, viewed Patty as a sissy, and she wanted no part of sissies. Freyda, who overcame weakness with sheer willpower, believed Patty had not pulled her weight but she had, and it was a life-enhancing episode. Barbara and myself saw Patty similarly, the cliché of the helpless female; we wanted no part of it or her. After we left Utah, the four of us—Freyda, Kathrin, Barbara and myself—kept in contact with one another and with many of the men . . . almost everybody except Patty. None of us ever looked her up or saw her again.

Kathrin found in her camping vacation an opportunity to let her budding machisma blossom, while the same vacation stirred Freyda's dormant sense of adventurousness. For each, the definition of what they experienced was fuzzy, and the sensation itself rose to the surface only because a compatible situation demanded it. Others are not content to wait. Like Jo in *Little Women,* they "never take advice" about staying warm by the hearth fire if they can help it. These latter-day Jos stamp their feet and say, as Jo did, "I like adventures, and I'm going to find some."

Two such women, an actor and a retail merchant, have nurtured their sense of daring much more consciously. Instead of stuffing adventurousness into a closet once an exciting trip is over, they each have let the spirit of adventure take over more and more of their lives. Their stories indicate that adventure can mushroom from being a largely inert portion of one's everyday life to being an overt style of enhancing that life, of carrying it to new extremes.

Carolee Campbell finds her thrills in white-water river-running. An actor by trade, she may be the only television star ever to miss the announcement of her Emmy award because she was deep in the belly of the Grand Canyon.

Carolee is that rare breed, a native of Los Angeles. She came east directly from Los Angeles City College, though, to study at the Actors Studio. The stage—New York theater—had been her goal since high school. Like a thousand actors before her, she waited on tables, got her share of small parts and prayed for the Big Break. Hers came in the form of an extra's role on *The Doctors,* a soap opera. She was so outstanding as Carolee Simpson that her character was written into the ongoing plot and for the next twelve years, Carolee Campbell had a steady gig. Early in that period, her life changed in other ways, as she met and married a noted actor, Hector Elizondo. With the two of them relatively rich (for actors) in time and money, they began backpacking, camping and rafting.

The turning point for her coincided with the approach of her thirty-fifth birthday. She joined a motorized boat trip through the Grand Canyon. The party was large, the engines noisy. But the sweep of the rapids and the grandeur of the canyon walls awakened in Carolee a need for new horizons, a passion for adventure that she suspected was the impetus behind her choice of acting as a career. Friends believed that Carolee deliberately courted danger. How many other women, or men, insisted on camping outdoors in Sierra grizzly-bear country? Yet in her own mind, the real risks were still to come.

Returning to New York after the first river trip, Carolee took stock. She was in the prime of life, a working actor as well as an aspiring writer and photographer. But first, she worried about her body, just as Ullyot had. Carolee got out of breath running for a bus. Craving exercise, she found at a Manhattan center for the oriental martial arts the sport that would hold her interest for the next decade: kendo.

Kendo is an exacting, one-on-one fencing contest with heavy sticks as the weapons instead of swords. It was not easy for Carolee, a narrow woman with hardly an ounce of extra flesh, barely five feet tall. But she fell in love with its formality, its offensive goals (unlike most oriental martial arts such as aikido and karate, which are taught as self-defense), its aggressiveness. It suited her; she *liked* to go in for the kill. There were moments when she would think to herself: *I'm never going to get through this class.* Then, like Freyda, she would discover how liberating it felt to push herself through what she thought were her physical limits. Carolee's body responded. She luxuriated in the soreness that was inevitable after a strenuous kendo fight. And as her body awoke, so did her dreams about another river trip.

Five years after her first one, she took a second Grand Canyon run, this time in a party of nonmotorized oared boats. She didn't tell her companions she was a television star, sensing that such a pronouncement unfairly colored other people's view of her. And no one could guess from the sporty image she presented. The river trip was slow, undulating. Carolee had time to become friendly with Irene, a woman from Tucson about her age. By the end of the trip, Carolee was a captive of the Southwest.

It was May. She called her husband and explained why she could not come home immediately. The commercial outfitter whose passenger she had been was willing to take her on another trip, as an unpaid raft apprentice. She simply had not absorbed enough of the canyon, of the nights sleeping on sand in an absurdly deep wedge of the earth's crust, of the giddiness that overcame her with each plunge over the rocks in the foaming water. "Do it," Hector urged her; "yes," he said, "I understand." Not until October did Carolee Campbell of *The Doctors*, now a river rat with a full season of experience under her belt, quit the Southwest temporarily to go home and work.

She started running and lifting weights to grow strong enough to meet a new goal: running rapids on her own, in her own boat, under her own oar power. It was all coming together for her—the Southwest, her impulse toward the outer reaches of adventure, a willing companion in Irene, her husband's approval. She was possessed. At forty, she felt she had spent her life thus far as a successful yet unfulfilled actor, obeying the direction of others. Now she would plot her own direction, on a different stage. If river-running was not quite a career or a way of daily living, it was at least a piece of the whole she had in mind. Her photographs, black-and-white portraits and landscapes in the tradition of Ansel Adams, landed her some one-person exhibits in New York. As soon as these outlines of her second life came into focus, she refused to renew her contract on *The Doctors*.

Her producer nearly fell out of his seat when she announced she would not re-sign. She had to convince him that it was not a ploy to get a raise. Her friends told her she was crazy. But Hector supported her, and he was the one who counted. Carolee and Irene each bought an Italian-made inflatable dinghy, and they spent weeks mastering their solo skills.

Although her apartment windows look out on a Manhattan cityscape, Carolee Campbell these days appears to be more a Southwesterner than a New Yorker. Her walls are papered with her photographs, and her jeans are adorned with a beautiful Navajo belt. Her voice still rings with an actor's dramatic inflections, but she talks about bigger rafts and wilder rivers, not about the theater. "I feel I've just tapped the surface," she tells friends when they compliment her on how daring she is. "When

I row down the Grand Canyon myself, *then* I will have done something."

Will it frighten her, a solo trip through the Grand? "I'll be scared shitless," she says—and laughs.

Like Carolee, Nancy Snell is a woman who yawns at the thought of sybaritic spas or lying on beaches. Her idea of a swell vacation spot? A war zone. Almost any war zone will do, but preferably it should be a "glamorous" one—like Israel when Middle East hostilities flared, or Vietnam.

In the sixties, she had helped blacks in so many civil rights drives in the South, had marched in so many antiwar demonstrations, that she couldn't stand the idea of *not* being there, where the action was. So, in the summer of 1974, Snell, a Minneapolis-born retailer then thirty years old and single, marched to her local travel agent in Aspen, Colorado and bought an airline ticket to Hong Kong. From there, she caught a flight filled with intelligence agents, war contractors and journalists to Saigon. On the plane, her male seatmate inquired politely, "you've got a husband over there?" She told him no, that she was simply visiting, that she didn't like to get her news second-hand from Walter Cronkite. He blinked and continued to be polite.

At Ten Son Hut airport, some fellows from Air America, the CIA airline, gave her a lift, not to a fancy hotel, but to the Gray House, where the agency pilots lived. When she arrived, her polite seatmate was already there. He looked at her in amazement. "Well, lady, you did it! You got off the plane!" he said with a mixture of disbelief and admiration. Snell spent three weeks in South Vietnam, talking to soldiers, wandering everywhere. More than once, she was taken for a prostitute. By that time, she was used to such mistakes.

Nancy Snell is a full-bodied blond woman who prefers to show off her attractiveness rather than hide it. Her green eyes are always carefully made up, and she most emphatically does not resemble the run-of-the-hill, rosy-cheeked collegiate Colorado ski bunny. She *does* resemble a successful merchant of

women's clothing boutiques, which she is. Having begun as a
saleswoman, she now runs and owns the two Mogul Shops in
Aspen, her home for the past fifteen years. Under one arm of
that fur coat she wears is an ever-present manila file of invoices,
and under that pile of Dolly Parton tresses is a cool, independent, smart business head.

Snell cheerfully owns up to her self-conscious streak of adventurousness. She is a self-styled "macho woman." Like so many
others, she ran away from home at least once as an adolescent.
At seventeen, she took a bus to the sleazier section of St. Paul.
She waited on tables in a strip joint where the men all wore
shoulder holsters and all the women were prostitutes. She didn't
stay long, but the rebellion confirmed what she had always taken
on faith: adventure was stimulating. "Maybe it comes from reading too much Hemingway as a kid," she once remarked. The stories of his she liked best dealt with wars.

Arriving in Aspen as a ski bum, she was able to work her way
up to store management. With the mind of a war correspondent
but without the skill, she *needed* to be where the action was.
Pressed to define that need, she smiled, showing even rows of
white Minnesota farm-girl teeth, and said straightforwardly, "I
crave fear. I thrive on a situation that's dangerous, so I seek out
danger. It's a physical high." Snell described its symptoms: her
body starts to sweat, her palms grow clammy and sometimes she
breaks out in prickly heat, especially when she is being followed.
Besides Vietnam, she has pursued that high in Portugal, hanging
out with anti-Salazar rebels during the early seventies. In Jerusa-
lem, she deliberately went to the Wailing Wall at night because
it was considered at its unsafest then. In Calcutta, the idea of
riding through the teeming multitudes in a taxi struck her as so
bourgeois that she ignored Indian custom and hitched a ride
with two Brahmins who were total strangers.

Snell did not go to dangerous places to risk her life; she went
to see others in the course of risking theirs. "I don't want to get
shelled," she told her seatmate on the plane to Vietnam, "I'm
going because I want to learn." The riskiness of a trip added the

necessary spice to her learning experience. She had such a refreshing honesty about her strange hobby that it did not sound weird or perverted, only eccentric. She was the first to agree: "I *do* thrill in being places most women wouldn't dare to go. I like being surrounded by people who aren't the same as me. I tend to gravitate to small cafés where there aren't any white people or Americans."

Snell was equally forthright about her looks. She could limit herself to a low profile, but her experiences would not turn out as they have if she dressed in jeans and a knapsack. A wider variety of people would converse with you in odd places, she found, when you were dressed as if you just came from brunch at the Plaza. She is amused, rather than annoyed, when she is visited by a hotel house detective who has mistaken her for a hooker. (Her business card or just a frosty smile is usually enough to chase him.) Nancy is proud of her buxom figure and almost theatrical appearance, with a pride that stems from the same root as her adventurous spirit. In Aspen, a resort town whose permanent residents occasionally seem overdosed on "est" and overfocused on their navels, she bubbles with a willingness to "go for it," as the sports cliché suggests. If she had come to Aspen a hundred years earlier, she might have been its leading madam, its most popular chanteuse . . . or its prettiest silver prospector.

4

THE TRAINING CAMP: OUTWARD BOUND

The scraggly line of running women emerged from the fog that hung over the rough path on the island. It was 5:30 A.M. Although the sun had not risen yet, the thirteen women had already jogged more than a mile through the woods, all the way to the dock that jutted into Penobscot Bay.

The afternoon before, the same women had hopped, skipped, jumped, and fallen their way through a terrifying obstacle course. The day before *that*, they had been stranded with no warning on an uninhabited island and had slept, bundled together without blankets, under a mosquito-ridden plastic tarpaulin.

Now, only a bit warmed by the run, the women, each over thirty years old, stripped to their swimsuits. A leader beckoned from a platform on the dock. Below, a good twenty feet away, freezing salt water slapped against the pier. "This is the dip," announced the leader cheerfully. Quaking, either with fear or cold or both, they leapt, one by one, off the platform into the

Maine mist, plunged into the murky water, and swam to a
nearby ladder. The two seconds it took from launch to splash-
down were ones I shall remember for a long, long time.

Welcome to Outward Bound, adult female division. This is
where thousands of adventurers-to-be enter basic training. Less
secure in their abilities, perhaps, than Carolee Campbell or
Nancy Snell, they are emphatically more conscious of their desire to test the waters of machisma than a Freyda or a Patty.
They know what is in store for them—a grueling survival skills
course. How astonishing it is, then, that in the ten years since
Outward Bound has run special programs for females only,
women have signed up in record numbers and now represent 40
percent of Outward Bound's students.

The majority consists of collegians, who take the twenty-six-
day courses open to anyone over the age of sixteen and a half.
But the shorter adult courses are becoming more and more popular with women who, having taken their first jogging steps, seek
a faster track, yet one with its boundaries carefully patrolled.
These women have felt too many tugs at their skirts by their
children lately. They yearn for a release from everyday pres-
sures, whether put on them by family or work. By joining a program at one of Outward Bound's seven "schools" from Maine to
Oregon, they are sending *themselves* to summer camp, for a
change. Or they are putting more distance between themselves
and their jobs than can be achieved on a quick weekend at the
beach.

The Hurricane Island Outward Bound school has honed a reputation as a veritable saltwater boot camp, where flabby grown-
ups can build character as they build fires and nurse their self-
confidence by navigating huge sailing boats. The organization's
literature makes promises much grander than one would antici-
pate from a mere adventure vacation. It promises "a unique
educational experience which leads to a new understanding of
yourself and the fact that most of your limits are self-im-

posed. . . . Some amazing things can happen. . . . Find out who you really are. . . ."

In other words, the goal is to discover your inner core by scaring yourself half to death. How ideal for the would-be macha woman! Except . . .

What relevance does jumping off a high dock into numbing seawater have in terms of "real life?" How does successfully sailing a boat through fog relate to making executive decisions back home? Does fasting for three days on a "solo" help make you a better mother or lover? Is it necessary for women who want to nurture self-reliance or daring to do it in an all-female group? Once embarked, do these women act differently than their male counterparts would?

I asked myself those questions as I guzzled a final beer in Rockland, Maine, one summer morning. For journalistic purposes, I was joining a dozen other women over thirty on a sailing voyage at the Hurricane Island Outward Bound school. Once underway, we would have no cigarettes, pills, coffee, meat or sugar—and no beer. The school's receptionist, when I had inquired about beer on board ship, had stared at me as if I had asked about heroin. "Gee," I protested mildly, "beer and sailing always seem to go well together." Her voice was stern. "This *isn't* just sailing." Forewarned is forearmed.

Before leaving the dockside office, women over forty had to take the Harvard Step Test, which measures heart rate under stress. "How did you do?" a gray-haired woman was asked. "Fair, but I think I'm better than that," she replied. "I think my anxiety got in the way." Her name was Mary Louise and she was almost fifty-eight years old, among the oldest ever to take the course. She would soon be known fondly as the Susan B. Anthony of Lindbergh Watch, the name given to our boat crew in honor of Anne Morrow Lindbergh, who lived among these islands while writing *Gift From The Sea*.

A number of women were brought to the office by their husbands and boyfriends. "Take good care of her," one man said, in the tone one would use seeing an eight-year-old off at a bus depot.

A flutter of nervousness was wafting like a draft through the room. How cold do you think it will get? ("It never gets really warm in Maine," someone warned.) Did you bring gloves?

The machisma factor was also operating. One woman, a hardy type, eased into the weather conversation by mentioning offhandedly that she had sweated when she jogged that morning. A younger one, ruddy with health, managed to slip in the fact that she had taken a punishing hike with her boyfriend the day before.

The next hours were spent dividing the twenty-four enrollees into two Watches—Lindbergh and Banana. Lolly, the muscular chief instructor, headed the latter bunch. Eliza, leader of the Lindberghs, took twelve of us in hand to collect camping and sailing gear and to introduce ourselves. First, she exhorted all of us to "appreciate every single moment, because it's going to pass very fast. Ten days is nothing. Appreciate the craziness—that's what you're here for."

As we sat by the edge of the office dock, each person told a little about why she was doing this. The previous year, Eliza had taught the first all-women's course at Hurricane Island. (Her earlier experience had been mainly in deskwork and public relations.) "It was the best one I've ever done," said Eliza, a thirty-two-year-old Rhode Island native, "and I'm looking forward to a very vibrant experience."

LeeLee, her deputy, spoke next. She had lived part-time on Hurricane Island for eight years because her husband was an instructor. Her first teaching experience had come the summer before this. In years past, she said, "I was either pregnant or taking care of an infant." Now that her two children were older, she found it more interesting to lead than to watch. "The idea of working with all women really turns me on," she concluded.

It was the participants' turn, and the majority were not too removed from LeeLee's earlier life. We ranged in age from thirty-one to Mary Louise's fifty-seven and a half. Nearly all worked full time. All but three were mothers, and four were single parents. Among us were several educators, an administrator, a garment manufacturing executive, a medical student and an artist. Our reasons for choosing Outward Bound varied—Mary Louise was there on a gift certificate from her husband!—but an overriding theme was the desire to challenge oneself.

Marie, a thirty-three-year-old Atlantan, stylishly dressed in jeans and expensive sweater as befitted a sportswear company manager, started off the exchange by revealing she had "great expectations" for the course. "I've been wanting to do Outward Bound for fifteen years," she said. The mother of a small child, she had been divorced for two and a half years. Next Mary Louise, a jaunty engineer's cap on her head, lifted the solemnity by repeating what a friend had told her: "If my husband gave that gift certificate to *me* as a Christmas present, I'd be suspicious!" She herself was slightly hesitant. "I guess I'll enjoy it once I get into it."

Harriet, a very large woman who worked for an Iowa insurance agency, eyed the rest of the group with actual fright.* "It's going to be the greatest challenge I've ever done. My husband's a farmer, and he told me, 'Harriet, no way!' But I've got to prove it to myself." Eliza tried to soothe her nerves, saying, "That's really the right attitude."

Ingrid spoke with a New York accent but she had lived with her husband, an anesthesiologist, in Anchorage, Alaska for the past twelve years. "For a city gal to go to Anchorage—I didn't know anything!" she laughed. At forty-one, she continued to enjoy challenges, having taken two other wilderness survival courses. She wanted to improve her sailing skills because sailing was her husband's avocation. At first, she had wanted her children to do Outward Bound. But they said, "Mother, you know how you push when you want to go on something yourself." So she came to test the waters before they did.

I explained that I hoped to write about the trip. I was among

---

* Her name and some details have been changed to protect her privacy.

the older participants and childless. Franny, sitting by my side, was, at thirty-seven, the same age as myself. A Cape Cod artist also involved in Jungian psychotherapy, she was here to get away from "my reality" for a while.

Susan, a mother of two, from Pittsburgh, offered many of the same ideas. She picked Hurricane Island of the Outward Bound schools because "the mountains of Maine sounded a lot smaller than the mountains of Colorado." Toni, thirty-four, another single parent, was a Maine resident. She had always thought of Outward Bound as "*those* people," the outdoor nuts, until she had been talked into trying the voyage for herself by a friend.

Carolyn drew a round of cheers; she was celebrating her thirty-ninth birthday that day. A New Yorker, she had almost picked a co-ed course, "because I figured there would be men there who would know what to do if something went wrong." Then she scolded herself, "that's the problem!" Lisa, thirty-three, said that during the previous winter, "I got stuck in a mothering, nurturing role. This trip is a physical manifestation of the changes I wanted to make in my life."

Pat, thirty-two, single and childless, was also making changes. She had quit a teaching job to start law school. "I want to learn to sail and I want to be with adult women," she said, concluding the opening ceremony.

There was genuine fear circulating through the gathering. Both Eliza and LeeLee, however, were reassuringly small, compact women, compared with the Amazonian Lolly. What was clear was that the students had sincerely sought this companionship of women, free from the intrusions of men. A few thought the trip might change their lives; most would be content to conquer the pervasive anxiety.

"The pointy end is the front." Thus Eliza, a pert, no-nonsense woman, introduced us to our home, a thirty-foot "pulling boat," so called because it is equipped with gigantic oars for rowing when the sea is becalmed. Having each packed a duffle bag of warm clothes, sleeping bag and toiletries, the Lindberghs climbed into the boat, and heaved long sighs as they rowed away from civilization. "Now I know why they call rowing aerobic," said Pat, a husky athletic woman, breathing hard.

We "gave way together"—dipped the oars in unison—until the boat was far enough into the bay to set up the mizzen and mainsail. Eliza employed a standard OB tactic by having one Lindbergh almost immediately take the tiller, asking the rest to figure out how the sails were to be hoisted. We would learn by doing. Within the first few hours, we learned the elementary principles of sails, compass, tiller. Leaders came forward right away. Franny, the Cape Codder, volunteered to keep the first-aid beltkit. Toni was among the first helmswomen.

For four hours, until nearly 7 P.M., we practiced sailing our rather clumsy sprit. We had been divided further into two sub-watches, which took hourly turns. Each had a "bow watch" who called out obstacles such as lobster pots or buoys, a helmswoman, a navigator, and several helpers who handled mainsail and windsail. While one group sailed, the other rested. A few women turned green with seasickness. The sun glinted off indigo waves; by afternoon everyone had smeared her lips with zinc oxide. We each wore a gray life jacket.

Personalities did not take long to surface. Harriet, overweight and underprepared, had persuaded herself after the first hour that she had made an awful mistake by joining up. She took the tiller without relish and was glad to relinquish it. She did not like the responsibility, she said. Others, though unschooled, welcomed the chance to play captain—Franny, Toni, Pat, me. "This is what we paid for!" Pat said. Franny was a natural go-getter, pitching in with good cheer whenever someone faded.

Toward evening we dropped anchor in an inlet, erected a huge plastic tarpaulin "tent" over the boat, and began to cook spaghetti and tomato sauce on a tiny camp stove. That was at 7:20. By 7:40, everybody was gazing hungrily at the still-stiff hunks of spaghetti. "If you were a group of seventeen-year-olds," said Eliza with a grin, "you'd all be yelling to eat this raw." Mary Louise quipped that we had waited so long, the meal should be called "brupper"—midway between supper and breakfast. When, at last, we dug our single utensil, a soup spoon, into the chewy spaghetti, it tasted as splendid as if it had come from Alfredo's of Rome.

The trip was to have unexpected jolts around every buoy. We knew we would sleep under the stars, but where? On the boat, we learned, in an alternating head-feet row of sleeping bags—with the *oars* as our mattresses. A medieval rack would have felt like a Beautyrest by comparison.

Before dawn, we were rousted and herded ashore to run a mile over twigs and tree stumps. Next, we were ordered to wade into the icy bay, naked, sea urchins spiking our feet, for a fifty-yard swim. The same morning, we plotted a sail with Banana Watch from one end of Penobscot Bay to the other. We had only one day under our belts, yet we were distinctly more confident handling the boat, and less shy with each other.

In late afternoon, we headed toward a rock-encircled island. Eliza, mischief in her mariner's blue eyes, explained we were about to be exiled on the island overnight while the two instructors sailed away. We could take a total of four items on shore—nothing else, except the clothes on our backs. "Come on," Eliza hurried us as we hastily conferred, "it's shipwreck time!" A tin of food and a gallon of water were unanimously chosen as the first two items. Third: the big tarp. But what else?

After spirited arguing, we decided on the bag of small tarps.

As soon as we hit the island, the women gravitated to activities they were familiar with. Lisa and Toni went foraging for edible plants. I was curious about Toni's reasons for joining the course; she was cryptic. "I fell into it. I almost wish I didn't know this place," she said, discovering many patches of wild beach peas. Pleasant memories of these very islands in years gone by had made her resistant to the Outward Bound experience. Toni was uncomplaining, but that night her conflicting emotions gave her an upset stomach. Strange: Toni was the type of woman who looked chic in her yellow rain mack and always had a moment to tidy her hair. She also turned out to be a fine leader and a natural athlete. If anyone had been voted "most popular" or "best all-around" after the trip, it would have been Toni. Yet her stomach was churning at the very moment she was finding us greens to eat.

Before it got dark, Toni got the idea of reading aloud passages from *Gift From The Sea*, which happened to be in the food tin. Lindbergh's thoughts got us discussing why it was acceptable for women like us to be alone in situations not acceptable to men. For instance, a woman is permitted to spend long hours in her home by herself, while a husband is at work and children are in school. It is normal for single women to spend evenings on their own, reading, but many men can't stand the idea. "They always have to be out with this group or that, playing their macho games," one person said, the rest agreeing wholeheartedly. Yet when a woman raises this subject with a man, someone added, she is told, "Aw, why don't you just go out and enjoy life?" Whoops of recognition greeted the remark. "God, I'm so glad someone else has heard that!" exclaimed Toni. What amazed me, even though I had seen it time and again, was how quickly a collection of women, strangers the day before, could hit upon intimate commonalities.

The mosquitoes were merciless in the lean-to Pat and others had constructed. The smaller tarps were spread as ground cloths. The ground didn't give an inch; shoulder blades and hipbones hurt as we curled into sleeping positions. Despite sweaters and rain macks flung over us like blankets, we got cold fast. Ingrid forced the mosquitoes away a few inches with a superstrength insect repellant. But as the night wore on, there were murmurs of "whatever possessed me to come on this . . . ?" Toni dragged herself repeatedly outside the lean-to. She said wryly that when her sons asked, "Mommy, what did you do on your vacation?" she would say, "I barfed!"

Harriet took almost no part; she had fallen and hurt a bad knee. Inside the lean-to, Franny tried to draw her out of her shell, asking why *she* had joined this course. "To prove to myself that I'm not as klutzy as I'm told I am," Harriet answered, bitterness showing. "I'm an office bod and a house bod. My husband's

very outdoorsy." Franny was not satisfied. "But now, here, with
as much support as you'll ever have, how do you feel?"

"People have to give me a literal kick in the ass," Harriet said,
dripping with self-pity. The rest of us felt some sympathy, but
also growing annoyance. We, after all, were trying to cope, too.

Morning arrived, not a minute too soon. Ingrid—the Lindbergh
with the greatest wilderness experience—spun tales of hikes on
the Alaskan icefields with her children as we hunched on the
rocks, trying to warm our aching joints. Ingrid's husband was a
workaholic, so the two of them went separate ways much of
the time. More than anyone else, Ingrid seemed most equipped
to handle this trip's hazards. Yet she was there for the most conventional reasons: to learn to sail well enough to please her man.
Was it part of a larger plan she had to renew a spark in their
marriage?

At about 9:30 our boat hove into sight. Eliza and LeeLee were
"blown away," they said, by the fact that we took no sleeping
bags with us. Most groups, faced with the choice of four items,
took as many as four bags to zip together, on the clever assumption that food was not essential for a one-day shipwreck. "Were
you cold?" they asked innocently.

The morning rendezvous with the Banana boat included an
"inspirational reading" from *My Ship Is So Small* by Ann Davi-
son. The passage was about courage and self-doubt. I liked the
sentiments but was embarrassed by the awkward insertion of
such a recital into the day as if we were on a camp schedule—
"9:30–9:45, Inspiration. 9:45–10:15, Knots and Ropes."

A hard, tacking sail deposited us that afternoon on Hurricane
Island itself, a conifer-studded outcropping with a small colony
of tents and weathered wooden houses. Our campground was a
sunlit outpost on a hill. The big tarp went up more smoothly this
time, for there was a tree to anchor it beside a flat open space.
Lunch was hot; so was the sun. Some of us dozed in the grass for
a few delicious minutes. Lest anyone have a chance to catch her
breath or contemplate what she had gotten herself into, however, the group was soon confronted with a challenge that for

several of us would be the most forbidding one of the ten days: the "ropes" course.

In the clearing of a dense forest, the first impression of it was that of an immense Jungle gym, with about twenty obstacles connected via trees to the next. First, a simple set of climbs and jumps on logs. Then, balance beams, both fixed and swaying. A series of rope swings, rope ladders, a rope bridge, a pair of logs with a three-foot gap between them hanging high off the ground that one had to span with spread-eagled legs. Ultimately, a long rope pull through the air, Tarzan style. A couple of the obstacles were so far above us we had to crane our necks to see them. Eliza, lithe and sure-footed, demonstrated the first half and Lee-Lee, falling once or twice, the second.

A haunted silence hung over the forest. No jokes this time! The entire course looked, to many eyes, completely impossible, yet the prove-yourself spirit prevented anyone from saying so out loud. No one dared to be "chicken" in front of the others except Harriet, who had already made up her mind to quit the trip. More importantly, no one wanted to run from her own fears without a fight. Toni, a math tutor in real life, broke the silence first, and perhaps silenced her personal demons as well. "I'd just as soon do it now than wait," she said evenly, hoisting a foot on the first log.

Toni was superb, falling almost as few times as LeeLee. With everyone watching in awe and envy, she swung from obstacle to obstacle, nervously but nearly always in control. By the end, the group was a tinge less scared. One by one, each Lindbergh set out on the same route. As darkness closed in, nearly all had attacked at least a portion of the course. That seemed remarkable in itself, given our initial thoughts. More remarkable were individual feats. Marie, hardly five feet tall and one hundred pounds, leapt into the final Tarzan swing with gusto—only to get entangled in both the rope and the safety cord linked to her waist. For agonizing moments she was suspended above the ground, the safety belt grinding into her midsection. In a flash, Eliza shinnied up the nearest tree, her woodsman's knife clenched in her teeth, and hand-over-handed her way along the rope until she could cut Marie free. Then there was Pat, a powerful athlete but, with her stubby frame and high center of gravity, not ideally built for balance exercises. When she fell twice on the technically most difficult obstacle, a narrow log twenty feet off the ground, leaning at a forty-five-degree angle against a tree, she stopped for a while to gather her courage. She then marched resolutely back to the beam, climbing it with arms flapping, knees knocking, teeth grinding—a picture of willpower in motion. She tottered breathlessly up the last yard to the safety of the tree and hugged it, her cheek against the bark, as if it were her lover. There was wild applause from below. (The struggle was an excellent illustration of Pat's temperament. "I have real trouble accepting failure," she explained later. "I was very afraid. I couldn't talk the fear out of my mind. I can draw strength now, knowing I did it.")

Finally, there was Mary Louise, the last person on the course. Every step was torture for the older woman. On the swinging balance beam, she slipped, falling into the arms of waiting supporters but turning her ankle badly. She burst into tears of frustration. "Damn it, I *want* to go on, please, please!" she begged. Eliza assured her she could tackle it again before we left the island.

That night in our big tent we made ourselves more comfortable in two rows of sleeping bags. Psychologically, the ropes course was the glue that cemented us. "I looked at that stuff today and for the first time I believed all the scary things I'd heard about Outward Bound," giggled Patricia, a medical student who had arrived late. The youngest among us at thirty-one, she had to summon as much stamina to run, row and climb as Mary Louise did.

The challenge that day also charged everybody's batteries. When I told the group I would change the names in anything I published to protect their privacy, Susan objected, "Oh, no! I want full credit!"

I had trouble falling asleep that night, still strangely anxious despite having kept up with everyone else. The ropes were the scariest physical test I had faced in a long time. Also, I had come to Outward Bound intending to participate, but to observe at the same time. Preserving my journalistic distance made me feel superior vis-à-vis my "subjects." Now there was no distance; the lines were blurred. These were my *companions*. I had no special privileges, no cover as an upperclassman at Assertive U. out to watch the freshmen struggle through their initiation. The women around me were accomplished, competitive, funny, smart. I, therefore, was as vulnerable as they were. It was a workshop of my peers.

Except for Harriet. The next morning, she tearfully announced her departure, blaming it on her bad knee. If she stayed, she said, she would not be able to participate properly. What she neglected to say was that she had not participated from the first hour. "This is something she's going to have to deal with by herself long after she's left," whispered Franny. Still, we lined up to give her comforting goodbye kisses, a gesture with which most men never would have bothered. Without Harriet, the group would be more closely bonded. Almost every team or expeditionary group has a "sufferer" who absorbs group anger and frustration. (That was Joan Firey on Annapurna, Patty in Canyonlands.) Harriet continued to be the Lindbergh Sufferer after she quit, but at least she was not present to feel our darts. Months later, a sportswriter reminded me that in pro sports, an injured man is shunned by his teammates, as if he has a contagious disease. No one wanted to be infected by Harriet's; she carried the germ of failure.

Those who were not fazed by the ropes course got a chance to brave *their* worst fears on Afternoon Four, on the rocks. "I stand on a rock in Central Park and I get dizzy!" mumbled Carolyn. In a corner of the island that was once a quarry, she stared at a set of progressively higher, steeper rockpiles, the kind you see "human flies" like George Willig splayed across on *Wide World of Sports*. A special male instructor was in charge. In soothing tones, he compared rock-climbing to ballet, a lovely analogy. His movements did flow as he demonstrated how sneakers against the rock created a friction that held the body without slipping. It helped banish from many Lindbergh minds the concept of rock-climbing as an act copied from gorillas.

Nonetheless, each rock face appeared menacing initially. On our first fifty-foot technical climb, climbers were roped together with one belaying the other for safety. Mary Louise slipped down the hard rock by accident, her fall stopped, as it should have been, by the belayed rope clipped to her belt. Without thinking, our elder stateswoman screamed, "Jesus Christ!" A second later, she muttered, "I don't know why I said that. I'm a Unitarian." Franny had an even better line. Finding herself stalled with terror on the rock, her knees shaking uncontrollably, she cried, "I must be seven centimeters dilated!" The natural childbirth veterans doubled up with understanding laughter.

Then came the step in rock-climbing that looked to some literally like their last: the rappel. Each climber teetered backward with nylon belt slung diaper-fashion around her rump, clipped at the pubic bone into a taut rope that she would play out slowly to control the speed of descent down from the top of a cliff. Franny and Patricia went before me, faces as pale as the sails on our ship. "Don't worry," I said, trying to relax them, "with that seat you're going to have an orgasm on the way down." They smiled wanly and disappeared over the jagged edge. Sure enough, at the bottom of the six-story drop, there were grins all around, not quite postcoital, but real. Rappelling happens to be fun, once you kick past the top lip of the cliff.

There was a final, colossal cliff, almost the height of the Statue of Liberty, to scale. Carolyn and I started on parallel lines of ascent. To me, climbing was like a physical chess game in which you had to plot three moves ahead. (If I put the right foot there and the left on that knob, will I be able to grab that crack with my right hand?) But to Carolyn, it was a foreign, terrifying affront to gravity. She tremblingly chattered her way up, shrieking, skinning both knees, clawing, demanding encouragement from the instructors. Many "I-can't-do-it!" yelps later, she scrambled on top of the ledge. (Later, she recalled that she had sat on the lower rocks for a long while before the last climb. LeeLee offered to lend her a hand, but she brushed it away saying, "don't be ridiculous." Carolyn knew she would have disappointed herself if she had not given it a try. What had she learned from the climb? "Being able to trust another person," the belayer responsible for the other end of the safety rope, she said. "That's very hard for a New Yorker.")

Walking back to our campsite, the Lindberghs agreed it had been a positively satisfying day. In the morning, there had been brief orientation talks about foraging for food, building fires and setting up tents from tarpaulins. Someone remarked how absorbed Patricia was in lighting her "hibachi" (two Number 10 tin cans with a twig fire built in the bottom one). The medical student replied, "When it's your first fire, you get *very* engrossed." Susan and I had paired off for the tent lesson; she had never put up a tent before. Franny expressed the group spirit when she said, "Wouldn't it be nice if we could learn as much in one day at home as we're doing here!" But one tired voice added, "Can you imagine going through this every day like professional athletes do?" The answer was a chorus: "No way!" However diverse we were in age, careers, families or hometowns, we kept discovering common ground in aches, laughter, terror.

On Night Four, Lolly brought Lindbergh and Banana Watches together for a chat about the "solo." "If you find yourself getting bored, what does that say about yourself? Maybe you're a boring person. So be creative," she urged. "Slow down. Find out about your island. How many of you have ever been alone for three days without a radio, a TV or a book? It's really a special experience."

The solo would certainly be easier than the physical stunts. Still, the solo was potentially the most dangerous part of the course. There have been a total of fifteen deaths in various Outward Bound programs (none at Hurricane Island) and many oc-

curred on solo. "You are your own safety feature," Lolly said.
"Take care of yourselves. Don't get fried." At the end of her talk,
she asked, "How do you feel about all of this? Excited?" Nods.
"Anyone apprehensive?" Vigorous nods. "Don't worry. No weird
lobsterman is gonna come and rape you." I looked at Lolly, with
her Amazonian body, and figured that if I were a lobsterman, I'd
worry about what she would do to *me*.

Lindbergh Watch was rambunctious that night. In our big
tent after the meeting, the "ghetto rats" (as those of us from
northeast metropolises had been nicknamed) started trading
barbs about the expedition. "$450 we pay so we can work like
dogs" . . . "Hey, dogs get treated better . . ." "I don't like the
Bananas' karma . . ." "Karma? Is that like chutzpah, only from
California? . . ." Soon everyone was screeching with the hilarity
that comes from getting through another day without a broken
limb. "My God, this is a slumber party!" hooted Franny after
some adolescent jokes. "Animal House!" shrieked someone else.
"No, it's premenopausal hysteria!" said Susan, a school administrator, who was revealing a marvelously caustic tongue. Whatever we called our outburst, we were certainly asserting both a
common and an individual sense of self. We quieted down only
when Toni led in the singing of "Good Night Ladies." (In retrospect, Eliza felt Lindbergh Watch had drawn together more
cautiously than other of her groups, retarded perhaps by Harriet.
But we had also manifested traits almost universal in group development on Outward Bound trips—annoyance at the group
solo, fear on the ropes and the rocks, apprehension before the individual solo. The main difference was, our apprehension came
through disguised in wisecracks.)

In the morning, we were permitted for once to eat breakfast in
the mess hall. So high-spirited that we practically threw bread
balls across the table, we had regressed to the behavioral level of
ten-year-olds. Eliza, herself a rebel—she had turned her back on
desk jobs in publishing after her graduation from Skidmore in
favor of a self-sufficient outdoor life, and was even now building

a home in Maine with her two bare hands—nevertheless scolded us. We were embarrassing her in front of other instructors.

The solo outing began on a pleasant note. We boarded a large motorized boat, each of us with one gallon jug of water plus a duffle bag stuffed with sleeping bag, tarp, sweater, hibachi cans, matches, emergency flags and a notebook. The weather was sunny and breezy; Penobscot Bay looked like a New England picture postcard. Each of us was dropped off on her own small island. Marie, still fashionable and clean while the rest of us wore clothes that appeared to have been used as kitchen mops, suddenly wrapped her arms around herself. Thinking about her son, she said, "I've got the hugging disease." The whole group was in need of comfort; we hugged and kissed one another before trooping onto the shoals of our islands.

Mine was named Little Rye. (In my notebook, I changed the spelling to Wry.) It was supposed to have clambeds—Eliza had taken note of my love of shellfish. Mussels were abundant, so I collected a potful before setting up my "bedroom" in a well-worn campsite. I took an approximate reading of the time by the tide and the sun, a seaworthy act that became routine in the next seventy-two hours. Like most of my companions, I was not afraid of the solo. However, the solitude was more meaningful to the single mothers, who had little of it at home. Besides, I had camped out alone before in the Sawtooth Mountains of Idaho. By comparison, this environment was tame.

The first night, lighting my hibachi fire with a single match, I steamed mussels in salt water, pleased with my camping skill. Sleeping was less successful. My tent and sleeping bag were fine, but the mosquitoes thought so too. A smoky fog swooped in that night, obliterating dawn views of nearby islands. Forgetful campers like me who had not covered their woodpiles were stuck the following day with damp, unburnable wood. The misery of being without a morning cup of cocoa (included in our "emergency rations") or anything else in my stomach put me in a foul mood. A booklet by no less an authority than Euell Gibbons enabled me to forage for such exotic raw greens as orach and grasswort. They tasted about as bad as their names, and they might assuage the hunger of a rabbit, but not mine.

When the third day dawned dark and rainy, my mood—and that of the others—sank. I fumed at the prohibition against bringing a book, since I had brought Joseph Conrad's short novels with me especially for the solo. "You can read Conrad without leaving New York City," Eliza had shrugged. I napped intermittently on the rocks that day. Meals of grasswort and plain water left me lackadaisical. At midday, I gave in and nibbled a piece of the emergency "brownie" that Lolly had referred to as "reconstituted bear-shit." I sang at the top of my lungs to amuse myself. My frame of mind, according to those notes: discombobulated, slowed down, but anxiety-free. Physical state: bruised and battered. Lessons learned: what the phrase "at a snail's pace" really means, by watching in fascination as whole armies of snails wriggled their way out of the low tide muck.

The group was glad to be reunited when motorboats plucked us each up in late afternoon, not because we had been lonely but because everyone was ravenous for a hot meal, a hot shower and a hot dry bed. Marie was weak from fasting. Passing the mess hall, we caught the tantalizing scent of meat loaf. "No, that's not for you. We have some hot veggies and rice made up for you in the boathouse," Eliza announced. At that moment, the whole philosophy seemed needlessly cruel. "Goddamn!" I exploded. Before the trip I promised myself that because I was there as a journalist, I would not impose my views on others. But right then, I could not restrain myself. "You're tough, Eliza, I've got to hand that to you!" I shouted furiously as we entered the boathouse for the gooey "welcome back" feast. Franny was also downcast. "I'm ready to pull a Harriet—bump my knee and go home," she said.

Eliza eventually relented and allowed us to troop, in the dark, to the showers. But the general mood was muted.* Toni summed

---

* Especially my own; word was waiting for me of a death in my family. I had to leave the next morning. I got a complete report on the final cruise afterward.

up the solo well by saying, "It was no big deal." In fact, it may mean more to youngsters than to grown women. Still, we had expected more of a reward upon returning.

Mutiny was in the air in the morning, the low point of the voyage. The weather was foggy, we were tired from the solo and we had been kept up late the night before. The leaders took a few women off to the ropes course at dawn, their last chance to finish it. The rest were supposed to run and dip, but they conspired to run, period.

The remaining three days turned out to be among the best. The Bananas and the Lindberghs negotiated a major sailing expedition through Penobscot Bay. Instructors acted strictly as advisors. The women, some of whom, just days before, could not tell a mizzen from a mainsail, now took firm control of both, piloting their boats through fog, rain and dark without a serious mishap.

There was a predictable blowup in midexpedition between the two boats over how distant a destination to aim for. Lolly's Bananas pressed for an all-night run to one site. The Lindberghs thought it was ridiculous, and refused. Some detected hostility between the two leaders, Lolly and Eliza. The Lindberghs got angry enough to wish that Banana boat would spring a leak until a compromise solved the problem. But within the Lindbergh family, the urgent sense of cooperation, apparent from the beginning, solidified. And without prodding, the women asserted true command of their boat. The camaraderie of the final sail—Pat on the bow watch calling out "lobster pot ahead at two o'clock" to Lisa at the helm, while Susan consulted the compass—was the flowering of friendships begun hardly more than a week before.

The most assertive of the bunch might have learned the most on the last voyage. Franny felt exhausted, seasick and sunburned after a ten-hour sail through blind fog. No one had the strength to lift the oars. Then, someone remarked how much worse it must be for the starved Vietnamese boat people. Franny heard a click! in her mind, linking her plight to that of a friend, a Vietnam veteran. She knew then that these "ordinary" women, so

privileged by contrast, could revive themselves one more time.
Carolyn and Marie learned from one another. Both were independent career women, eight years apart in age. Carolyn had
been an army bride in West Germany who managed to hang on
to army jobs after she and her husband split up. Even with the
burdens of a single parent, she also managed to earn a pilot's license. Marie had been uprooted by *her* husband from North
Carolina with little warning early in her marriage. On her own
in Atlanta, with her baby boy, she still made a name for herself
in the high-powered world of merchandising. Yet upon first seeing Carolyn, Marie thought, "Mmm, fortyish, housewife." And
Carolyn was equally patronizing at first about Marie: "Mmm,
Southern belle." On the final night at sea, a thunderstorm blew
off the big tarp that protected the sleeping crew. Marie's sleeping bag got drenched. Shivering, Marie knew the only sensible
solution was to share a sleeping bag. Carolyn saw her standing
in her underwear and figured, "what the hell!" She promptly
shed her inhibition and invited Marie to crawl in with her. It
was an epiphany for everybody.

At last, the Lindberghs sailed triumphantly toward the Rockland dock. On that final day, the women left behind their remaining inhibitions, revealing innermost secrets to one another
about their children, their jobs, mental health, marriage, divorce.
There were no outpourings, no tears. But the departure from
Rockland was a series of farewell meals, hugs, and fervent agree-
ments to keep in touch. As one of them put it, "I'm different
now, and it's because of whatever it is that talking to a bunch of
women for ten days does to you." We were proud of each other's
resiliency. The majority felt the trip had invoked a new pride
and self-esteem by making them master their fear of physical
workouts like the ropes course and the freezing swims. A deeper
satisfaction, though, came from the extraordinary bonding. It
seemed astonishingly coincidental that nearly every woman got
her menstrual period during those ten days. In fact, it is a common phenomenon among women who endure stress or simply
live together.

When Susan got home to Pittsburgh, it struck her that she had never become so close with a group of women so quickly. Her husband was very proud of her, although he kidded about sending her to Fort Bragg next for airborne training. After Carolyn told her "war stories," her seventeen-year-old daughter asked, "If I start saving now, can I go next year?" That delighted Carolyn no end. Ingrid, who came to learn her husband's sport, impressed *him* no end when they went sailing together afterward. But what literally made him sit up and take notice was another of her new skills. The family spent the summer constructing a two-story cabin on the ocean. When her husband needed a good perch in order to set the glass in the upstairs windows, Ingrid rigged a harness seat and belayed him off the roof!

No one said Outward Bound fundamentally turned her life around. One woman felt much calmer, more able to "tell a crisis from a hassle." Another reinforced her belief in accomplishing hard tasks. A third came home ready to accept a man with whom she had been having quarrels that she now felt had stemmed from false self-doubts. Still another thought she was "carrying around a little of the cool" she took away from the voyage.

No one knew how long these emotions would last. But Marie had a calligrapher draw her a sign that expressed the lesson she wanted to apply "every goddamn day, whether it's people or business, jumping off a dock or rappelling off a mountain." The sign read: "Go for it!"

Franny, whose reasons for coming were a complex mixture of goals that typified the group, put her reactions down on paper. "For years, people have been telling me how strong I am, how resourceful I am," she wrote. "For years I have been defining myself with precisely those definitions—the ones that others have made for me. I was not certain who/what Franny was about. Oh, she survived all right, because it was necessary. Never less than two jobs. Making art until the dawn of the next day. Providing the children with the best of experiences. Being very self-denying. When I closed my eyes to see my own image, there was nothing specific. Franny was a protoplasmic fuzz." The trip helped her understand herself, and others. She understood her Vietnam friend's "platoon love and loyalty," in another context. "Outward Bound was not a war," she continued. "Perhaps, though, it was a personal 'incident' for each of us. And each one of us advanced, then 'took a hill.'" She gained priceless personal insight: "That I must think primarily, guiltlessly, about myself. We all did. Then, after each of us had managed to take good care of herself, she was able to return to the group and give the necessary support." Franny proved to herself what friends could never hammer home—that she *was* a winner, one with humor, spunk and joy . . . and she had plenty of company.

Some of us had reservations. It was disturbing that Harriet was not screened out of the program before she joined us. On a more mundane level, Mary Louise and I both questioned whether certain hardships were truly necessary—the lack of a foam pad under one's sleeping bag, the "dip" in freezing water, the starvation diet on solo. "Sometimes I wondered why I was punishing myself so, proving myself for the sake of telling someone about it," said Mary Louise. "There were times I counted the days, thinking, 'well, people survived Stalag 17, too!' I don't think it made me a better person."

Nor a worse one either. Placing yourself in just such an all-female course is a statement of your need for challenge that goes beyond pleasing a husband or a child. Women invariably hang back at first, in OB mixed-gender groups. Men thus lead by default. That's more like real life, unfortunately, since most of us operate in a male-dominant world. And real life *is* more complicated than plucking grasswort for breakfast on a New England island. The exhilaration of mastering challenges, as we did, fades fast without frequent refresher courses. Such courses, whether Outward Bound or improvised ones, are not easy to come by. Like est and TM, Outward Bound often has been overpraised.

My group happily rejoiced in the sailing, the sharing, the sisterhood. That was more than worth $450. For months, Lindberghs kept in touch by means of xeroxed letters, phone calls, visits, and even a "slumber party" at Lisa's house in Massachusetts. As Marie remarked, "we've made lifelong friends." Maybe women, more than men, need artificial adventures. Programs similar to Outward Bound, such as the less structured camping jaunts sponsored by Women in the Wilderness, a California group, are proliferating. A burgeoning number of women long for such primitive, all-female romps that so many missed as children.

Artificial or not, Outward Bound permitted us to fill our sails in female terms that might be unthinkable in a mixed group, no matter how "liberated" we might be. I can't picture men taking turns sewing odd patches of cloth together for an expedition flag. But Lindbergh Watch did. And I, a woman who wouldn't be caught dead sewing a button on her own jeans, spent half a day during my solo, stitching my part of the Lindbergh flag on, just so.

5

THE CRUCIBLE: ORGANIZED SPORTS

A touch of the macho spirit has always been an asset to men in organized sports. So it is with women, as female athletes come into their own. If Outward Bound is a tutorial program for ordinary women who want to learn adventuring skills, then organized sports is where extraordinary women collect their doctorates.

Throughout the seventies, the most famous professional athlete in the world was also the most voluble, the most controversial and the most quotable—Muhammad Ali. Not too far behind him was a woman, nearly his equal in volubility, quotability, controversy and charisma—Billie Jean King. Tote up their shared qualities; the sum is a superstar who blows his or her own horn for all its worth. Certainly, there are self-effacing superstars whose relative quietude stands out as much as the brashness of others. For every Reggie Jackson, there is a Hank Aaron, for every Darryl Dawkins a Larry Bird, for every Billie Jean King a Chris Evert Lloyd. The stardom of the quieter ones is not at issue. What *is* at issue is why sports thrives on the brash heroes, why the public accepts aggressive women more readily in sports than in everyday life, how the fighting spirit is thrust on pioneering sportswomen whether they like it or not.

Most female athletes who have charged through the pack to become stars in recent years have received good "ink" (newspaper and magazine coverage), usually in proportion to their price tags. Naturally, looks count, but they counted as much for Ben Crenshaw when he was golf's newest sensation as they did for Nancy Lopez. Joan Joyce, the Cy Young of women's softball, has not received the recognition she deserves, but she has gotten more than any *male* softball player alive. Billie Jean King taught male sportswriters that women athletes can make six-figure salaries and make good copy; her effectiveness has paid off for the tennis stars who followed in her footsteps.*

The impact of the written word on the acceptance of women athletes has been important, yet small compared to the explosive impact of television. Television's unsparing eye is good to female athletes. It displays them as personalities, not as freaks.

Athletic competition, viewed in person or on television, puts a premium on personality. Thus, while being macho or macha might be regarded by some as inappropriate behavior or as a personality defect in everyday life, it is usually an asset in organized sports. An extraordinary woman may use it as a positive element in flair, or as a cover-up for a lack of inner security. However it is used, we take it for granted—in a flashy wide receiver as he spikes a football after a touchdown catch, in Virginia Wade as she twirls her tennis racquet and arches an eyebrow while awaiting an opponent's serve. Putting a little extra into one's act is an accepted part of performing in sports. One reason Chris Evert Lloyd was rarely the crowd's favorite during her reign as tennis queen was that she was perceived as emotionless

---

* Interestingly, male sportswriters have reserved their cattiest criticism for women *reporters* who dared to compete for their jobs, while treating athletes with more respect. It was not the sanctity of the locker room they really worried about, it was the threat of journalistic competition.

—not colorful enough. Flair, style and color serve to enhance an athlete's image off the playing field as well.

Athletes are encouraged to manufacture a winning, flashy personality if one does not come naturally. In the novel *Goldengirl*, later a movie, a talented blonde runner is programmed by scientists to capture gold medals in the Olympics. A key feature of her training is, of all things, how to conduct a postvictory press conference. She practices her "ad-lib" repartee with an imaginary press corps in order to enhance her marketability. For example, one "reporter" asks:

"Doesn't all this training mean sacrifices?" She raised her eyebrows. "Sacrifices? Like not going out with guys? There are still some hours left in the day for that. You can't do trackwork after dark, but other things aren't impossible." She paused, waiting for the laughter to die in the loudspeakers. "Like reading books and listening to music. . . ."

"I believe you're six foot two, Goldine. Would you say your height gives you an unfair advantage over other girls?"

"I admit I can spot a good-looking guy at fifty yards, yes."

"What are your plans for this evening, Goldengirl?" . . . She was fully in command . . . smiling, getting to her feet and putting a hand up to shield her eyes as she peered into the limbo beyond the lights. "I've nothing arranged. Get yourself stilts, mister, and you might have a date."

These answers might seem smart-alecky on paper, but in the film, Susan Anton, playing Goldengirl, put them across as appealingly and as realistically as any sassy jock might. Although the book is fiction, the idea of drilling an athlete in off-field activities is certainly possible. And some stars need no coaching to come up with one-liners like Goldengirl's. Inge Nissen, the six-foot-five-inch Danish-born basketball star, is an example. During one game for Old Dominion University, she got trapped in a scramble for a loose ball and wound up on the floor, writhing in pain. Later, at a press conference, I asked where she had been hurt. She looked down at me from beneath black mascara-shaded eyes, a wicked smile on her face. "There'll be no loving for a week!" she said, pointing to her lower groin. "Next time I wear a chastity belt."

What about star quality? How is it related to machisma in a female athlete? Flair, style, wit, toughness and talent are implicit in definitions of either. But machisma also implies a woman jock who keeps the upper hand, who can tease as Nissen or the Gold-engirl character did, who is extroverted to the point of showing off. Nancy Lopez, the golfer, for instance, projected "star quality" from the moment she captured headlines as a rookie. There is nothing show-offy about Lopez, however. A warm personality who does not denigrate her skills, she sticks to her business on the links, beaming a grin when she hits a particularly good shot, frowning when she misses. She is friendly with her crowds, not bantering. Off the course, she can put forward an air of honest humility. To see Nancy paired with JoAnne Carner, a leading golfer who is over forty, is to watch Nancy's sunny star quality play off JoAnne's bouncy machisma. Carner's style involves a wiggle of body English here, a club thrust triumphantly in the air there, an occasional wink for her gallery. Lopez is self-contained; she plays "within herself," to borrow an athletic cliché. Carner plays more openly to the crowd. There is room in sports for a variety of styles, and fans clearly enjoy those of both Lopez and Carner.

For athletes such as Suzy Chaffee and Diana Nyad, who excel in sports that do not have a big spectator appeal, the cultivation of an extroverted, plucky personality can pave the way to a successful professional career. Skiers and swimmers rarely parlay their amateur glory into a lasting fame, with the exception of a few Olympic gold-medal winners. Chaffee never won an Olympic medal and Nyad never even swam in any of the games, yet both have maneuvered themselves into the limelight on the strength of their showmanship. Younger Olympians, professional in everything but name (and in what the athlete is allowed to declare as income), are increasingly taking their cues from personalities like Chaffee.

Janet Guthrie has great talent and showmanship. But she had to maneuver through an early rebellious phase, one which was born of a less liberated time. And once Guthrie devoted herself to her chosen sport, she found, to her dismay, that her fellow drivers were determined to resist her entry into the field no matter how many times she proved herself. In order to cope, she evolved a style of quiet but smoldering determination, the style of a pioneer.

Tall and composed, with loosely curled light-brown hair that sets off piercing green eyes, Guthrie, at forty-one, strikes reporters as a great deal more mature than most athletes, regardless of age. She is a sophisticated woman who unfailingly goes sightseeing on a road trip (athletes in general are more inclined to stay in hotel rooms watching soap operas on television), who cooks gourmet dinners for guests when she is home, who listens to classical music. She has weighed the risks of a career as a race-car driver and committed herself to it only after considerable soul searching. An interview with Guthrie is not the usual staccato question-and-answer session, but a meditative dialogue. She is that rare species, a performer both shy and daring at the same time.

In 1978, she became the first woman to complete the Indianapolis 500, despite the fact that she had to drive with a broken right wrist. Mobbed by the press after her ninth-place finish, she said flippantly, "If I weren't a woman, you wouldn't be paying all this attention to me, and I could be back in the garage now having a beer with my crew." Remarks like this were, in a sense, cover-ups to hide the real Janet Guthrie, a sensitive, death-defying person who burned inside with a stubborn tenacity.

During one interview in her New York high-rise apartment, I asked her to list the words that most accurately described racing and her attitude toward it. The adjectives she picked were "challenging, demanding, adventurous, very difficult." She was also "stubborn, tough, insistent." But "tough cookie?" Wrong. "Lady race driver?" Worse. "I like being called a lady," she explained, "but I don't like being called a lady race driver because there isn't any such thing. There are just race drivers, period. I like being called feminine because I think I am, and because the assumption sometimes tends to be that a woman who does this kind of thing must be otherwise. I *like* being a woman."

Indeed, her hobbies include traditionally female ones, such as cooking and sewing. Still, there is another aspect of her personality that is so nontraditional she plays it down: her daring side. In a practice run once at California's Ontario race track, she revealed this side to the amazement of racing veterans. Guthrie forced her car to lap the oval so close to the outside restraining wall that a six-inch metal rod jutting out from the passenger side door scraped the wall itself. Her object was reasonable enough. Drivers who are used to road races must learn, when they do enclosed oval races, to accept the presence of that wall. It is not easy; some Grand Prix drivers who have come to Indianapolis have made a few circuits of its walled track and turned right around to quit. Guthrie was determined not to let an oval's wall intimidate her. "At first, as many rookies do, I was having trouble adjusting my line," she said. "So I got a piece of welding rod and stuck it on the passenger side door. I just drove around the track tickling the wall with this 'curb tickler' until I got used to the feeling." She spoke as if describing a Sunday outing in the country rather than a gutsy move few other rookies would have tried.

Yet Janet Guthrie's natural athletic impulse was the side of her personality that she rebelled against early in life. She grew up in Florida, in the fifties. "My object was to avoid sports completely," she said. It was an era in which athletics were not regarded as ladylike. Her father, however, was a commercial airline pilot. Whatever adventurous spirit he had must have rubbed off on his first-born child. Janet was always taking off for parts unknown, running away about as far as her bicycle would carry her. Her favorite reading matter was World War I stories about flying aces. From the age of three, she was taken for sky cruises in DC-3s. By the time she was thirteen, she had coaxed her father into giving her a few turns at the controls, and by sixteen she had made her first (and last) parachute jump. Flying was her first love. She scraped together money for flying lessons by working summers at a local airport. Automobiles, on the other hand, were simply a means of transportation at that stage. Guthrie, the woman who broke the sex barrier at the Indianapolis 500, *failed* her first driving test as a teenager because she didn't bother to stop for red lights.

The conventional sex stereotypes of the day prevented Guthrie from setting her sights on an airborne career. As a substitute, she entered college as an aeronautical engineering student, later switching to physics. Upon graduation from the University of Michigan, she applied for the NASA Scientist-Astronaut program, and was one of four women to get through the initial screening, but her lack of a doctorate eliminated her. So Guthrie came east to work for Republic Aviation. She bought her first car, a used Jaguar XK120, on account of its handsome looks, not its power.

As Guthrie remembered it, she "sort of slid" into racing. Living on Long Island, working for Republic, she entered her Jag in local weekend road races for fun. Then came a Jaguar XK140; this one she modified for racing. By the late sixties, auto racing had its hooks in her. Bored with physics, she left Republic and did well in numerous endurance races. When she ran out of money, she went back to work as a technical magazine editor, resigned as soon as she was solvent again and returned fulltime to the world of speed. She racked up impressive victories before she became famous, including the North Atlantic Road Racing Championship in 1973.

The more of a threat she became to the male racing establishment, the more the men resented her, and her battles to enter oval-track races over their objections propelled her into sportspage headlines. Women were not even allowed in the pits at U. S. Auto Club Indy-style races until 1971. It was 1976 before Guthrie and Arlene Hiss became the first two women to obtain USAC racing licenses. That was the year the car builder Rolla Vollstedt, specifically seeking a woman to gain publicity for his stable, asked Guthrie to test his Indy "Championship" car. The name Janet Guthrie thus became synonymous with female Champ car pioneering.

Ironically, as far as Guthrie was concerned, auto racing was one of the few sports in which men and women could compete as equals. Factors other than gender were responsible for keeping women out of the field. First, a woman either had to have her own money to buy a car and maintain a crew, or she needed a very rich patron. (Guthrie was able to turn pro thanks to the hefty salary she had drawn in her years as a physicist.) Second, of course, was male chauvinism. It was an opponent that Janet did not seek, but it "came with the territory." Before she had a chance to flash her "Champ car" entry card, Guthrie was attacked as an amateur by Bobby Unser, an Indianapolis 500 winner, who declared that no woman could "hack it" in his two-hundred-miles-per-hour universe. Or maybe any woman could; he was always contradicting himself. "I could take a hitch-hiker, give him a Corvette from a showroom and teach him to drive faster than Janet Guthrie," he snorted. Guthrie's sanguine response? "Male chauvinist pig." They fought one another in the press while she proceeded to pass the rookie test at the Indianapolis Speedway with flying colors. Then, Vollstedt's car developed mechanical troubles that kept her out of the 1976 big race after all. She did drive competitively in other oval-track races that year to shut Unser up—for a while.

Guthrie came right back in 1977, qualifying again for the Memorial Day Indy 500. It turned out to be the biggest calculated risk of her career. Her Lightning-Offenhauser was fast but unpredictable; the driver got no advance notice when it was about to spin out. "I can't find the edge," she complained to Roger McClusky, who had driven it the year before. Neither could he. During one practice, she spun out and crashed, suffering minor injuries but major jitters. She learned how little warning the Lightning conveyed. "A microsecond of a little feeling," she said, "like the tires have just turned to bubble gum." The damaged car was patched up, but it remained "squirrely," according to Janet.

By the time Memorial Day arrived, she was "spooked." But she would be damned if she'd admit it. "I knew that if I didn't put the car in the show in '77 it was all over. I was never going to get another chance and that would be the end of my racing career," Guthrie said. When the gentlemen started their engines, Janet Guthrie started hers, too. She knew the machine could squirrel out from under her at any second. For four laps, she kept the car on the edge of a spin-out, refusing to play it safe. Then, engine trouble forced her into the pits for good. "I was breathing hard when I came in," Guthrie said dryly.

She held the edge the next year, 1978, broken hand and all. But Al Unser, Bobby's brother, won the race. After a few beers, he suggested to some reporters that Guthrie had not had the guts to drive her car flat-out, and that her injured hand had made her a menace to the rest of the pack. "Bullshit!" fumed Guthrie in her living room months later, her green eyes hard as marbles. "To do something like finishing ninth at Indianapolis, and then to have the winner dump on it, was probably the single rottenest thing that's happened since all this started."

As we talked, Guthrie had one ear cocked toward the telephone. She had just returned from racing in Texas, but she was hoping for a hurry-up call to fly to Florida to join a team in the Sebring twelve-hour race that weekend. Midway through our discussion, she discovered that she had accidentally knocked her phone off the hook. A quick call confirmed that the Sebring deal had come through. Within minutes, Guthrie was pulling the rollers out of her hair, muttering, "I've got to decide which of my afternoon appointments to keep and which racing suits to throw in the washing machine." She dragged out a white, satiny one-piece suit smeared with grease. "Hmm," she said, sniffing it like a housewife in a detergent commercial, "it stinks."

The sight of the outfit triggered another crisis. She had forgotten to mail her measurements to a manufacturer for a new racing suit. The form was on her dining table, next to an eviction no-

tice. (She had also forgotten to pay her rent.) The eviction notice could wait. The suit could not. She handed me a tape measure and I turned seamstress, marking off her inseam lengths. The
rest of the interview would have to be postponed. "You know," I
said, finishing the measurements and heading for the door,
"what you really need is—"

"—a wife!" she completed the sentence for me with a telling
laugh.

Two weeks later, Janet seemed less tense. Sebring had not
gone badly. Her team had finished seventeenth in the endurance
contest. But as soon as she resumed talking about her role as a
female sports pioneer, her jaw tightened. She had mixed feelings.
She had not set out to be a pioneer; she simply wanted to be a
racing driver. "I can't deny that there is a little enjoyment in
being the first woman to drive at Indianapolis, because everybody wants to make a little mark in history, carve initials on the
tree trunk. What I am getting very tired of," she said, "is the
continuing flak." Her jaw was stone by now. "The flak ought
to end. I have a record. The record is a good one. The fact that I
am a woman doesn't make any difference. I am just tired as hell
of the fact that everybody doesn't accept it yet."

Guthrie, a graduate of Miss Harris' Florida School for Girls,
does not ordinarily pepper her sentences with profanity. When
she curses, the effect is startling. She was angry because, while
waiting to register at Sebring, two crew members on line with her
couldn't resist needling her. As Guthrie told it, "son-of-a-bitch if
the first thing that comes up isn't, 'well, I don't know if you girls
are going to have strength enough for this Ferrari.' Oh shit! I
thought. Not again. Here I have been driving Grand National
stock cars on high bank half-miles as well as on super Speedways
for three years, the Champ cars, everything else. I thought I had
wrestled this damn strength question to a standstill." Her voice
was filled with fury. "Why, after seventeen years in racing, is
some cheap mechanic *man* still telling me I don't have the
strength to drive his fucking race car!"

Couldn't she laugh in their faces? Not quite. These men were responsible for seeing that her car ran right over the coming two days. So Janet gritted her teeth and told herself, "they'll find out better." But another voice within her asked plaintively, "why don't they know better already?"

Incidents like this had boxed Guthrie into a corner. She did not like the idea of "out-macho-ing the men," even if it appeared that she was trying. No, she claimed, she was merely protecting herself, "trying to keep some of the shit off," in those moments when she executed supercharged practice laps, or when she dodged reporters who asked about fear. What *did* it feel like at the wheel of an Indy car going full tilt? It was hard for her to answer honestly. If she did, she was certain the next morning's headline would read, "Janet Guthrie Scared of Race Cars." Male drivers, she insisted, can admit such an emotion. "They *do* admit that Champ cars are scary; they *are* scary," she said. Her memory skipped back to that first Champ car practice with Vollstedt in 1976. "I wouldn't admit it for, oh, a year, year-and-a-half afterward, but every time I stuck my foot down on the straightaway, and played at getting through that next turn a little faster, I was saying, 'I want to go back to the garage and suck my thumb for a while.'"

Janet leaned forward, serious but no longer angry. "You're trying to attain a respectable speed, okay? The watches are on you, and naturally you're going to go very fast at first." So she worked like crazy to reach the car's maximum achievable speed. "That," she concluded, "basically means you just scare the socks off yourself."

Was this the feeling that egged on a race car driver to return, race after race? Was it thrilling because of the risk or in spite of it? Guthrie groped for the correct words, the honest ones that would not trivialize the act to which she had dedicated her life. She said slowly, "Somewhere, the fact that risk is involved operates. But exactly how, or in what way, is really strange . . . peculiar. I don't entirely undertand it. The fact that there is risk involved is part of what makes it worthwhile." While a driver is standing in the pits waiting for a practice, fear is *not* the motivation. It is rather the opposite; a driver knows how frightening it can be and could invent a dozen excuses to avoid a run.

But if you don't do it, Guthrie continued, if you let the fear talk you out of driving, by the end of the day "you're climbing the walls, absolutely twitching." The reason? "You haven't done what you're really about," she said, her palms turned up as if to show how hopeless words were in explaining. What mood came over her when she gave in to the fear, on those days that she did not make the practice run? She grinned. "Go on a junk food binge. I eat corn chips. Pork rinds. M & Ms. Drink beer."

Yet when she finally did lower herself into the little spaceship of a car, snapped down the windscreen on her helmet and gunned the spaceship into asphalt orbit, the twitching stopped. There was no adrenalin rush. There was no craving for corn chips. There was only the driver, the car, the road. "Part of the essentials for a racing driver is emotional detachment," she said. "I mean, you just don't feel excitement when you're on a race track. You've got that all under control. You can't *allow* yourself to become wildly excited." No chuckles at passing A. J. Foyt, either, not for a pro. As with most professional athletes, Guthrie's anxiety reached its peak directly before the event, then dropped precipitously during it. "The pleasure comes when you know that you have gotten that car through that turn as fast as that car will go. The fact that the penalty for error can be high—it operates somewhere. But it's not the essence of the thing. The essence is getting that car balanced on that beautiful edge."

She paused, rearranging the sentences in her mind, capping her dissertation with scientific precision: "It's a combination of competition and exercising a skill in an environment that does pose certain hazards." Nothing, she emphasized, so crass as to be considered "showing off."

Aside from racing, had she taken another kind of risk recently? Janet Guthrie broke into a wide smile. "I really overextended myself in cooking. First excursion with a new Cuisinart. Made quenelles. Sure tasted awful!"

Of all the team sports, basketball is the showiest. It is a game in which close cooperation among team members does not inhibit individual flair. Charisma is easy to spot because there are fewer players on the court. The pace of the game (compared to either baseball or football), the relative intimacy of a gym, and the scantiness of the uniforms—these elements appeal to a crowd on a number of levels. Basketball is marvelously sexual, as any woman who has rooted for Walt Frazier, Rick Barry, Julius Erving or Magic Johnson would gladly acknowledge. It is a game that gives the shooter, the passer, the strutter plenty of room to display his talents. As played by women, the very same showiness attracts the same spectator response. Women's basketball is an inherently macha sport.

Why, then, has it not captured the spotlight earlier? Simply because of sexism and its archaic structure. Until 1970, there were six players to a side, most of them restricted to a half-court game. Once schools switched to the five-player, full court game, with its premium on speed and aggressiveness, girls' basketball took a quantum jump in excitement.

After *Parade* magazine began picking All-American teams in 1977 it was just a matter of time before entrepreneurs packaged an eight-team Women's Pro Basketball League (WBL). It made its debut in 1978.

A six-foot-two-inch New York player, Althea Gwyn, knew what it was like to play during the league's first year in remote college gyms rather than in Madison Square Garden. She was used to the skeptical, often sexist remarks from ignorant men. ("Why don't you get a sex change?") But she understood that the opportunity to play a major team sport could change the life of a female ghetto kid just as it had transformed the lives of Willie Mays, Roy Campanella, Jim Brown and Elgin Baylor years earlier.

She grew up in Amityville, a Long Island town with extremes of rich and poor families. Hers was poor. Her father tried to support the family on two jobs, and her mother, often sick, had to leave Althea unsupervised a great deal. She began hanging out under the rim of the schoolyard basketball court when she was nine. Maybe the affinity was hereditary; her mother had been a high-school star and had even been offered a college scholarship, unheard of in the fifties for black women athletes. But the local preacher had talked Mrs. Gwyn's father out of allowing the girl to accept it. She stayed home, got married, had children. Althea was her first child.

At nine, Althea also adored football and softball. On the half-court concrete basketball court, though, she could more than hold her own with the boys. If they initially tried to exclude her, a few lay-ups convinced them to change their minds. If they were recalcitrant, she could beat them up. She was six feet tall by the end of the sixth grade and she was very good—at sports. Socially, she was very, very bad.

Althea was a proud member of a gang called the Scooters in junior high school, and she had trouble with everybody—her family, her teachers, her neighbors. "I used to be real wild," she said with a grin that showed her pointed, gleaming teeth. "I was drinkin', hangin' out, beatin' up people, that kind of wild. The code of our gang was to be tough." In the ninth grade, she was about to fail physical education, of all things, when her gym teacher made an unusual proposition. The teacher challenged her to a game of one-on-one. "She said if I beat her, she'd give me a passing grade. If not, I'd have to repeat the ninth grade all over again." Gwyn won. Basketball was sending her unmistakable signals.

She came close to ignoring them, however, at Amityville High School. "I'd go to school Monday, get suspended Tuesday," she recalled. Once again, an interested teacher, the basketball coach, intercepted her. "It took her a year, year and a half. I guess she played my psychiatrist, my mother, my friend and my coach all in one." The coach, Patricia Burns, acted on more than simply humanitarian instinct. The minute she saw the gangly fifteen-year-old shoot a few baskets, she said to herself, "we're gonna be champions for the next three years." Sure enough, they were. Burns did such a good job of channeling Gwyn's street-fighting

ability into playmaking that her star center won both ball games
and acceptable academic grades. Competing in softball and volleyball along with basketball, Althea drifted away from her
gang. She was awkward, suffering the humiliation of feeling like
a freak, of going to parties with boys a head shorter than she.
But sports gave her protection. "I wanted to feel needed,"
Althea admitted. "At least I knew I wasn't gonna be teased, not
to my face." By her senior year, college coaches were scouting
the Amityville wonder, who could grab every rebound and in
one game score 49 of the team's 58 points. She enrolled at
Queens College, where Lucille Kyvallos, the highly respected
coach, took over the dual role of mentor and guardian.

Overwhelmed at first by the new freedom of college, Gwyn
cut so many classes that she was in danger of flunking out.
Kyvallos settled her down. Gwyn tried to coast on her reputation
by skipping practices. Kyvallos suspended her from the team,
insisting she learn discipline. On the court, Gwyn was too much
of a "teddy bear"—worried that she might accidentally hurt
someone. Kyvallos taught her sporting aggressiveness. They had
long talks, and Kyvallos explained that if an opponent bounced
off her in a scramble for a loose ball, it was not Gwyn's problem.
By the end of her four years at Queens (she is lacking some
credits toward a degree) Gwyn emerged as a complex personality: a tiger on court, a mature young woman off. "I'm really
proud of her," Lucille Kyvallos said years later. "This girl turned
her life around."

She played professionally in Belgium for a few months, then
returned home. The WBL had just been established, and the
New York Stars welcomed her. She became an instantaneous
leader on the team, averaging 23.2 points a game, leading the
league in its first year with 17.3 rebounds per game. At twenty-
three, Althea Gwyn was the defensive anchor of the Stars, elbow-
ing her way under the boards, directing teammates, intimidating
opponents. It was a big leap for the once-ferocious Scooter of
Amityville.

According to some players, the pro game is far more "physical" than college basketball, and no one exudes its physicality more than Gwyn. "I seem to have the quality of making people afraid of me," she remarked, flashing a disarmingly innocent smile. "I'm not scared of being hit, because I've been hit all my life." Scowling like a Doberman, Gwyn demanded respect. When it was not forthcoming, opposing players soon discovered the consequences. In one game, an Iowa Cornet crowded Gwyn from the opening jump-ball. Annoyed, Althea kept shouting, "Doris, get off me!" But Doris stayed close a bit too long; Gwyn jammed an elbow between the Iowan's ribs, sending her to the floor. She was out cold for seven minutes.

Although the WBL had its reverses (several teams including New York went out of business) and was unable to draw big crowds, its players were grateful for the opportunity to earn money playing the game they loved. The good feeling was reflected back by men like Dean Memminger. "I don't coach girls, I coach athletes," the Stars coach would say, paying them the highest compliment of all.

In amateur basketball, the most ballyhooed contest of recent years was held not at Madison Square Garden, but at the Scope arena in Norfolk, Virginia, before ten thousand wildly partisan fans. The game pitted the Russian national women's team, acknowledged as the world's finest, against Old Dominion, the American collegiate champions. The pivotal U.S. star was a white, Jewish, redheaded girl who grew up not too many miles on Long Island from Althea Gwyn. Her name was Nancy Lieberman and she was out to prove it could become as recognizable some day as Larry Bird's.

Nancy Lieberman presaged a new era in women's basketball. Her one-time teammate on the New York Chuckles, J. T. Thomas, five feet three inches, embodied the first generation of small, fast guards. Lieberman, at five feet ten inches, was also a guard, not only taller, but faster. Lieberman excelled on both offense and defense. She could snake inside for a lay-up or shoot from the corners, snap a pass to one teammate while feinting toward another, steal, rebound, run—and promote sales of season tickets. Barely twenty-one years old, still in college, she was crowned by coaches and writers alike as undisputed ruler of her domain—the first truly complete female player. She had no qualms about playing "hot dog" or "dirty"; intimidation was among the first lessons she had learned in the schoolyards of Harlem, where she perfected her technique. Besides, by Nancy's senior year (1979–80), all the really good college players were "physical."

Furthermore, Lieberman did not hope for recognition—she worked for it. No single person could put women's basketball on the sports map the way Billie Jean King had tennis. But Nancy had an unswerving vision of her own role. It was a vision that crystallized after a typically tomboy childhood, with its classic rebellion against adult strictures. Lieberman was no ghetto child like Althea Gwyn. Yet her early years were unhappy enough for her to see basketball, too, as her salvation.

Lieberman was born in Brooklyn but raised in nearby Far Rockaway, a section of Queens. Her parents were divorced when she was small. She rarely saw her father, a real-estate man, whose approval she craved. She fought constantly with her mother, a sincere Jewish mom who only wanted her second child to play with dolls, be feminine, marry a nice Jewish boy and maybe become a nurse or a secretary. Nancy, however, lived in the playground and as an adolescent referred to herself as "Mr. Tough Guy." If she wasn't bullying some unsuspecting boy into one-on-one basketball, she was scooping up grounders in softball. Once, in desperation, her mother punctured her basketball with a screwdriver; Nancy stormed out and got more balls. Another time, Nancy announced she was off to Harlem to play a night game. "You can't go to Harlem!" her mother yelled. Nancy scampered out the door and outran her mother to the subway station.

Admiring black teammates on the Chuckles in Harlem gave the redhead from Far Rockaway the nickname "Fire." She could penetrate the defense to get to the basket and she could mesmerize an opponent by dribbling with what seemed like six hands.

Competitive? "If we were playing blackjack, if we were flipping pennies, I'd want to beat you," Lieberman said. "If you're aggressive and assertive, people pay attention."

Except for sports, high school was a trial for Nancy. Later, her mother would watch her play basketball wearing a glassy-eyed but proud stare, as if she were thinking, "that's *my* daughter?" Earlier, though, Nancy's family made no bones about the fact that they felt she was wasting her life. "They would say, 'you're not gonna grow up to be anything.' And here I am, going to college on a scholarship, flying around the world, winning awards, winning championships, getting exposure. Now I hear, 'Nancy, we've been behind you all along, we think you're super, can we have two tickets for the game at Madison Square Garden.' Well, the hell with them," she laughed, tentatively. "They caused me a lot of grief. I wasn't stealing, or taking drugs, or sleeping on corners. I was doing something enjoyable and healthy. *Now*, they think it's all right. *Now*, it's nice to be a woman athlete."

Luckily, she had a best friend who sided with her when no one else would—the first baseman on their softball team. Nancy, a shortstop, had such a strong arm that when she whipped a ball across the diamond, most first basemen (and the fans sitting behind her) would instinctively duck. Barbara Wood didn't; she simply refused to catch a ball unless Nancy threw it well. Nor did she tell Nancy she was crazy. "Just do what you want to," she kept urging her friend. Nancy accepted a basketball scholarship to Old Dominion, comfortably distant from her Far Rockaway home, while Barbara won an academic scholarship to Adelphi in New York. They visited often during college, and Barbara never hesitated to criticize Nancy, no matter how much applause her friend got in the ODU fieldhouse.

Actually, she did not garner the applause easily. There was plenty of the "playground rat" left in Lieberman when she entered ODU, tucked away in the Tidewater area of Virginia. "I was very strong-headed," Lieberman reminisced. "It got to a point where if you said 'red,' I'd say 'blue.' My freshman and sophomore years I was very egotistical, very cocky, 'cause I was defensive. That was my way of protecting myself. I came out of high school labeled Olympian [she was the youngest member of the 1976 team in Montreal], Bionic woman, the greatest. It was very hard. I had more publicity before I ever put on a uniform at Old Dominion than anyone! They were ready to retire my number before I ever played a game. Every time my teammates opened the newspaper, there was my face. They didn't understand me, I didn't understand them." As her college career progressed, Nancy acquired a trace of a southern accent and an inner security she had never known before. The victories she helped ODU collect, culminating in the national championship in 1979, cemented a new friendship with her teammates. "I grew up, I think," she said one day in the middle of her senior year, a mischievous look in her blue eyes.

Along the way, she majored in marketing. With coaches and teammates, she made the rounds of local rotary clubs, luring local people to games with free tickets, begging them to let the ODU women show how terrific they were. In her freshman year, a lot of listeners laughed. By her senior year, four thousand fans would be standing in line in the snow outside the ODU fieldhouse to buy tickets to a Lady Monarchs' game. "It's just a matter of time," Lieberman said confidently, just before her college career ended. "Basketball is not a fad. It's gonna go. It's in the limelight. All the publicity I get, it reflects on my teammates and my sport."

But there would always be a touch of the playground rat in Nancy Lieberman's character. In freshman training camp, someone dared her to push the head coach, who had a reputation for being stern, into the swimming pool. Nancy sauntered over to the coach, pretending to admire her watch. When the coach handed it to her to examine, Nancy nudged her into the pool, fully clothed. Even the coach had to laugh. By Lieberman's senior year, although she was passing behind her back less and giving up the ball more to her teammates, she was still irrepressible. She got herself a hot Chevy Camaro to cruise around in, and, as

she liked to tell people, "I'm leading the league in speeding
tickets!" A new nickname also had been bestowed on the redhead known as "Fire" in Harlem. Her Virginia friends hailed her
as "Super-Jew."

6

THE LABORATORY: DAREDEVILS

Daredevil is a risky term. Hearing it, we think of people who deliberately expose themselves to dangers either beyond their capacity or potentially fatal. We think of stunt men and women, of skydivers, of Philippe Petit walking a tightrope between the two World Trade Center towers, of Evel Knievel, of the demolition derby. Most of us react negatively. The stunts are silly, the odds long, the compensation small. These people are show-offs, clowns. They are not serious.

Daredevil women are, of course, risk-takers. But some are mighty serious about what they do, and doubly careful. A handful of daredevils of both sexes have performed "stunts" so glorious that it made them into heroes, such as Charles Lindbergh and Amelia Earhart. What private satisfaction daredevils derive from their stunts often is what counts most to them, not competition, money or applause. Their inner-directed attitude is part of what separates them from competitors in dangerous sports, like Janet Guthrie. Also, they thrive on escalating risk, long after they have proved themselves, which separates them from one-time amateur daredevils such as the Outward Bounders.

They do share similar emotions with ordinary women. Daredevils often commit themselves to their activity *despite* the danger, not because of it. Danger then lifts them to a higher emotional peak, and it is there that the satisfaction swells. In many ways, their motivation resembles that of the Annapurna mountaineers. Like climbers, daredevils usually dislike the word "daredevil" because, as experienced risk-takers, they prepare thoroughly enough to enter a self-defined safety zone once they begin their "stunt." For example, to a trained diver, a double-somersault half-twist high dive into a small swimming pool is risky, but hardly life-endangering; an untrained diver could crack his or her head on the edge of the board attempting only a single somersault. If you are Janet Guthrie, you can take a Champ car through a racing oval easily at one hundred miles per hour; if you are a Sunday driver, you could easily spin out and crash on the first turn.

As women progress from jogging, to game-playing, to vacation adventuring, to professional sports, the logical next step can be physical thrill-seeking. Scuba diving is a borderline "thrill" sport, hang gliding, a central one. Sky diving, white-water rafting and ice climbing all fall into the same broad category. In 1970, there was not one "serious" high-flying female hang glider. By the decade's end, there were an estimated twenty-five or more. Thrill-seekers, daredevils—however we label them—are multiplying as the horizons for women expand.

It is mostly a twentieth century phenomenon. In the American daredevil sweepstakes, there never has been a woman to rival the number one position of the legendary pilot who was first dubbed "Lady Lindy": Amelia Earhart.

Amelia Earhart spent her professional flying life—and lost it—trying to live down the suggestion that her first historic flight was a mere stunt in which she was just a passenger. Opening her career as a true daredevil, she ended it as a larger-than-life hero, a mystery, a role model.

Earhart was born in 1898 in Kansas. Like Dorothy in *The Wizard of Oz* she took to the air to escape the humdrum flatness of the Middle West. In her pre-Atlantic flight days, she was a daredevil barnstorming pilot who made flying more of a show business than a commercial one. She was "discovered" by a press agent at the age of thirty in 1928, when it seemed that her flying days were over. A wealthy woman named Amy Guest longed to become the first woman to fly across the Atlantic, but she was deterred by her family. Guest, who owned the plane, sought a substitute of her own sex, who would be a passenger; the plane would actually be piloted by a man. Struck by Earhart's resemblance to Lindbergh, the press agent enlisted Amelia with the "Lady Lindy" hook already in mind.

Earhart knew, as she made the flight, that she was rather a fraud. It didn't stop her from being thrilled, and she expressed her excitement at one point in a wonderfully female phrase: "I am getting housemaid's knee kneeling here gulping beauty," she wrote, crouched behind the pilot. Amelia became an instant celebrity. Few knew that embarrassment with her initial role motivated her to smash flying records with her *own* hands on the controls.

Deeply romantic, she stirred romanticism in others. After she disappeared, Walter Lippmann, the leading political pundit of the day, observed:

> The best things of mankind are as useless as Amelia Earhart's adventure. They are things that are undertaken . . . because someone, not counting the costs or calculating the consequences, is moved by a love of excellence, a point of honor, the compulsion to invent, or to make or to understand. . . . They have in them the free and useless energy [that] cannot be . . . weighed by the standards of utility or judged by its social consequences. It is wild and free. . . .

Lippmann's elegy could be the perfect epitaph not just for Earhart, but for adventurers like the Annapurna climbers Alison Chadwick and Vera Watson.

Even though feminism languished in the years following her disappearance in 1937, Earhart's star never dimmed. Rumors circulated that she had been on a secret spy mission for President Roosevelt. There is no evidence that was so, but the rumors did nothing to tarnish her luster. In the sixties and afterward, Earhart was quickly enshrined in the pantheon of feminist heroes. *Ms. Magazine* put her photo on a cover; inside, Pete Hamill wrote of his daughter's fascination with the Earhart legend; Judy Chicago inscribed her name on the floor tiles of her "Dinner Party" sculpture; Joni Mitchell celebrated her in song.

Earhart deserved the adulation. When she wed G. P. Putnam in 1931, she wrote an informal marriage contract, long before such documents were in vogue. The contract said they could have an "open" marriage (though it didn't use that phrase). "Please let us not interfere with each other's work or play," she wrote. "I may have to keep some place where I can go to be by myself now and then, for I cannot guarantee to endure at all times the confinements of even an attractive cage."

Considering her fame, the most astonishing thing about Earhart was that she did *not* spawn a flock of daring female flyers who would then take over as pilots or executives in the post-World War II commercial aviation boom. Her contemporaries, such as Jacqueline Cochran—a spirited friend and competitor of Earhart's—helped organize the two-thousand-member WASPs. (The Women's Airforce Service Pilots flew important military noncombat missions during World War II.) But, as with so many professions infiltrated by women in wartime, men reasserted their supremacy in civilian flying after their military duty was over. Jacqueline Cochran herself became better known for her cosmetics line, and the Earhart name lived on most visibly as a brand of luggage.

Will the name Nyad (Greek for "water nymph") mean something to daredevils or feminists years from now? Will it be a swimwear collection, a condominium complex in Florida? Whatever, the woman who carries that name so proudly—even though Nyad is the name of her stepfather, not her natural father—is bent on securing her place in history. Pete Hamill made the point that Earhart "worked on being a hero." A half-century later, no one has worked harder at that task than Diana Nyad.

Nyad wrote her name in record books as a swimmer of marathons, one of the hardest and dullest endurance sports. She single-handedly transformed it into a daring event. Imbued with the quest for heroic goals, she chose her swims and promoted them with a hustle that was impossible to ignore. "I am an extremist," she proclaimed (as if there were any question). And she could spin intricate webs of philosophy about her obsession, entwining friends, reporters and television crews in the process, even though her "feat" was to dip one arm after the other in the ocean, hour after hour after hour. She has approached each swim with an intelligent, infectious hype that is captivating.

Her first big splash was her record-breaking swim around Manhattan island in 1975. When reporters asked, before she dove into the sludge off East 89th Street, what her aim was, she answered, "fame and fortune," a quote guaranteed to win the hearts and microphones of any journalist. Later, she pointed out that the Manhattan swim was one of the easier ones she had done, but she gleefully accepted the reward. "Twice! I made the New York *Times* front page twice!" she crowed, with the savvy of a candidate in a tight primary race.

Actually, Nyad never did conquer the English Channel, never swam in the Olympics, never completed the Cuba-to-Florida marathon. For the first quarter-century of her ambitious life, she was just another Fort Lauderdale kid to whom the ocean was a second home. Her earliest victories were won in pool races, swimming laps in lanes like anyone else. (The mantel of the bedroom her mother still keeps for her in Fort Lauderdale is ringed with trophies.) Not until she was eliminated from the 1968 Olympic tryouts by an untimely illness at sixteen did she take a second look at the marathon swimmers she had always regarded as blobs of blubber.

She was trained in the early sixties, when Olympic-minded coaches first began breeding early-teen automatons via mindless hours of pool time. Diana hardly needed encouragement; she was a glutton for discipline. Her description of herself as a child reveals a spine of Teutonic zeal, softened by a layer of Latin romanticism. When her high-school swim team came down with a bronchial infection, the coach told everyone to stay in bed and take Vitamin C. Diana awoke the next morning as usual at 4:30 and climbed a fence in order to get into the locked gym pool. Her drive had what she came to believe was a terrible effect on her younger brother, "a skinny little intellectual, not a macho kid," and an inhibiting one on her younger sister. As the eldest, she would order them around, demanding that they obey her rigid schedule. If they protested, Diana would become "a dictator, and beat them up, either physically or verbally." Her brother later chose to be a full-time religious mystic. Her sister got married, had children and became a homemaker. Nyad's adoptive father, a Greek "macho type, a con man" involved in real estate, bolted the family when Diana was twelve. (She did not learn until the night of her high-school graduation about her natural father, whom her mother divorced when Diana was two and whom she never met.) Diana had once ended a dinner-table confrontation with Nyad by dumping a salad bowl in his lap. In her view, until she was nearly thirty years old, she "didn't believe in any sort of compromise, whether it was in friendships, relationships, and certainly not in my ambitions."

She was also an industrious student of literature and philosophy. An early hero was George Sand, the French novelist. "She wore men's suits and she smoked cigarettes and she had lovers among all the interesting men in Europe. Those ballsy type of women appealed to me. It was hard to have a man as a hero. I tried having Jim Thorpe for a hero when I was much younger, but I realized it was different," Diana recalled. She dedicated her autobiography to her mother, "my first hero," but what she admired was not so much her mother's life but her character, her steadfastness and ethics. (Her mother, a Frenchwoman, is still

Diana's biggest supporter, sheltering her in Florida when she trains there.)

At the same time that Diana was a reader, a jock and "an animal for training," she was a complete daredevil. In high school, on a dare, she jumped off a canal bridge near her home that was many meters higher than the highest Olympic diving board. She had to be fished out of the canal, half-conscious, by incredulous friends. For kicks, in her freshman year at Atlanta's Emory University, she leaped out of a fourth-floor dorm window with an open parachute on, nearly breaking both legs. She got a kick out of it all right—a kick out of school. As a young adult, she terrorized friends by driving at night the wrong way on freeways at one hundred miles an hour, while cars coming toward her scattered like frightened cockroaches. Even now, she will deliberately stand next to ornery characters on the New York subway at 4 A.M. and will spit at a sidewalk Lothario who mutters obscenities at her.

She nevertheless was a keen student at Lake Forest College in Illinois, the only place that would accept her after the Emory fiasco. She majored in comparative literature and made Phi Beta Kappa in her junior year. "If I wanted to be good at something," she said, "there was no such thing as a day off."

Although a love affair taught Nyad some forms of compromise, the two extreme sides of her personality—the Teutonic and the Romantic—remained. She would train six months of the year on land and six in the water to keep her standings as a marathon swimmer and as a top-ranked amateur squash player. Along the way, she put in long hours playing the clarinet, got entangled in consuming relationships, took hallucinogenic drugs to explore her unconscious, kept a diary of her dreams and memorized the poetry of the German Romantic writer Rilke. (In her teenage years she would barricade herself in the bathroom and have imaginary conversations with the poet.)

In short, Nyad was a bundle of charming contradictions. She was one of those rare athletes who openly embraced celebrity: "I want a filled stadium," she said. Yet she pursued celebrity in marathon swimming, knowing full well that while it might be the national pastime of Egypt (fans line the Nile to cheer competitors) it was a national yawn in her home country. No matter; she had the talent, the physique and the endurance for practice that ordinary mortals would regard as masochistic. That was enough.

For years before her name made the *Times'* front page, Nyad traveled the world, participating in swims in the exotic waters of the Indian Ocean, South America, Africa. But the publicity she reaped from her Manhattan swim changed things. (She had moved to New York to do postgraduate work at New York University, eking out a living as a part time bartender in some of the city's raunchier gin mills.) She saw, at last, a way to end a swimming career that was growing stale and earn herself that mythic "filled stadium" to boot.

The way was the Cuba swim—an unheard-of one hundred and thirty miles. Protected from sharks by an underwater cage, accompanied by an America Cup navigator and an NBC television crew including former Olympic swimmer Donna de Varona as commentator, Nyad set out from a beach near Havana in August, 1978 to compel sports fans everywhere to take notice.

The swim failed, but Diana succeeded. The seas were so choppy that after forty-one hours of nonstop swimming, a remarkable achievement in itself, she was miles off course, seasick, and headed in the general direction of the Yucatan.

And she was a household name.

Still, Diana was not ready to write an end to her epic until she devised a more dramatic finale. The following spring, she returned to her mother's home in Fort Lauderdale to resume pool practice. It was rolling the stone once again up the hill. After two months of indoor workouts, she moved to the Royal Biscayne Hotel, a beach resort that she had talked into providing her with a suite for herself and her trainer, plus rooms for visiting aides. In October, she announced, she would make her second attempt at the Cuba-to-Florida swim. With the help of a Washington-based middleman, she had received permission from the Castro government to use its shores as a takeoff point again. She had signed with a new manager. She was working the syndicated column and product-endorsement angles. An early $2,500 contribution from Dannon yogurt was all she needed to rev up the training mechanisms once more. The October swim from Cuba to Florida was estimated to be at least sixty-five hours. In early July, she was already putting in twice-weekly "long" swims of six and eight hours. When I visited her that month, she was on the eve of a progressively harder swim: eleven hours, from Key Biscayne north to Fort Lauderdale.

"Daredevil." Nyad frowned a moment, staring into space in her Royal Biscayne room. "Daredevil—that could have been a middle name for me," she said grudgingly. But, playing with other words—cocky, bravado, risk-taker, arrogant—she reckoned that "daredevil" was more descriptive of her as a teenager and young adult, when she was "immature." The "daredevil" tag did not take account of the months of discipline, much of it painful, that she coped with in order to pull off a single marathon swim, sharks or no. The more she pondered "daredevil," the less she liked its implications.

She *was* a show-off, she conceded. She hungered for the world to applaud her swimming feats. But that was not the root of her desire to perform the Cuba swim. "I am very reverent about it. A daredevil doesn't do a serious athletic event." How did she distinguish between that and a stunt? "Evel Knievel is a stunt. But Lindbergh was in the same vein as someone who wants to win Wimbledon. Climbing Mount Everest isn't a stunt." Knievel definitely had guts, but to what end? Lindbergh, however, "showed what could be done in aviation and for a person. I think that to show that a human being can swim the distance between Cuba and Florida is in keeping with the old primeval sense of the human capacity. It's having a long-term vision, like a Lindbergh." Or, she might have added, an Earhart.

But there was an inevitable follow-up question. Why another try at the Cuba swim? Hadn't Diana made her point with the first try, even though she never reached her land target? Margie Carroll, Nyad's twenty-one-year-old trainer, attempted to explain. "I knew as soon as it was over that she'd want to do it again. Diana and I knew she could make it." Symbolic efforts, "nice tries," added up to zero in Nyad's arithmetic. Moreover, she had the knack of inspiring people like Margie to adopt her extremist arithmetic as their own. Margie was a student who had met Nyad while at Barnard College, where Diana was coach of the swim team for two years. A graduate of the Bronx High School of Science (perhaps the most highly rated public high school in New York) and an economics major at Barnard, Margie was a faithful follower, but not a slavish one. She had acted as trainer on the first Cuba swim, and had put off another year of college when Diana asked her to play the same role the second time. Her principal duty was to keep Nyad company in a boat on the ocean swims. At the hotel, she had an adjoining room. A true city kid, Margie spent as little time as possible in the Florida sun, preferring to stay indoors watching television. She dressed like a latter-day Dead End kid, jeans slung low on nearly nonexistent hips, her hands jammed into the back pockets, swaggering rather than walking. Margie was physically strong, and like many swimmers, including Nyad, she worked out regularly on Nautilus equipment. But in terms of mental strength, she insisted she was no match for her mentor.

Had she tried to talk Nyad out of the second attempt of the Cuba swim? Margie chuckled. It was like asking Gunther Gebel-Williams if he had tried to coax his circus tigers into skipping dinner. "You can't talk her into, or out of, anything," Margie said with finality.

On the humid Saturday morning chosen for the Key Biscayne-Fort Lauderdale tune-up, Diana reigned over the breakfast table in plaid pajamas. With her were Margie and two male friends who had flown in from New York just to accompany her in Margie's rubber dinghy. Steve Germansky, a husky lawyer, had helped on the abortive Cuba swim. Stu Goldstein, the number two professional squash player in the United States, was on his first venture in Nyad's game. Between bites of scrambled eggs, orange juice, Roman Meal toast and milk, Nyad was relatively quiet, meaning she talked a half-mile instead of a mile a minute.

"I feel nervous. I didn't sleep well last night. It's not a pleasurable experience, swimming eleven hours in the ocean fast," she said. She toyed with a jar of Phillips motor oil that was on the table.

"A little oil to grease you up?" inquired Stu.

"I drink a quart of it a day," she joked.

Margie, who would crew the dinghy, packed an ice chest—a six-pack of ginger ale, sandwiches for the three crew members, a stash of vanilla yogurts for Nyad's water feedings. "I don't want to build up any debts today," said Diana, standing and windmilling her arms. She was referring to energy debts. "I want to eat at two and a half hours, four and a half hours, six, seven, nine and then ten. Can you remember that?" she asked the men. (Much has been written about how marathoners of any kind handle food right before a race. These discussions are about as interesting to the layman as a baby's feedings are to childless adults.) Diana changed in the bathroom, slipping on two tank-type swimsuits.

Her hotel room could have been mistaken for that of a newspaper correspondent rather than the typical athlete. Strewn about were a portable typewriter, a week's worth of newspapers, piles of manuscript pages, nautical charts, *The Powers That Be* by David Halberstam, and, on the chest of drawers, Thomas Mann's *The Magic Mountain*. (Nyad rereads the latter every few years.) The only sports clues were a ten-speed bicycle, a swimming kickboard, and a Mickey Mouse hat from Disney World with "Diana" stitched in script across the front.

Outside a cabaña on the beach, Margie and the men inflated the dinghy. Diana smeared Vaseline on the skin around the edges of her suit. "Just for chafing," she said. The water temperature was about eighty-five degrees, so she would not need the heavier grease swimmers use for warmth in water like that of the English Channel.

"The breeze is right," she rambled on in her contralto voice, which always sounded on the verge of a head-cold. "South-easterly. It's almost continually that way this time of year. That was what was wrong about the Cuba swim in the summer. You want a westerly breeze for that." As she tucked her short brown hair under her cap and adjusted her goggles, she jumped along to small talk about Superstars, Gloria Steinem, Key Biscayne. She was still talking as she strode toward the waves. "Have a nice day," she called over a shoulder. She waded up to her hips, fiddling with the goggles. Then, in one graceful motion, she did a standing dive into the surf and began the methodical two-miles-per-hour crawl stroke, head cranking left toward the dinghy. It was 8:05, five minutes off Margie's planned starting time and soon the slap, slap, slap of her arms was lost in the whirring of the boat's Evinrude.

Another woman and I then drove two cars to the Nyad family home, a large ranch house in a wealthy area of Fort Lauderdale near the famous oceanfront strip. Diana's mother was away. We were to wait until Margie collected Diana out of the water, beached the dinghy and called for us to pick them up. The point of the swim was simply for Diana to put in eleven straight swimming hours. Fort Lauderdale had been chosen as the target because both Diana and Margie were bored with other practice routes. If, at eleven hours, Diana had not reached Fort Lauderdale, the plan was for her to quit and ride the rest of the way in the boat.

Margie had not called by 7:30 P.M. We knew Diana must be out of the water, but what if the boat were in trouble? An hour later, with darkness closing in, the phone rang.

We reached the beach in a few minutes. Any notions that this was all precision evaporated at the comic sight before us. Steve, Stu, Margie and Diana were shivering in swimsuits in the dusk. They were ignored by the hundreds of cars on the strip filled with beer-swilling teenagers who apparently still believed that Fort Lauderdale was *Where The Boys Are.* The wet quartet hopped up and down on bare feet, waving frantically. The dinghy, its pontoons now deflated, rested on the sidewalk. I looked around in vain for Paula Prentiss and Jim Hutton.

Diana, with a T-shirt pulled over her suits, was puffy around the face and her teeth were chattering. It was always like this, she sputtered, since even an eighty-five-degree sea was not as warm as her 98.6-degree body temperature. They had been delayed because the water, smooth as glass near Biscayne, had become rough further north and the tide had turned against them. Her teeth clenched, Diana told of having to change her feeding schedule, of feeling ill after eight and a half hours but regaining enough strength to "sprint" the final minutes. Although subdued physically, she was mentally hyperactive. I could barely imagine anyone walking under her own power after eleven hours of steady swimming, much less providing a full commentary on the trip afterward, but Diana was doing both. She marched into her mother's house, immediately turned off the air-conditioning and stepped into a long steamy shower.

For dinner, Diana, Stu and Steve slapped together sandwiches while Diana continued her nonstop talking jag. She kidded Stu about getting seasick, but her comments returned, again and again, to the mishaps of the first Cuba swim.

With no trace of malice, Nyad related the story as an incredible tale of mismanagement, laziness and neglect of her wellbeing by the oceanic experts she had brought to Cuba. Her navigator, she contended, knew the sea was choppy and unsafe the night before she stepped into the water. She had specifically asked him to do what any responsible navigator would—to sail at least ten miles out and take his own reading of the conditions. Later she had learned that he never bothered to make that check. Instead, he told her the choppiness would disappear further from shore. On that bad advice, she made the mistake of trying her big swim on a totally hopeless day.

But there was more. The navigator had visited her at her Manhattan squash club months afterward with another story. The night before the swim, he said, Cuban officials informed him that the Nyad party would be allowed only one more day in Cuba, no matter what. That was why he had let her swim under such terrible conditions. Nyad's own theory was that the navigator felt so guilty over his failure to check the seas that he had concocted the "get-out-of-Cuba" cover-up. I found the entire thing shocking. For all her public relations, Nyad's swims seemed put together with the nautical equivalent of spit and baling wire.

After she finished this yarn, Diana grabbed a jar of sour pickles. "You know, until about a year ago, I never knew these things started out as cucumbers. I mean, I thought they just grew like this in someplace slimy and salty." She grinned at her own naïveté.

For risk-takers, the afterglow of achieving a goal (such as swimming eleven hours) keeps adrenalin flowing long beyond the end of the activity. It is the same as the "cool-down" a distance runner must go through after a race, or the restlessness that affects an intense artist, writer, businesswoman or anyone at the completion of a concentrated task. When Nyad's adrenalin finally did stop pumping, she slept for twelve hours. The following day, she did nothing more vigorous than drive back to Key Biscayne. Her body became "broken down" during an endurance workout. Regardless of how rested she might feel, she had to permit it to regenerate itself. She also had to eat to regain the eight or ten pounds she'd lost during the swim. The following weekend she would do an even longer tune-up. All this, week in, week out, for one more shot at that treacherous strait from Cuba to Marathon Key.

Masochism! That's how I viewed Nyad's training before meeting her. Not the whips-and-chains kind, but . . . didn't one have *some* enjoyment of pain in order to throw herself into such a regimen at thirty, well past the age when an athlete is supposed to know better? Was a marathoner, a daredevil, a show-off also a bit of a masochist? Was that entwined with her love of discipline? Her obsession with will power reminded me of Nietzsche. "Yeah," she agreed, "I guess there's some of that in me." The two personality traits she identified in herself most strongly were courage and discipline—the latter as an end in itself. "I am often caught up in doing things that are beyond what I need to do, but want to go through it just to see if I can make myself. There is good pain and there is bad pain," she continued. "A fine line. I wouldn't want to burn myself. I try to stay away from needles. But the kind of punishment you take on a swim—the eleven hours, for instance. It's true that I'm only doing it to get ready for the Cuba swim. But it was interesting in itself in that the mind goes through so many variations of wanting to quit. It's only trying to help you! It actually hurts. After about the fifth hour, I constantly have lulls of thinking, 'What am I doing this for? I'm going to get out! I'm going to pull a tantrum!' Very manipulative stuff. If I get in the boat, who is going to throw me back in? It's my choice whether I quit. I found that it was interesting to push through those few barriers."

Her torment was comparable to what she had seen professional writers go through, although she would not label it masochistic. "Masochism has no positive end to it." Her swims were only temporarily painful. "The physical pain is going to go away," she reasoned, "the mental pride and the emotional feeling is going to stay with me my whole life. The body heals."

Indeed, hers did. Several weeks afterward, Diana tried swimming from Bimini in the Bahamas to Palm Beach, both as a tune-up and as a reminder to the public that she was still in there, plugging. For twenty-nine miles, over twelve and a half hours, she was on course. Suddenly, a Portuguese man-of-war, whose huge, nasty tentacles can paralyze a person with their sting, nipped her on the neck, arms and back, disabling her completely and aborting the swim. The swelling from the stings had barely receded when she tackled the same swim again two weeks later. She completed the gutsy eighty-nine-mile haul from Bimini to Juno Beach, Florida in twenty-seven hours, thirty-eight minutes. She had no protection against stings except for a coat of latex paint that peeled away from her skin early, and several volunteers who kicked underwater ahead of her, beating off schools of jellyfish with sticks. The feat won Nyad another "first" and another photo on the front page of the New York *Times*.

Meanwhile, she had dramatically increased the risk offered in the planned second Cuba swim. She made the decision not to use an antishark cage.

Nyad maintained that it was not bravado but a matter of comfort. In open seas she bounced around so much that she often hit the sides of the cage, a wire basket beneath her attached on one end to the boat she swam alongside. There had been a point in her life when her attitude was, "screw the sharks, they'll have to get out of my way." But she had grown "mature" enough to worry about them slightly. The compromise was an antishark force field, an electronic device that would not harm Nyad but would repel sharks entering its path.

She did not get to use it in October, 1979. Despite the success of the Bimini run, Diana ran out of money by late summer. She vowed to try again or attempt instead a marathon across the Aegean Sea. Whether she accomplished either seemed almost a moot issue. Nyad was a classic case, doing what she did best: upping the ante on daring.

The first impression Mary Kaknes makes is that she could be Diana Nyad's opposite. She is as unknown as Nyad is famous, as blond and fair as Nyad is dark and tanned. Her high-pitched voice is placid in contrast to Nyad's throaty "guess-what-happened-to-me!" delivery. Her speech is laced with broad New England A's, her manner that of a plain-Jane, twenty-eight-year-old widow who runs a shop to support her two children. About the only thing the two women would appear to have in common is their Greek ethnicity.

But these strangers are sisters under the skin. The daring that Diana performs on the sea, Mary exhibits in the sky. She is a professional hang glider.

Hang gliding has been tagged by the media as the fastest-growing "thrill" sport in America. More than twenty-five thousand persons are now estimated to be entrusting their lives regularly to the aerodynamic swoops of multicolored Dacron kites. Not coincidentally, it is also perhaps the riskiest. In 1974 alone, according to the count of the gliders' own national association, forty-three people were killed in gliding accidents, although the association said better equipment and instruction brought that number down to fourteen in 1978.

Women were involved right from the start of the boom. But there were very few in the early seventies and there are very few now. Still fewer make their living through gliding, as Mary Kaknes does. With a male partner, she runs one of the best-known glider sales and instruction shops in the Northeast, Aerial Techniques in Ellenville, New York. She has also attended numerous competitions, weekend get-togethers and beer blowouts at which glider pilots from California to Cape Cod convene. Glider pilots form a close-knit fraternity. Reputations get around —who is brave, who is crazy, who knows wind, whose opinion you can trust. Mary has a very good reputation.

It is a well-earned one. You cannot appreciate the terror of hang gliding until either you do it, or you stand on top of a hill next to someone who is in the act of doing it. On a rain-soaked lump of a hill in northern New Jersey one afternoon, with winds so chancy that the wind socks and tell-tails planted at strategic intervals fluttered in schizoid disarray, I stood next to Mary Kaknes as she prepared to fly. Of the two of us, she was undoubtedly the more frightened.

Hang gliders are "sneaky-macho" types, and Mary was no exception. She spoke lyrically of the freedom of nonmotorized flight, the oneness with nature, the ecstasy of thermals. But she also worked into the conversation every detail of every broken bone she had suffered in pursuit of these ideals.

Hang gliding, for Mary Kaknes, brought into harmony a rebel attitude harbored in the face of strict parents, and her love of athletics. She was born in Greece, coming to the United States at age eight. After graduating from high school in Lowell, Massachusetts, where her father was a painting contractor, she chose marriage over four years of premed at college. "Greek fathers like to have their daughters bring home Greek men with mustaches, and that's what I did," she said as we sat in a car in New Jersey, waiting for the rain to stop so the gliding exhibition could begin. But her husband turned out to be just as adventurous as she. With him, the once-sheltered girl who had not been allowed to bicycle or even swim learned motorcycling, skiing, and, finally, hang gliding. Along the way, she gave birth to two daughters in quick succession and her husband became a charter airplane pilot.

One day, they were watching *Wide World of Sports* on television. Gliders were soaring off cliffs in Hawaii. The sight gave Mary goosebumps. "What's that?" she asked. It was the most picturesque sport she had ever seen. The Kakneses, unfortunately, lived a continent and an ocean away from regions like Hawaii, where glider groups were easy to find. A full year later, Mary noticed an advertisement in *Popular Mechanics* for a $600 used glider. With ten equally intrigued friends, the Kakneses chipped in $50 apiece and bought the thing, not having a clue how to maneuver it.

A hang glider pilot can get killed on a hill as low as 7 feet. They started out on a hill of 1,200 feet. Almost every one in the group finished the first day of gliding by landing in the hospital.

That first time, Mary hooked herself in the kite, ran down the little hill a bit, was lifted straight up, and then plunged straight down 75 feet to hard ground. Damages: a concussion, a dislocated jaw, a small broken bone in the neck. Verdict: "I thought it was the greatest thing that ever happened to me," she said with no exaggeration in her voice.

Somehow, she knew this was to be her adventurous métier. "I figured that if I could get up the guts to do it again, it was for me. It had licked me right off the bat. I wanted to do it until I got it right." It was not the risk that hooked her, Mary emphasized. It was the thrill of those few seconds in the air, hearing nothing but whistling on the glider cables, the wind in her face. Retelling the story, she sat silent for a minute, twisting one of her long pony tails in her hand, peering dreamily through thick glasses at the hill she would ascend as soon as the rain stopped.

Three months after her maiden flight, less than three months after being released from the hospital, Mary was back on the same hill. Each time she climbed to the top, her teeth chattered involuntarily. "I was scared to death," she giggled. So she retreated, kite in hand but feet still on the ground, to collect her lost daring. At last, a day arrived when she was tired of rolling the kite up the hill and back down again. She grabbed the control bar, ran, took off, flew for a few seconds, and smashed feet first into a boulder, spraining her ankle so badly she could not walk properly for a month.

Another three months passed. "I've got to do it!" her inner voice told her. This time, her iron determination was tempered by some preparation. She and her husband went to a few competitions, talked to people, read books, learned about the effect of terrain and clouds on wind, and all the rest. "You practically have to be a micro-meteorologist," she concluded. She hang glided regularly from then on everywhere in the Northeast, occasionally finding herself the only woman bunking in a dorm with twenty-five men. As a mother of two small children, she rationalized the risk she took by becoming what she regarded as a "supercautious" flier. Like the typical daredevil, she would not accept the idea of her sport as a deadly one *for her.* She would take off only under optimum conditions, and only in a kite already tested by someone else. Still, accidents happen. In one, she smacked her breasts against the control bar while coming in for a landing, causing a fibrocystic condition to flare up. It required surgery to correct. In 1978, her husband, then thirty-one years old, was killed in an airplane crash. Mary was left with little money, two daughters under the age of ten, and half-ownership of a glider shop in Ellenville, in which her husband had invested. She had never seen the town.

Had Mary Kaknes not been a "daredevil" personality, she might have stayed in Massachusetts, resewn her kites into pinafores and gone back to work as a laboratory technician. Instead, she moved to Ellenville, took her share of responsibility for the

shop, kept flying . . . and was about to teach her favorite sport
to her eldest daughter, now nine.

Like Nyad, Kaknes flatly refused the term "daredevil." "If I
thought it was too dangerous," she argued, "there's no way I'd
let my little girl fly. It can be just as natural as driving a car. If
that's being a daredevil, maybe we all are."

But, but . . . the mind sputters like a car engine that won't
turn over. Every other sentence out of her mouth was contradictory; didn't *she* almost kill herself the first time out? Even the
worst drivers don't usually do that badly. There is far less room
for error in flying as a mode of transportation than driving.
Would she snap herself into the bindings of a pair of skis for the
very first time and schuss down an advanced slope without instruction? Yes, she probably would. There are times when arguing with a risk-taker is no more fruitful than debating a Moonie.

The rain had let up. Pilots were trudging up the treeless New
Jersey hill, pushing their gliders ahead of them on the two
wheels at the bottom of the gliders' triangle control bar. The
wind socks and streamers flitted ever so slightly up the hill—a
hopeful sign. Soon, the first brave soul at its crest hunched his
shoulders through the control bar so the kite was resting on his
back, ran downhill a dozen steps as fast as he could, and was
lifted into the humid air by the wind catching his sails. He
soared for a few minutes, then descended slowly into the bog
100 feet below.

The hill was a beginners' one, somewhat like a novice slope in
skiing, except that the glider hill was steeper. As more pilots took
off, Mary's companion and Ellenville partner, a short, wiry man
named T.J. who had greater gliding experience, lifted his new
Moyes kite and flew a test flight. He crash-landed, unharmed,
while trying to make a U-turn too close to the ground. Everyone
hooted, laughing.

Mary felt the time was ripe. A student carried her new Seagull
glider up the hill for her, joining the line of big primary-color
birds awaiting their turns. (This glider weighed about forty

pounds. Neither Mary nor anyone else, male or female, turns down someone's offer to carry it up a hill.) The Seagull had never been tested, but Mary sensed its good feel. She slipped into a blue dacron harness that looked like a large, padded kitchen apron with extra ties around the thighs. The harness was to be hooked to the top of the kite so that she could hang prone, belly down, while flying. The prone position was the preferred one of late, because it gave the pilot more flexibility and stability. The old seated-harness position made the pilot ride like a child on a playground swing. Mary had learned to glide in the seated position; this would be her twelfth outing flying prone.

Halfway up the slope, she paused for breath. "This is the hardest part, especially if you smoke as much as I do," she said, having chain-smoked all morning. Reaching the top, she called to T.J. with a tinge of nervousness, "does this glider fly slow?"

"It's fine," he shouted back. "Just go with it, Mary!"

Her blond pony tails hung below her helmet like a white squaw's. She wore a plain white long-sleeved shirt, jeans, and old hiking boots. Mary stood for a minute at the top, inhaling and exhaling air deep into her lungs, fiddling with the harness and the control bar. She said nothing. T.J. silently tipped the front point of her glider upward until it was parallel with the ground. Mary's face was pale. She pulled the kite onto her shoulders, took a few frantic running steps . . . and she was off!

She sailed a couple of feet above the slope that was slowly dropping further away from her. "Fly straight, baby," T.J. whispered as if it were a prayer. Maneuvering the glider slightly downward by pushing the control bar down and toward her body, Mary did fly straight, for several long seconds. But when she tried to complete a right turn before landing, she lost the wind. The kite stalled before she could get her body adjusted so that her knees were bent and her heels were jutting out in the correct landing position. The glider flapped and fell quickly, and Mary landed (as most had before her) in a belly-flop.

Unhurt, she lugged the kite back across the open field to the mass of vans. "Should've reached for the down-tubes sooner," she was saying, "but I've only made one stand-up landing in twelve prone flights. It takes a lot of practice." T.J. gave her a congratulatory kiss anyway. The rain began again and everybody retreated to their vehicles until the weather improved.

Nearly an hour later, a twenty-year-old New Jerseyan, Penny Jacobsen, made an impressive flight in a prone harness staying aloft for nearly a minute, then making a smooth turn before landing on her midsection. Pounding happily on her instructor's back, she asked, "Did you see me? Did you see that turn?" To another pilot she boasted, "I got off real well and made a *turn*, my first flight in full harness!"

Penny was five feet eight inches and one hundred and forty-five pounds, among the heftier women at the gathering. She had taken a mere three lessons so far, along with her boyfriend. Scared? Not on your life, she insisted. Having raced Hobie-cats in the ocean and ridden 650-cc motorcycles, she was not going to let hang gliding intimidate her. "Hell, I haven't tasted the *real* thrill," she said, "like jumping off the edge of a cliff."

Penny and Mary had the identical philosophy: "I'm only gonna live once, so I might as well enjoy it." Mary's was formulated after her best friend died at the age of twenty-five, while pregnant, from cancer. That, and her husband's death, brought home a message Mary was still carrying. "I want to do whatever I can in the short time I have left," she said. "I don't ever want to say I wish I had done something when I was younger. I want to get enough out of every day. If I go, I don't want it to be 'natural causes.'"

With their cocky live-for-today stance, women glider pilots are modern versions of early aviators such as Earhart, the original "barnstormers" who flew stunts for the fun of it and for the glory of it. As for myself, I had never regarded my athleticism in the same class, nor had I ever had the extremist ambitions Nyad had. The one sport remotely connected to "daredevils" that I ever experimented with was rock climbing. There, however, safety devices for breaking one's fall were built in via the be-

layer. Besides, although rock climbing is risky, it was not terrifying to me. Scaling a rock seemed too logical to be categorized as
"thrill-seeking." The Outward Bound ropes course *was* terrifying, and I would not have deliberately sought to test myself
there.

So it was with trepidation—let's be frank, with fear—that I
ventured to Ellenville one weekend to learn hang gliding at
Mary's school. Standing beside her on the hill in New Jersey had
not been enough. I needed to feel which muscles quivered like
guitar strings before a person took those first steps on take-off. I
needed to see whether I would lose my lunch later, or my appetite first, whether lessons relax a pilot's sense of terror. I wondered what it really felt like to ride the wind on Dacron wings.

To begin, I saw what only the most daring pilots see: a high
cliff that was the Northeast's favorite runway for expert kite-
flying. It was an outcropping of the Shawangunk Mountains
1,000 feet above a flat valley and the Nevele Country Club
golf course. I also saw, in Mary's phrase, "half of what hang
gliding is all about—waiting for the wind." Upon our arrival it
was blowing straight downhill. Anyone who dashed off that runway under those conditions would smack into a stand of trees a
few hundred feet below. A group of pilots waited the entire afternoon, but the wind sock never bent anywhere but directly down
on a line with a Nevele sand trap. At sundown, the pilots, thoroughly frustrated, trudged back to their vans instead of flying.

The following day, Kim Sherman, a twenty-two-year-old instructor, promised that I could be airborne after four hours of
lessons. He drove not to the cliff, but to a 100-foot baby hill
in someone's backyard, a less frightening one than even the
little New Jersey hill from which Mary had flown. A dozen
intermediate students were setting up kites, though the wind
sock again drooped sorrily like a wilted flower. It was hot and
humid, not a perfect day for gliding, by any standard.

Kim emphasized that it was important to know what you were
doing and why. Once a pilot is in the air, he pointed out, "there's
no guy in a black-and-white shirt, no referee taking the ball

away from you, if you do something wrong." Nice analogy. I was
growing more petrified by the minute. As we set up a glider,
Kim noted that the only moving part would be the pilot. "Hang
gliding is a body falling through air, with a wind that converts
the falling movement into forward movement," he explained.
(Wasn't that Newton's law or something?) A glider is inherently
stable, he stressed, so that if its nose is pulled up by a wind draft
and the glider starts to stall, the nose will automatically try to
dip to interrupt the downward movement that the stall has
started.

The wealth of flying data that Kim packed into an hour and a
half was reassuring. Next, I climbed into a prone harness and
helmet and Kim suspended me from a "simulator," a rotating
metal gismo with a triangular control bar that gives some of the
feel of gliding. The prone position is superior to the seated one
because it makes it easier for the pilot to adjust the kite in the air
and offers less wind resistance. "Superman flies that way, so it's
got to be good," Kim said.

When he kicked away the wood step, leaving me to swing
from a carabiner (metal ring) as my hands gripped the horizontal part of the control bar, I felt more like Lois Lane getting herself into one of those foolish situations for which reporters have a
penchant. By pushing the bar out, I edged the nose of the imaginary kite above me upward, thus slowing it down. By pulling it
toward me, I was dipping the nose, picking up speed. A shift of
my body to the left, and I was making a left turn. It felt very peculiar. The simulator had the same relationship to gliding as the
steering wheel of a make-believe race car on a track projected on
a game-room screen has to actual driving.

After lunch, I was still scared, but willing. The wind was not. I
lugged the glider on my back, realizing how heavy a forty-five-
pounder felt before lift-off. But Mary and Kim, thinking of my
health and their reputation, decided that conditions were not
good enough for a beginner's flight. The intermediate students
on the hill were flying, or rather imitating Big Bird with a bad
case of arthritis. They were, in fact, demonstrating more varia-

tions of the Flying Belly Flop than I would have believed existed. Later, some experienced pilots risked one soaring trip off the high Shawangunk cliff, and *they* looked beautiful. I closed my eyes and imagined myself among them, the wind in my face, the roar of pure air past my ears, aloft and lost in the infinity of space.

I could have returned on a better wind day and completed my beginner's course. I never did.

There are some daredevils who do their capers primarily to pay the rent. Jeannie Epper, Hollywood's premier stuntwoman, thoroughly enjoyed crashing through glass as the "double" for television's "Wonder Woman" and sliding off the roof of a speeding car as the "double" for Charlie's latest Angel. But she has been bouncing around on movie horses for twenty-one years. Now thirty-nine, she has three children who themselves are professionals in the stunt business. Jeannie comes from the first family of the stunt world; both her parents and her five sisters and brothers have worked in the trade. In her best year, she might earn more than $30,000. "I'd like to be making more money with less bruises," she said seriously on a recent day off from *Charlie's Angels*.

It was a profession that her father, a Hollywood stuntman for forty-five years, did not urge her to enter. As a teenager, she was sent to a Swiss finishing school to learn to be "a lady." But even though she became one, falling off a horse was, for Jeannie Epper, well, as easy as falling off a horse. Older stuntwomen such as Patty Elder and May Boss were her idols. She could not stay away from the back lots. Soon, like the rest of her family, she was falling off horses for a living.

When Jeannie Epper slipped off her first saddle in 1959, there were few women in stunt work. Often, directors used stunt*men* in wigs to handle a fall down a flight of stairs supposedly happening to a woman. It took Jeannie, her sisters and women who followed to prove that "the ladies" were as capable as men (Kitty O'Neil, a deaf stuntwoman, is renowned for her driving and her "high falls"). Occasionally, Jeannie would give a director a "feminine" angle on a stunt—"a man who is shot at the top of a flight of stairs will just fall, while I'll react like a woman and scream more," she explained.

As adamant as she was about being "a professional," a wife and mother, Jeannie Epper owned up to the fact that she could have opted to be simply a dancer or a homemaker. But she always had the thrill-seeker inside her as well. Professionally, her job was to set up a stunt, make it look realistic, then walk away without a mark on her, even if she has been thrown off a car or simulated a fist fight in a saloon. Emotionally, however, each stunt was an "adventure," a sense of accomplishment, a perfect performance under pressure. "There's an ego that wells up, like when the crew claps at a good stunt," she noted. "I always say to myelf, 'go all the way, do the ultimate.' You gotta go for it. I get scared less than most people. It's a gift from the Lord—a sense of fearlessness. I don't like to think about a tough stunt beforehand. You can lay in bed the night before and say, 'I-can-I-can-I-can!' but what you're actually thinking is, 'can I *really* do this?'"

Jeannie found out early on that she *could* do it, sometimes without the anxiety the night before. When she became a born-again Christian a few years ago, the Lord helped, too. She would pray before every stunt, giving herself to God. "An awareness, a calmness comes over me. When you're in that corner and the lights are on you, you're there with the camera and the Lord. After I'm through, I thank Him." She defined her mental state as "crazy under control."

Like Mary Kaknes, who hang glided with her husband and then with her partner, Epper got a charge from working in tandem with her sisters and her pals. (She and two sisters had the pleasure of beating up Paul Newman in the movie, *Judge Roy Bean*. Jeannie elbowed him in the stomach; sister Stephanie feigned kicking him in the groin. The two of them kidded one another, saying if they slipped up, Joanne Woodward would never speak to them again. They did not slip up.) But unlike Mary Kaknes, who would be pleased to see her daughters hang glide, Jeannie Epper had conflicting emotions about her children performing stunts.

"My 'mother' side is protective, and on the other side I'm excited my daughter wants to follow in my footsteps," she said. "I know my kids know how to take care of themselves. And I want to make the work better for my daughter and people like her. I want them to be less hassled by coordinators, by directors."

The result was inevitable. That week, Jeannie was doubling for Charlie's newest Angel—and her eldest daughter, nineteen-year-old Eurlyne, doubled in the same episode for Jaclyn Smith. Jeannie's stunt was to flip herself off the top of a speeding car. Eurlyne's job was to stand motionless as the car aimed straight for her, and then bail out of the way at the last minute.

If Jeannie, whose only visible scars are stretch marks from bearing three children, was nervous about the welfare of her first-born, she did not show it on the set. When the director called for action, mother gave daughter a straightforward nod and told her, "you're on your own, kid!"

One measure of a daredevil is the emotion he or she feels when the daring act is done. An amateur who does something physically risky is likely to feel anxious before, frightened during, relieved and elated after. A true daredevil, however, experiences the elation in the midst of the act itself, and determines that this "rush" or "thrill" is worth the risk again. The enormity of the thrill far outweighs the fear. Even the terror of dying shrinks in the face of the mind-expanding insights the activity releases. When the elation wears off, depression can engulf the daredevil, a depression relieved only by the preparation for the next attempt.

Jacqueline Cochran had a standard answer for those who asked why she continued to take risks in flying. "I might have been born in a hovel, but I determined to travel with the wind and the stars," she said, revealing the romanticism that underlies most daredevils.

Earhart, before her fateful final trip, told anyone who would listen that she felt she had "just about one more good flight left." The implication was that she had no choice but to take it. And long before that, Earhart sensed that only by taking risks in a plane could she *become* herself. An accident might mean death, but not failure. In letters that were to be opened if she had died as Mrs. Guest's designated hitter across the Atlantic, Earhart articulated this notion brilliantly: "Even though I have lost, the adventure was worthwhile. Our family tends to be too secure. . . . I have tried to play for a large stake and if I succeed all will be well. If I don't, I shall be happy to pop off in the midst of such an adventure." An Earhart biographer declared, in more realistic terms, that within daredevils like her, there is "something addictive about glory."

Once is not enough. Adventure can be an end in itself. Self-discovery is the secret ingredient that fuels daring. Nyad's obsession with longer, more dangerous swims suggests many of these characteristics. Diana is a student of dream theory and the bi-lobed functions of the brain. During a long swim, she thinks one half of her brain falls asleep, while the other half keeps repeating, "one-thousand-one, one-thousand-two, I'm gonna make it, I'm gonna make so much money on my finish, I'm gonna break the world record, I'm the greatest, I don't care what the waves are." The nonrational side of her mind keeps her going. Occasionally, she has had hallucinations. On one long swim she suddenly began beating her arms around her head, convinced that giant birds were attacking her. She goes through cycles of "incredible highs, incredible lows" as her arms mechanically slap against the water.

For these reasons, she was able to say, a mere twelve hours after she had been pulled out of the sea on the aborted Cuba swim, "It was the greatest experience of my life, the furthest I ever pushed, the best I ever knew myself." In a more mellow mood, she was still unequivocally pleased she had made the attempt. "I knew that I was pretty tough before, and that I had a lot of willpower, but I had no idea that I had that much," she said. "I really impressed myself."

After twenty-one years, Jeannie Epper was still as proud as ever of her body and the stunts it could accomplish. "I feel pretty good for an old lady," she said with a chuckle, pointing out that she kept in shape with exercises and spent off hours playing softball for her church team. "I'm five-foot-eight and one hundred and twenty-five pounds, just like I was in school, and I can still put on an evening gown and look like a lady," she boasted. Competitive? "Oh, yes! I don't do something halfway. I don't want anything because I'm a woman. I want it because I'm good. I want to be the best."

The wellspring of self-esteem in daredevils rarely runs dry. They never appear to lose their nerve. More often, they lose their interest, or turn to another expression of the desire for daring. (Or they die. Dying, however, can signify a mistake brought on by the waning of interest. Dying can also be seen as the furthest extension of daring, not as failure. Cochran said of Earhart's disappearance: "One can mourn her loss but not regret her effort. Amelia did not lose, for her last flight was endless.") Even while training for the Bimini swim, Nyad was seeking a fresh outlet for her boundless taste for risk; she was writing a screenplay about "a female Rocky" who had every ounce of the courage of Sylvester Stallone's film character. Nyad's Rocky, naturally, was a swimmer.

And whom did she have in mind to play the lead?

"Me!" she yelped, delighted at her own chutzpah.

There is a classic, though shallow, pop media analysis of such women who do stunts, fly, sky dive, rock climb, hang glide, swim shark-infested waters, or kayak through foaming white water. According to the analysis, these women either have been freed from traditional mothering roles, or are trapped like their male counterparts in dull jobs. Bored by the lack of challenge in their postindustrial, easy-street American lives, they are in search of the quick "fix" that comes from plunging into an alien environment and emerging unscathed. As one skydiver said, "I don't fly to defy death, but because I enjoy living so much." *Newsweek* referred to them, men and women both, as "the thrill-seekers," whose "patron saints range from Icarus and Ahab to Evel Knievel." Their motives, the magazine said, stemmed from "a zest for life enhanced by the real and chilling possibility of injury and even death."

To judge by women like the Annapurna climbers, Guthrie, Nyad and part-time adventurers, this analysis is simplistic but not terribly off the mark. A psychologist who has pioneered in the study of adventurous people sees the "thrill-seekers" as one category within the wider context of "sensation-seekers." Along with other researchers, Dr. Marvin Zuckerman, a professor of clinical psychology at the University of Delaware, identifies "sensation-seeking" as a "general trait" made up of cultural factors, heredity, hormonal distribution and the chemistry of the brain. Sensation-seeking, numerous scholarly reports contend, is neither gender-related nor intelligence-related.

After measuring more than ten thousand subjects over more than a decade on a "sensation-seeking scale," Dr. Zuckerman and his colleagues have reached certain conclusions applicable to women as well as men. Those who score high "are likely to have not just one but a number of adventurous tastes, from an eagerness to try risky sports such as sky diving to a desire for variety in sexual partners." They also "rate the dangers of such activities *lower* than those who generally seek less stimulation." [author's italics] And even when they agree they're taking their lives in their hands, "the highs contemplate the activity with more pleasure than anxiety."

The data further suggests that between half and two thirds of the "variability" in daredevils is related to heredity. This, in turn, leads to hormones and brain chemistry. Daredevils tend to have high levels of both types of sex hormones—androgen (male) and estrogen (female). Less definitive studies indicate that the brain chemicals governing mood, such as noradrenaline and dopamine, and the brain chemical that *blocks* the action of those two—monoamine oxidase (MAO)—also play a major role in leading one person to be a "thrill-seeker" while another is a stay-at-home.*

Now we are on truly risky ground. The brain chemicals mentioned are the same ones related to manic-depressive illness. Are daredevils really manic crazies who have found exactly the right stimulus to scratch their itch for excitement? Conversely, are they really melancholics who hang glide their way out of depression? Are they sex nuts? Thrill junkies?

Er, well, um, here the scientists hedge. Dr. Zuckerman flatly states that "there is no correlation between sensation-seeking and neuroticism." At the same time, he does see a high correlation between some sensation-seekers and recreational drug use. There is also evidence that some out-of-control sensation-seeking corresponds to manic behavior.

Dr. Gerald Polin, another researcher of such trends, intimates neuroticism by describing thrill sports as "the adolescent anti-depressant" and "a symptom of the depression of our times." Dr. Ari Kiev, a psychiatric expert on suicide, extends the theory by suggesting that "some, but not all" daredevils do use risk-taking to "ward off depression." In an attempt to re-create the "natural high" of a daredevil sport, they "escalate the risks" until they deliberately threaten their lives, "increasing the emotional stress and reducing the elation." At some point, Dr. Kiev concluded, such already-depressed daredevils become "overtly suicidal," a pattern also seen in some drug addicts.

Let's not jump—literally or figuratively—to hasty conclusions. This brief summary of research does *not* mean that the next time you, I, your daughter or your mother takes a fling at white-water kayaking, we are trying to commit suicide. It does not mean Diana Nyad is addicted to jellyfish bites. In the words of Edward Stainbrook, head of the human behavior department at the University of Southern California, "thrill seeking expresses an almost desperate need for *assertive mastery* of something. In some cases the aggressive defiance can be overdone and become a dis-

---

* See Chapters 8 and 11 for extended discussions of "sensation-seeking."

guised suicide drive. But more often, it's just a quest for control of the self—and for doing rather than thinking." [author's italics] Even among depressed persons, Dr. Kiev wrote, "the underlying motive for undertaking high risk activities . . . is the need to gain mastery over oneself by gaining mastery over one's responses." A basic incentive in all thrill-seeking is, as Dr. Kiev put it, "the elation that comes from tapping one's inner strength to overcome physical stress, and the sense of achievement from accomplishing something which singles out the individual as distinctive."

Perhaps it comes down to how a woman interprets that inner voice when it hisses, "I dare you."

7

THE PROFESSION: ADVENTURING FULL-TIME

Odysseus established the pattern. In the greatest adventure story ever written, he got to roam the world for ten years, dallying with Calypso and Nausicaa and Circe, confronting strange cultures like those of the lotus-eaters and meeting weird creatures like the Cyclops. By taking the long way home to Ithaca, Odysseus—man, husband, father—was permitted a voyage of outer- and self-discovery. His wife, Penelope, of course, got to stay home and take care of the children. From ancient Greece through the present, the most stirring tales of explorers always seem to feature men.

Not fair! Nor is it entirely a male-exclusive world, when one looks closely. There have been daring female explorers in the past and there are more, such as the Annapurna climbers, today. Beyond the Outward Bound novices, beyond the weekend thrill-seekers, apart from the serious athletes are women for whom ad-

venture is a full-time occupation, a way of life as well as a way
of earning a living. Not surprisingly, the majority of contemporary women are in the pay of a government, often in a military
service, as men have been from Columbus to Neil Armstrong.*
Equally interesting is the handful of women who operate free-
lance.

"Adventurous professions" discussed here are limited to those
in the narrow dictionary-definition sense: professions in which
women undertake "dangerous or unknown risks." Whether they
are in pure exploration, travel, police work, the armed forces, the
space program, espionage, crime or field anthropology, their
"jobs" are quite different from white- or blue-collar jobs.
(Women who act adventurously within the parameters of more
conventional businesses will be examined later on.) Long before
working women became commonplace, there were hardy souls
who disobeyed the mores of their cultures to venture into distant
lands, exotic civilizations, exciting work.

The most hospitable location for female adventurers was the
British Empire during the Victorian Age. This was *not* because
the Queen happened to be a woman, but because it was an ex-
pansionist era, and the scope of the Empire gave explorers huge
realms in which to wander. For Americans, the Victorian age
coincided with the gold rush and its aftermath. Following the
Civil War, men and women alike joined the final phase of the pioneer thrust westward. The least heralded pioneer woman had
to be as brave as her man in the untamed American West; cov-
ered-wagon treks and sodbusting required back-breaking labor
of both of them. In addition, the pioneer American West and the
Victorian Empire attracted more than their share of female adventurers whose odysseys have never been given enough credit.
(The one woman who *was* given her due in the United States
was Sacajawea, the Shoshoni scout without whom Lewis and
Clark would not have crossed the Louisiana Territory in 1804.
But despite her fame, her role has usually been portrayed as that

* See Chapter 8 for a discussion of women in the military.

of a supporting player, the faithful aide, a female Tonto.) One thing these women had in common was their lust for the unknown; another was their habit of masking their gender in men's clothing for both comfort and safety.

In the American pioneer West, two female "Charleys" stand tall, both in male attire. One was Charley Parkhurst, a New Hampshire native born in 1812 who is thought to have spent her adult life without revealing her true sex.

Primarily a horse trainer, this Charley headed west during the days of the Forty-Niners. Until her death in 1879, she was recognized as a crackerjack stagecoach driver who plied the rough roads between mining camps and supply towns.

Then, there was Mountain Charley, alias Elsa Jane Forest Guerin, whose story (perhaps embellished in her autobiography) reads like a pulpy melodrama of the times. In fact, there were so many accounts of such a woman in the feverishly active Colorado mining regions between 1855 and 1859 that scholars speculate there may have been several "Mountain Charleys," women who sidestepped the taboo against independent females by pretending to be men.

The Mountain Charley who wrote her autobiography adopted men's clothes as part of a vengeful hunt for the man who murdered her first husband. The killing occurred in St. Louis, leaving fifteen-year-old Elsa Jane a destitute widow with two children. To escape prejudice, she sortied out as a "cabin boy," working the Mississippi steamboats. In 1855, gold lured her to the West. She led cattle drives, tried mining without success, and finally opened the Mountain Boys Saloon in a new boomtown called Denver.

Throughout the years, she had been on the lookout for her husband's killer. Once in St. Louis, she had stalked him in the street, wounding him with a shot from her revolver. But he lived and escaped. Then, in Colorado, while riding alone in the foothills of the Rockies, she met another rider on a narrow path. With a single glance, she recognized her hated enemy. At almost the

same moment, he recognized her. They reached for their re-
volvers; Mountain Charley was a second too quick for him. She
emptied her gun firing at him. Amazingly, he survived, and
thereupon he revealed to all of Denver that she was a woman in
disguise.

The fascination of Mountain Charley lies both in her precarious life-style and in the psychological confusion it created inside
her. Elsa Jane was a vivacious and physically capable individual.
When she discovered the freedom that men's clothes entitled her
to, compared with the confinement endured by most women, she
refused to give up her disguise completely. Her autobiography is
rife with poignant references to her separations from her children. But it is also filled with allusions to the challenging extra
dimension her life as a "man" allowed her. "I could not wholly
eradicate many of the tastes which I had acquired . . . as one of
the stronger sex," she wrote. These included excursions to the
theater, onto steamboat decks, into saloons, "in short, any and all
places to which my curiosity led me." (She does not elaborate.
Did she go to whorehouses or all-male cabarets?) After Elsa Jane
was unmasked in Denver, she stayed to marry her bartender.
Eventually, she returned to Missouri. But she never returned to
crinolines and silk, choosing pants—with all their symbolism—as
her dress for the rest of her life. Later reports indicate that
"Mountain Charley" enlisted in the Union Army during the Civil
War, putting her dual-gender experience to work by becoming a
quick-change spy.

Mountain Charley was not the only woman attracted by the
gritty fun of the pioneer West. Prostitutes, dance hall girls, saloon keepers and lady bandits added spice to the frontier. Let us
not forget Martha Jane Canary, the "Calamity Jane" of the Dakotas during their gold rush, or Lillie Hitchcock Coit, a belle of
old San Francisco who served in its volunteer fire company. Coit
also played poker with the boys, masqueraded as a man on
camping trips and waterfront pub crawls, and had a bloody boxing match staged for her personal enjoyment in her Palace Hotel
suite. (Coit Tower on Telegraph Hill is named for her.) Nor can

we forget Belle Starr, a rustler as ugly as she was mean, whose gang rode wild through the Oklahoma Territory right up until she was killed in an ambush in 1889.

These adventurers, with their dime-novel lives, stand out as classically American. Their Victorian counterparts overseas were, with some exceptions, classically English. Most of the Americans were guttersnipes; the Englishwomen clouded their bravado with a smokescreen of upper-crust gentility. Often, the English traveled with a retinue of servants and wrote "literary" travelogues minus Mountain Charley's emotional overtones.

No matter. They were spiritual sisters. Luree Miller, in her biography of five female explorers in Tibet, describes the three Victorian Englishwomen—Annie Taylor, Isabella Bird Bishop and Nina Mazuchelli—as "indomitable," with "a lively curiosity, calm judgment, practicality and courage." They "proclaimed a *joie de vivre* seldom voiced by unconventional females in any age." Nina Mazuchelli became the first Western woman to behold Mount Everest. Taylor, "aflame with Christian zeal, made a wild dash over treacherous mountain passes to carry the Word to innocent Tibetans." Bird, on her own, explored and wrote about the American frontier, besides making arduous journeys to the Far East. When she returned to England she was inevitably plagued by serious illnesses, yet on her expeditions she was as strong as an ox. Nearing sixty, she climbed an 11,000-foot pass in Kashmir and felt "increasing energy and vitality." Still later, she took to concealing a loaded revolver in her pocket. She and Fanny Bullock Workman, an American explorer, were the only women of their time to address the chauvinistic Royal Geographic Society of Britain.

Workman embodied the competitive spirit that nestled in the hearts of these intrepid travelers. After another woman claimed to have toppled Fanny's altitude record on a mountain climb in the Andes, Fanny dispatched a survey crew to scientifically prove the other woman had miscalculated. Armed with the information preserving her record, Workman immediately notified

Scientific American that she was still Queen of the Mountains. She was hardly shy about her politics, too. She posed for a photo atop a glacier proudly holding up a newspaper with the headline, "Votes for Women."

The greatest female explorer, however, probably was a Frenchwoman of a slightly later era, Alexandra David-Neel. Starting as an opera singer, she traveled through the Orient her first time with a theatrical troupe. She later became famous through her books, especially *My Journey to Lhasa*. In this account of a 1923–24 trip she told how she went overland to the isolated capital of Tibetan Buddhism. She began in her usual imperial style, with an entourage. But she switched to the dangerous role of a beggar woman, protected only by a faithful young lama who posed as her son. She penetrated the Dalai Lama's fortress, the Potala (totally off-limits to Western women), and got the British government agent in Tibet to certify her visit to that country in case anyone doubted her word. All this at the age of fifty-six.

Like Isabella Bird Bishop, David-Neel grew to think of the road as home. She confessed in a letter to her husband, whom she almost never saw, "I am a savage. . . . I love only my tent, my horses, and the desert."

I first heard of Alexandra David-Neel from Sarah B. Larrabee, contemporary American adventurer par excellence. For a time, I believed Sarah might be an updated version of both David-Neel and Mountain Charley. Intrigued by a visit in Wyoming with this New England-bred nonconformist, as well as by the Annapurna expedition, I followed her to the Himalayas. In one sense, neither the scenery nor my companion disappointed me. In another, the latter let me down profoundly.

August, 1976: The ranch was in the high scrub sagebrush country of Wyoming. Sarah was straining curds of cottage cheese in the farmhouse kitchen. A Wellesley graduate, a Himalayan trek leader, and a dealer in Eastern crafts, she was spending a month at the prosaic job of farmhand. Why? Sarah laughed a tickled-to-death giggle that was her trademark, an unnerving sound from someone I had envisioned as an ethereal mystic. "I never worked on a ranch before," she said. "I'm an experience freak."

Few women of her generation had honed their wanderlust to such a fine point, or had patterned their lives into such a mosaic of happenings, as had this twenty-nine-year-old. She was already preparing to leave Wyoming in the summer to lead an all-female trek to the base camp of Mount Everest. For Sarah, the trek would be old hat; she had made the strenuous journey three times before. The first time, it was by herself, in sneakers. The second time, she guided American Youth Hostelers. The third time, she headed a group that she had organized herself, cooking eggplant parmigiana along the trail and baking a birthday cake for a companion out of yak butter and Chinese noodle flour.

Sarah "knew the territory," as folks say in Wyoming. But merely noting that she was a veteran "trekker"—the British word for people who tramp through mountainous regions—didn't do her justice. A catalog of her accomplishments would have to include the recording of Tibetan chants in a remote Indian monastery . . . working as a snake charmer in a circus . . . teaching yoga . . . caring for disturbed children . . . cooking in a health-foods hospital . . . selling jewelry in Aspen . . . and living in a commune with eight men.

The trouble was that this list made Sarah seem like a typical hippie. Not so. Her jobs did evolve as a means of financing her wanderlust. At the same time, she communicated sincerity in calling her trips "spiritual pilgrimages." Her urge to travel began when she was a child, she explained as we drove to a mountain lake. "I was 'exoticized,'" she continued, taking a minute to strip to a swimsuit and plunge into the lake. The water was absolutely freezing; I eased my body in slowly, my jaw rattling like one of those Halloween false-teeth clappers. How could I know that this dip was a prelude to a far more emotionally charged wilderness bath two years later?

At the age of twelve, Sarah went to a lecture by Sir Edmund

Hillary, conqueror of Everest. She asked why his wife hadn't
gone on his famous ascent. Sir Edmund laughed and told her the
climb was so hard Lady Hillary would not have enjoyed it. The
rest of the audience laughed with him, but Sarah was crestfallen.
Soon after graduation from college, she turned down a marriage
proposal in favor of her first "spiritual pilgrimage," a year-long
academic world tour. It changed her life. India, with its teeming,
starving millions, was almost too much for the young philosophy
student to bear. "Bam! There you are in a place where all the as-
sumptions about life are foreign to us," she recalled. She visited
her first Buddhist monastery, where each monk could chant
three notes of "om" at once, she spent a night in a wayside shack
sleeping between two yak skins, and she slept another night in a
bed said to have been the Dalai Lama's.

Although she returned to New England, the pull of the East
would not let go of her. She could take "stasis" for only a few
months. She went back to India and Nepal. On impulse, in
sneakers, she set out from Kathmandu toward Everest base
camp. Two young men joined her, but soon dropped out. Sarah
continued alone until the last few towns, when an aged Indian
man making his first such trek became her companion. As they
approached base camp, the old man embraced her, tears streaming down his cheeks. "Oh, my dear, it is only because of you that
I am here!" he exclaimed. A month later, Sarah came back to the
United States thirty pounds thinner, though laden with ivory
bracelets, embroidered cloth and other items she could sell.
There was a new period of "stasis," then the American Youth
Hostel tour to Nepal. Of twelve trekkers, three gave up before
reaching base camp and one became sick. Sarah swore she
would never take novices on trek again. On her next trip, she
came to know leading Sherpas and learned to speak a little Nepalese.

Sarah had never contemplated traveling as a profession. But in
the United States, people kept introducing her as "the person
who leads treks through the Himalayas." She originally resisted
the tag, until she realized it made sense. So she formed her own

company, Wind Over Mountain. The name is from the I Ching
hexagram that means "gradual progress." Trekking, she emphasized, was a sacred as well as physiological act: "the higher you
go, the closer you get to God."

It had been a long while since I had heard a non-Moonie
speak of such things. There was a serenity about Sarah that startled me, coexisting, as it did, with her zest for rodeos and other
down-to-earth fun.

The following day, we climbed a bit of a mountain near the
ranch. Sarah marched straight up, rather than along the marked
path. I was breathing hard after a few steps. She wasn't. She
showed me the "high altitude rest step," in which you straighten
out your knee on each steep step before taking another step. As
we looked out on a vista of Wyoming valley, she remarked that
one would never have a wide-angle view like it in Nepal, since
Nepalese mountainsides rose so sharply from narrow valleys.

Did she ever have the urge to keep going from the Everest
base camp up the two miles to the top of the world's highest
peak? Not really. Mountaineering, she maintained, was a macho
sport, very different from trekking.

"The highest mountain is a geologic symbol for the cosmos,"
she said seriously. "I'm in awe of the mountain, and I'm not sure
you should walk all over it." We climbed down to our car, Sarah
swift and sure-footed in moccasins, I, less so in hiking boots. We
had not gone far up. But the air was crisp with the promise of
fall; we had made gradual progress, and it felt good.

December, 1978: Nawang Gombu, an elf with a backpack,
sprinted ahead of me, darting off the gentler trail to an alternate
one that pointed directly up the mossy hillside.

"Look! We take short cut! Not far soon!" he said, trying to act
encouraging. Having panted up his previous "short cuts," I could
barely mumble a negative grunt as I kept plodding on the
gentler trail.

Once, in what seemed like eons past, I had stopped trekking,
taken in the sight of the narrow green valley below, sucked the

Sikkimese air into my lungs, and marveled at the beauty of the
Himalayan ridges dappled with a light so strange it made the
scene dreamlike.

How many hours, how many steps ago was that glance? My
eyes were now dully fastened upon my boots and my breath escaped in spasms. I was certain millions of my brain cells were
keeling over in exhaustion with each step. All the emotions that
had welled up earlier—the anticipation, the awe, the anger, the
psychic pain—had long since been erased. Remaining was a
slightly bloated body lurching up and up and up, in despair of
ever seeing the rest of my trekking group.

At last, suddenly, a cabin loomed above me. One more turn
and I was at a wooden fence. Behind it, in a gravel "yard," sat
Sarah Larrabee on a chair, her tanned legs propped up on a
fence post. She munched a hard boiled egg, chatting gaily with
the others. Her face was tilted toward the sun. She did not acknowledge my arrival for a moment. In that moment, a fragmen-
tary wave of feeling washed over me. I wanted to kill her.

Feebly, I pulled my camera off my shoulder, extricated myself
from my tiny daypack that now felt as though it weighed a ton,
and semicollapsed. "Do I get to eat now?" I asked. It was 2 P.M.
Since breakfast at 6 A.M., I had put away nothing more solid
than Tootsie Rolls. A barefooted porter bobbed in front of me,
pouring hot coffee out of a hand-painted Chinese thermos. My
lunch—oranges, sardine sandwich, sweet rolls, egg—was in my
daypack. As I sipped and nibbled, my brain started to receive
coherent messages again. Sarah, in an effort to cheer me up, announced we would just hike another hour or so after lunch. It
was obvious from the way she said it that my tardiness had
forced her to lower her goal.

But that was not all of the information now filtering through
the gauze of exhaustion.

*If this is what you mean by spiritual pilgrimage, lady, then I'm
the Dalai Lama.*

This trip, which has cost much of my savings and which I

looked forward to with such eagerness, is not a dream; it is a nightmare and there is no escape.

Grace, you sniveling crybaby, you are a worthless person who did not deserve this thrill and thus will not be permitted to enjoy one of the world's greatest spectacles.

Sarah, I was ready to follow you to the end of the earth; now that I have, why are you abandoning me?

It was our first day of a Larrabee special trek through a corner of India's picturesque province of Sikkim. Our Sirdar was the famous Gombu, the best in the business. The trek was supposedly tailor-made for me by Sarah's Wind Over Mountain agency, which itself had thrived after my article about her in Wyoming was published in a national magazine.

And here I was, Sarah's most fervent admirer, hunkered over a sardine sandwich, my eyes again fixed on my boot tops, feeling about as frightened and miserable as a yak in quicksand. I wondered how I would pull out of it, much less make the climb to our destination, the base camp of Kanchenjunga, third highest mountain on the planet.

The trip had sounded so adventurous three months before—a priceless opportunity to see an incredibly foreign nook of the East in the company of an expert. Sarah was excited, as well. She still thirsted for more treks, and while her crafts trade was faring well, her travel business could use a boost. Earlier that autumn, she had led one trek to the Everest base camp, then had come to Darjeeling with one other Everest trekker. The three of us would trek in Sikkim at Christmastime. Afterward, the plan called for Sarah and me to continue on to Kathmandu and Nepal's Tiger Tops game preserve resort.

Sarah's catalog description of our trip was a unique blend of travelogue hype and prayerful sincerity:

The lush Western Valley of Sikkim, leading up to the base camp of . . . Kanchenjunga, has recently been opened to Westerners. . . . Nawang Gombu, the only man ever to have climbed Everest twice, will guide us. . . . Our Sikkim pilgrim-

age takes us to the beautiful Tibetan monasteries of Pe-
mayangtse and Rumtek. . . . Darjeeling . . . Calcutta. Oh,
Calcutta!

Calcutta! I dreaded the possibility that I would get stranded
there. My adventurism, I was discovering, had limits. I was very
unsure of myself, despite many travels in America, Europe and
North Africa. But when I reached the Calcutta airport to catch
another plane toward Darjeeling, my nightmares dissolved. After the interminable New York-London-Frankfurt-Teheran-New
Delhi flight, after the endless 3 A.M. customs lines in the filthy
Delhi airport, the comparatively airy Calcutta airport held no
terrors.

The plane from Delhi to Calcutta earlier, at dawn, had flown
parallel with a ragged white line on the horizon. I blinked, and
blinked again. The lenses behind my eyes focussed. The Himalayas. I was *seeing* them. Annapurna, Everest, Lhotse, Kanchenjunga . . . they were not figments of Arlene Blum's or Alexandra
David-Neel's or Sarah Larrabee's imaginations! Content, in my
jet-lagged state, with that thought alone, I had dozed off.

Miracle of miracles! At the Bagdogra airport on the dusty Indian plains below Darjeeling, a taxi, a driver and a guide sent by
Sarah were awaiting my arrival. The guide, Tshering Dhonchu
Andustang, a Tibetan woman with a kind manner and knowing
eyes, settled me in the back of our black British touring car for
the three-and-a-half-hour drive to "Darj."

Along the winding road that climbs steadily 8,000 feet from
the plains to Darj, Tshering handed me two miniature, succulent
oranges, a regional delicacy. "Are you a Buddhist too, like
Sarah?" she asked, her lilting Anglo-Indian accent sliding up and
down the musical scale. I confessed I was not. Tiredness over-
took me as the scenery changed from brown flatness and shabby
shacks to forests of huge trees clutching pitched mountainsides. I
was fast asleep when we pulled into the carpark in the higher,
tonier section of Darj.

The town, still a tea-growing center although the British are no longer in charge, is a series of wedges cut into the side of a steep mountain. The finest houses were built in the highest wedges, and it was said that during British rule, dark-skinned people (in other words, native Indians) were not allowed beyond this very carpark. Above it stood the building that was once the Ritz among the colonials—the Darjeeling Club, Ltd., or Planters Club for short. A slightly down-at-the-heels hotel that was "private," the Planters Club would make you a temporary member for a few pounds, er, rupees. This was where Sarah stayed.

She was waiting in her "suite," her blue eyes as penetrating as always, merriment crinkling their corners. Her long light-brown hair was neatly parted and combed. She wore an ankle-length Tibetan dress, with its distinctive woven apron around her waist. We hugged, both of us glad the rendezvous had gone well. Sharing the suite was Leonard, a thirty-year-old bearded Florida banker, the Everest trek veteran. As I was the newest recruit, I got a suite to myself that night.

The next day was for resting before our journey to Sikkim, another long auto ride north. In the morning, I stepped outside my room and was confronted by a stunning, washed-windows view of Kanchenjunga's five white peaks against a sky the color of Rocky Mountain lupines. The air was nippy, fresh. A small brown man in white servant's clothes jumped out of nowhere, bowing and scraping; such servility pervaded the Club.

The street below the verandah was clogged with people, yet almost no cars. The Club was eerily quiet and deliciously British. Hot water was dispensed to tubs in each suite for a mere hour or two. Fireplaces stoked with coal warmed the bedrooms, barely. A toy brass cannon was mounted near the Club's entrance, pointed with menace at the shoe store and the Dairy Piggery restaurant across the street. At dinner, Sarah chuckled at my astonishment over the fawning waiters. "Coming here," she said, "you find out that you're treated like a great Raj. It's catching! You'll get to love it, too!" It was not just spirituality that brought her back to India. It was also the opportunity to live like a Raj for a paltry sum.

The previous month's Everest trip had gone badly. Many of the dozen trekkers had disliked the fast pace and the awful food. Leonard, the banker, had gotten so feverish it was amazing he made it to base camp; he was now twenty pounds thinner. When I brought up the Everest fiasco with Sarah, she conceded that the food and the outfitting had not been up to par. The Sikkim trip, she assured me, would be professionally guided and staffed. There was no mention, however, of eggplant parmigiana on the trail.

Forewarned about "Delhi belly," I had come with all kinds of gastrointestinal medications. I felt equally prepared for our physical labors. Altitude had never seriously hampered me. As Sarah had suggested, I had jogged to get in shape until I could run two flat miles easily. What didn't dawn on me until later was that everyone—Gombu, his mountaineering daughter Rita, the porters, our two Darjeeling-based guides, Sarah, Leonard—was already trek-hardened.

Everyone except me.

We met Gombu, Rita and their family at dinner at their house before leaving for Sikkim. After pouring us Tonba, a strong fermented millet concoction, Gombu briefed us in his imperfect but understandable English. "Kanchenjunga means five treasure houses of snow. Each peak is made out of gold, silver, turquoise and coral," he began. A compact, jolly man with skin the color of teak, Gombu directed the Himalayan Mountaineering Institute in Darj. He also knew Sikkim intimately. Our final pretrek night would be spent at the Institute's hostel in Yoksum, where the porters would be waiting. He pointed to the town on a detailed plastic climbers' map, tracing our hike with his finger. There appeared to be not a quarter-acre of flat ground for scores of miles around Darj, Sikkim, Nepal or the border of Tibet. The fact that our trek into the mountains to the tiny town of Dzongri and then to base camp looked short in terms of miles gave no inkling of the spine-pounding jeep rides and hours of steep trekking ahead of us.

Rita, nineteen and sturdy, spoke such rapid-fire English it was hard to understand every word. She was a highly trained climber, yet her most prized possession were not pitons nor ropes but a pair of genuine American Wrangler jeans, which her dad had brought back from a summer in Washington state. Gombu and Rita gave me renewed confidence that I was in safe hands.

The next day, a cloudy mid-December one with temperatures in the forties, we all set off in a Land Rover toward Sikkim with duffle bags and gallons of bottled water. Our driver, a cigarette dangling from his lips, deserved a chance at Monza for the daring with which he negotiated the pebble-paved roads up, down and around the hillsides en route to Gangtok, the Sikkimese capital. (The roads were about wide enough for a single truck, so in order to pass the many army trucks lumbering in our path, we were in a continuous game of "chicken," teetering on the brink of sharp cliffs.)

Sikkim is a crucial outpost for India—the lynchpin that separates the subcontinent from Chinese-occupied Tibet. There have been skirmishes on the border between the Chinese and the Indians. Thus, Sikkim is carefully monitored by the bureaucrats in Delhi, and heavily fortified with troops and tanks. Foreign tourists need a special visa to enter Sikkim. Ours had mistakenly been stamped as three-day tourist passes, instead of two-week trekking passes. We expected to quickly clear up the mistake in Gangtok in order to leave room for a full ten days of hiking.

After winding through a cascade of terraced hills, matted with tea bushes that resembled gorgeously patterned green carpets, we descended to a bridge that was the Sikkim border. Less than thirty yards away was the first liquor booth, where we stocked up on Sikkimese rum at $1.00 a fifth. It was a jolly Rover indeed that entered the city of Gangtok a few hours later.

Shangri-La, I kept thinking, as each bend in the road brought a dazzling view of the lush hills and Kanchenjunga's peaks. Most of us first heard of Sikkim in the early sixties, when an American,

Hope Cooke of Sarah Lawrence College, became the tiny country's Gyalmo (Queen) by marrying its ruling Chogyal (King), a widower named Palden Thondup. Stories of their wedding conveyed the image of a fairytale romance in a kingdom that could have been lifted directly from James Hilton's novel. But history was not kind to this Shangri-La. With India perceiving China as a growing threat, the Indians took over the government of Sikkim and toppled the Chogyal. Hope Cooke and her children fled to New York. The Chogyal was under house arrest in his Gangtok palace. He had made an unsuccessful suicide attempt. Still, as our Rover entered the palace grounds through flower-bedecked streets, the Shangri-La image refused to disappear. The palace was a decorative two-story pagoda. On its broad lawn, boys were having an archery contest. One young man in a black robe watched passively. He was the Chogyal's elder son by an earlier marriage. Behind the closed doors, we knew, sat the melancholic Chogyal, his toy country taken away from him because of the exigencies of twentieth-century global politics. Perhaps, I thought, the Shangri-La image would still be intact in the hinterlands.

But that image was further damaged when we tried to extend our incorrect visas. Impossible, the chief of police declared. Three days and be gone! Shocked, we retreated to Gangtok's one charming tourist hotel to plot strategy.

The next two days were spent sight-seeing and fuming at Indian bureaucracy. Sarah, Leonard and I rode to Rumtek to be guests of an important deputy of His Holiness, the Karmapa. The deputy, a tall, handsome, cultured man, warmly greeted Sarah, who had met him on her first pilgrimage in search of Buddhist knowledge. Over tea, he quizzed us for information on two news items he had heard over his short-wave radio: the Guyana People's Temple Massacre and the presidency of Jimmy Carter.

"Isn't he beautiful?" asked Sarah with a giggle that night. Leonard and I agreed. But the communal guest room he put us up in was not beautiful. Did we mind a hovel with orange rinds on the floor and moldy blankets on wooden beds? I minded a lot, but had no choice. Sarah was finally on her own turf, showing off the exotic East as well as her own durability in the face of hardship. She had entertained us on our jeep rides by describing her exploits on previous adventures. A few years before, she had been in Afghanistan when she met seven British climbers about to do a "real macho number": they were to climb, in a single day, a mountain that would take them from 7,000 feet up to 14,000 feet and back down. She insisted on joining them. Condescendingly, the leader asked, "have you ever climbed before?" She decided not to disclose her experience: "I just matched them stride for stride." Upon reaching the peak, the male climbers were huffing and puffing and retching. Sarah was just fine, and silently triumphant. She told of another incident in Afghanistan when, alone on a road, she was challenged by an Afghani bandit, who held a gun and had a cartridge belt slung over his chest. He demanded "bakshir" (the pervasive bribe money). The implication was, her money or her life. Sarah had no money with her. She refused to lose her composure. First, she offered her shirt, but the bandit shook his head. She opened her pocket to prove she was penniless. Then, he pointed to her camera. She pretended not to understand. Bluffing her way out, she said, "all the best in peace and happiness to you," smiled and walked off resolutely. He remained rooted to the spot. "I was convinced that if I turned to look at him just once, it would be a sign of weakness and he'd plug me!" she recalled. Sarah finished the tale by adding that she had a passionate affair with one of the macho climbers. She happily defined her adventures as a blend of the carnal and the mystical.

Shivering in the Rumtek hovel, Sarah was cheerful as usual in the morning, ignoring my dour temper. We were ushered by monks of the Red Hat sect into the Karmapa's more comfortable visiting room. He sat on a couch, barefoot and cross-legged, spitting phlegm, as was the custom, into a copper spittoon he held in one hand. We sat at his feet.

For a holy man second in importance in Tibetan Buddhism to

the Dalai Lama, he was a jovial guy, especially after Sarah handed him a prayer shawl in which was wrapped our collective offering—about $25. "I am so happy to be here, Your Holiness, because you took me in three years ago," Sarah told him, her eyes glistening. The Karmapa's caged canaries chirped wildly. He blessed each of us and slipped a little circle of knotted crepe paper over each of our necks for luck on our journey. For a full hour, he then made small talk through an interpreter, showing distinct curiosity about Leonard's bank.

Our permits were still not corrected back in Gangtok. I had come halfway around the world to trek, not study Buddhism, and I was furious. Sarah decided to take matters into her own hands.

With Leonard and myself, she marched into the office of the Gangtok police chief, her jaw set. The chief, a pinch-faced civil servant in a western suit jacket, was ensconced behind a desk containing two telephones, neither of which worked very well. In a nervous voice, Sarah told him how important it was for his country—and his job—to allow us to trek. "We have been waiting patiently, and we were assured by officials in Darjeeling that the three-day visa was a mistake. You must correct it. Please understand, we have fourteen persons at great expense now in Yoksum. I lead many trips in your country," she said. "And these are not ordinary tourists. This man is an important banker. This lady is a journalist." With each reference, she arranged business cards and brochures like trial exhibits on his desk.

It could have been a scene out of *The Mouse That Roared*. The chief, annoyed at anything unusual, tried to shoo us out of his room. We sat quietly, refusing to budge. Sarah talked his ears off, keeping monumental control over herself, wearing him down. "Only Delhi can change permit," he insisted after twenty minutes. "You must go back to Delhi!"

Sarah pounced. "I have already been there and seen the minister of tourism and he assured me all was in order. May I suggest you call him and confirm this!" After more wrangling, his secretary tried the call. We three held our breath. At first, the line to Delhi (the only direct one in Gangtok) was busy. Then it was garbled. Then busy, again and again.

Success! The Delhi minister was on the line, hearing the chief complain about three Americans cluttering his office. "He wants to speak to you," the chief said to Sarah, resignedly handing her the receiver.

It was her moment, and she milked it for all it was worth. Shouting over the static, she improvised an Anglo-Indian singsong accent to make herself more understandable. "MR. MINISTER, THIS IS SARAH B. LARRABEE! I SPEAK FROM GANGTOK! DO YOU REMEMBER ME? GOOD!" Jabbering from the other end. Sarah continued shouting in her hilarious accent, "OUR PERMIT IS WRONG. YOU MUST TELL THE CHIEF TO CHANGE IT. IF NOT, I MUST CALL THE AMBASSADOR!" For five minutes, the receiver was passed back and forth between Sarah and the chief like a relay baton. Finally the man in Delhi left a decision up to the man in Gangtok and rang off. Sarah's eyes bore into the little chief.

Was he down for the count? Not quite. He sparred a bit more about trekkers, dialed a superior bureaucrat, slid his glasses on, and stared, downcast at our papers. With defeat in his voice he asked, "how many days will you need?"

TKO.

Sarah flashed a winner's smile. "Ten." He scribbled eight on the corrected papers, meaning we would have to cut down our actual trek. But we were grateful for anything. Practically ripping the permit from under his pen, Sarah thanked him effusively and we rushed out into the halls of the Gangtok police headquarters, yelling, "We got it!" We were the first American trekkers to be permitted in Sikkim in years.

Eight hours later, long past sunset, we trooped into the lodge at Yoksum. Our crew—two guides, one cook, one assistant cook, one waiter, nine porters—was as happy to see us as we were them. We celebrated with a bottle of Sikkimese rum and slept soundly on the wooden beds in the hostel, the last beds we would see for seven days.

It was in that spirit of having overcome adversity, thanks to
Sarah's bravura performance at the police station, that I followed
the others at dawn from Yoksum to the trekking trail. It was
three days before Christmas, my birthday. We began at an altitude of 6,000 feet. The air, no more than fifty degrees, was perfect for hiking. Sarah was in shorts and torn sneakers, even
though her pretrip bulletin had specified boots. The trail was like
the Sikkimese roads, paved with pebbles and loose rocks. Looking over my shoulder, I saw rows of Himalayan oaks, whose thick
trunks were topped with clumps of contoured branches that
gave them the appearance of bonsai plants.

Kanchenjunga was nowhere in sight. After an hour's trekking,
neither was Sarah.

The trail was startlingly steep. I could feel the strain, not on
my lungs, but on my legs. Soon my T-shirt was soaked with
sweat and my Fabiano boots felt like they were made of solid
Italian marble. I fell behind, the porters gliding by me despite
gigantic wooden food crates strapped to their backs.

"I can't seem to pick my feet up." During the lunch break,
that was the one coherent thought I managed to scribble in my
notebook to recall my morning of agony. The roller-coaster trail
had taken us from 6,000 to 9,000 feet. Luckily, the afternoon
climb was a mere 500 feet further up, over exposed root systems
of high oaks, Japanese evergreens and a few stands of bamboo.
At Choka, a primitive Tibetan village, our two-man tents were
put up by our guides. They were Darjeeling college students,
one short and stocky and dark, the other tall, thin and tan. Their
names were Sukesh and Mukesh, like a Hindu vaudeville team.

"It is harder than you thought," Mukesh said, smiling compassionately from under his dark mustache.

"Is the rest this bad?" I asked, accepting a hot cup of tea with
trembling hands.

"Do not worry. We climb less now," he replied.

Sarah said nothing to me, compassionately or otherwise.

For dinner Dowa, our Tibetan cook, served fried chicken, veg-
etable chow mein, curried eggs, fried rice, chips, and sliced

apples in cream sauce. My misery dissipated as I scoffed down the meal. Imagine having a Tibetan version of Chef Wang on an expedition instead of tasteless commercial freeze-dried backpack specialties! My tent, shared with Rita, was made up with a thick mattress, down-filled sleeping bag, and—bless colonial training— real pillows. Lying in head/foot formation, insulated from the wintry night, Rita and I fell asleep by 9 P.M.

At seven the next morning, a porter woke us, steaming cups of tea in hand. The sky was clear, the sun harsh. We hit the trail before eight. At 9,000 feet, we were in an other-worldly land-scape of massive, gnarled tree roots covered by moss. Clouds moved in, but the nip in the air was welcome because we were struggling and sweating. Up, up and up, we used the roots like stairs. Patches of snow showed on the ground at 10,000 feet. Bunches of moss clung to huge hemlocks, which soon gave way to high rhododendron bushes. The leafy branches of the rhodo-dendrons hung over the trail like a bower. Feeling somewhat recovered from the day before, I told Sarah I had never seen such entrancing oriental woodlands. She seemed less hyperac-tive, and even kept to my pace for a half-hour during the after-noon. While I moved with more confidence toward our 11,000-foot lunch spot, Leonard had spells of dizziness from the altitude. Rita, however, was breathing easily, sprinting ahead and then stopping to join me for a chat about college.

By early afternoon, we were beyond the tree line, ascending a rounded pinnacle of coarse yellowish grass. As I approached the crest, I saw tall Buddhist prayer flags staked at the top. Drenched with sweat, light-headed with altitude and joy, I tum-bled into a heap of my companions for a group photo. This was Dzongri, 13,500 feet—the highest point of our climb.

I've done it! I said to myself. *I've passed the test.* Surely we had been through the toughest part. Sarah chuckled as Rita, Gombu, Mukesh, Sukesh, Leonard and myself made faces for the camera. I held the Chinese thermos aloft like a victor's trophy.

Dzongri. With a rush, I realized precisely where in the world I was standing. Had I been almost anywhere in the lower forty-eight states, I would have been looking *down* at the scenery. Here, I was gazing *up*. A panorama of peaks that rose nearly three more *miles* high was spread out ahead of me in a one hundred and eighty-degree arc. The spiky, snow-capped mountains seemed so close that they sent a tingle down my spine. Wisps of clouds swirled around their tops. Sukesh drew an outline of the vista on my pad as Gombu recited the names: Kokthang. Frey. Ratong. Kabur South. Kabur North. Kabur Dome. Kanchenjunga! I wanted to snatch her five treasures in my hand. I stared and stared until my eyes watered.

We scrambled down the far side of Dzongri to a windswept campground. It was time for ski gloves and down parkas. Rita and I were well-matched tentmates; we were both night readers. By flashlight, she read *The Other Side of Midnight*, I *Dog Soldiers*, until the cold drove us into our sleeping bags. I slipped my trail flask, filled with hot water, under my feet. On this, only our second night on trek, we slept ten hours.

It was so cold at dawn that we let the first rays of sun heat the tent before we slithered out to gulp some coffee. Our trail now was short and comparatively flat but treacherous, because the coarse grass hid partially frozen ground littered with slippery rocks. Crossing an open valley in the shadow of Kanchenjunga, we had to hop from rock to rock, over the ice. A few times I tripped, skidding into calf-deep mud. My raw emotions bubbled to the surface, magnified by fear and the effect of high altitude. I roared curses when the slime seeped over my boot tops. We reached our next camp, Ooblathong, after four teetering hours. The air became so chilled once the sun went down that Rita and I could not read by the fire. Wind howled through the valley in the blackness, straining our tent's sturdy flaps.

This time, we slept for twelve hours. But we were not awakened until past 8 A.M. This was our "easy" day. It was Christmas.

On my pillow lay a birthday card with a lovely drawing of the mountains. Rita had secretly designed it on the trail. Outside our tent was a miniature Christmas tree that Sarah had fashioned from hemlock branches. She had assembled a stocking for each of us, filled with such "presents" as toilet paper, Tootsie Rolls and trinkets. Once again, my spirits rose. My thirty-seventh birthday would certainly be memorable, provided I managed to get back down the mountain.

Our plans were revised. Instead of aiming for Kanchenjunga base camp, we would stay at Ooblathong for the day, then turn around and head back. Gombu decided to take Rita, Leonard, Sarah and me on a rope-climbing excursion. But trouble loomed when we could not locate a good place to cross a rapid, wide stream to get to the rocks. Suddenly, we were playing the Outward Bound game: ford this rushing stream no matter how terrifying it looks. The tide was so strong that Gombu, the first to cross it, was bent almost parallel to the water. One by one, we knotted our boots around our necks, rolled up our jeans, and hobbled across the frigid snowmelt-water with the aid of a walking stick. As always, I was last. I paused, shivering in fright before stepping into the icy, swift flow. My legs became frozen after a few steps and I was sure I was about to be swept downstream. An eternity passed until I could grab Gombu's outstretched hand and step on the first dry rock. Pain flooded my feet where they had been numb under water. Without saying a word, Rita and I both sobbed uncontrollably.

"I didn't think you were going to try it," Leonard said with a grudging smile. Sarah said nothing.

The rocks we wanted to climb turned out to be dangerously loose and moss-covered. Gombu decided to head back to camp. This time, he scanned the stream for a better crossing. He thought he found one, and stepped into the water, but with no warning the tow pulled him off balance. He fell, then dragged himself upright before we had a chance for more than a second of horror. As he stumbled to the other side, Gombu was soaking wet and angry. Sarah, using a walking stick in each hand, managed to cross without completely falling. Then it was my turn.

At midstream, I realized the undertow was far stronger than I was, and I was sliding inexorably sideways, off my feet. Seeing this, Sarah did not hesitate. She waded back into the stream to-

ward me, hip-deep in the water. Her powerful arm locked under
mine, jerking me upright and hauling me across the remainder of
the stream. Tears came to my eyes again, brought on by grati-
tude as much as by pain.

We trudged back to camp. The faint voice of my logical self
whispered: *why?* Fording the stream twice had been among the
hardest, most unnecessary trials I had ever put myself through. I
could have said "the hell with it." But it had seemed a matter of
pride to follow the others. *Stupid!* the voice whispered. In the
back of my mind I saw a quick flash of Sarah, in Wyoming, in
the freezing mountain lake. Either she was showing off, or she
really had an affinity for ice water. For no discernible reason, I
wanted to test her again.

"Sarah," I called. "You said earlier you wanted to wash your
hair. I dare you to wade back into that stream later. A dinner in
Kathmandu says you won't." How crazy was she?

Very. Within the hour, she marched to the stream, shampoo in
hand. She shed her towel and slid, naked, into a freezing eddy.
While I watched, she calmly lathered her long hair, sending
Revlon bubbles to float deep into the heart of Sikkim. She
grinned the entire time.

That afternoon, she had saved me from a bad soaking. Now,
she was performing her Bionic Woman act. Yet with each new
feat, I liked her less. In a transference I could not comprehend,
her acts of bravado were diminishing *me*. In her eyes? Probably.
But also in my own.

Christmas dinner was grand—soup and roast duck at 12,000
feet in the Himalayas—and so was the astonishing dessert. In
Darjeeling, Sarah had snuck off to a bakery. Now, her purchase
was placed before me: a frozen, honest-to-goodness layer cake,
with "Happy Birthday" spelled out in pink on white frosting.
How could I harbor nasty feelings about a woman who thought
of everything?

The trek took on a surreal quality the day after Christmas.
Howling winds during the night had signaled a winter storm on

its way, and the winds were still fierce in the morning. Nevertheless, Dowa had prepared breakfast, so with my back to the wind I huddled over a cup of coffee and a piece of bread, trying to put something in my stomach before our trekking order was issued. Sarah told me to hurry; the winds would be against us and she and Gombu had decided to double the day's planned trek in order to escape the weather. "You'd better walk faster today," she said. "Nobody wants to stay behind with you." Her remarks blackened my already dark mood.

"You know, you make me feel like a real idiot," I retorted. "Like I'm holding everybody back." She did not dispute this; she was on her way to the trail. I tossed away my breakfast and scurried after her. Actually, I felt like a novice skier who had been put accidentally in an expert's class. There was no way to keep up. With my chin tucked into my neck, head down, I plunged into the biting wind. From the first steps, my body told me that spending four days at altitudes over 10,000 feet had taken a serious toll. My stamina was gone. Meanwhile, I was spilling over with a fury new to me, outraged at these "companions" who showed no pity for their weakest member.

It was my turn to play the unenviable role of The Sufferer, as Joan Firey had on Annapurna, Harriet on Outward Bound, Patty in Canyonlands. The fact that I normally saw myself as a leader, a Capricorn, a mountain goat, a step ahead of everybody else, made my depression that much worse.

Sarah was as furious with me as I was with her. Was she ruining my trip? Well, I was ruining hers. "Come ON," she shouted as we reached an arduous, snow-laden slope. "You've GOT to move faster!"

I was gasping for breath, fighting the wind, battling the uphill climb and sinking in the squishy snow all at once. "I'm-doing-the-best-I-can!" I panted. The higher we got, the more often I was forced to rest after every few steps. Above me, Sarah babbled instructions about breathing in and out with each step. Damn her! If I could have willed yogic breathing, I would be doing it. Surely it was obvious that, left on my own, I would make it any way I could, except quickly. On the other hand, she grew convinced that I was slowing down on purpose.

The conflict came to a head as we twisted up another sharp incline near Dzongri. I was slipping so often on the snow that I started to shake with fear. Remembering the "high altitude rest step" shown me so long ago in Wyoming, I straightened my knee as I brought one foot beside the other, slowing my pace even more.

Infuriated, Sarah whirled on me. "You're a spoiled brat!" she screamed when I came abreast of her. With that, she grabbed my arm and began dragging me by it up the hill.

"Stop, STOP!" I screamed back. "You're pulling my arm out of the socket!"

"I'm going to get you up this hill if I have to carry you," she hissed in my ear. "You're giving the whole trip bad vibrations!" With a single yank on my arm, she had me on her shoulder in a fireman's carry, my one-hundred-ten-pound frame draped across her back like a heavy rag doll.

My feet were off the ground. Freeing a hand, I pounded her. "Put me down, damn you!" I cried, on the edge of hysteria. "Leave me alone! I'll do it my way! LET GO!"

A couple of steps further, she did. Tears would have rolled down my cheeks but the wind plastered them to my lids. I was worn out, battered, humiliated. Sarah was shaken. She did not glance back at me and disappeared quickly over the next ridge.

Resting long enough to gather fresh air into my lungs, I didn't bother to compose myself. I just staggered ahead, alone.

My memory bank vaguely recalled stories of how high-altitude climbing frequently triggers bitter battles and emotional upheavals. But for the rest of the day, my brain registered little else. It was as if I were dropping a few notches down on the primate scale; I felt like a Cro-Magnon disguised in a down parka, creeping dumbly upon the Himalayan tundra. When I reached the others at a lunch spot, I noticed that I had lost my gloves and that my hands were red with cold. But I could not

summon the energy to make small talk. Sarah and I did not look
at one another. The afternoon was endless. We were hiking
straight down under threatening skies. Still shaky, I moved as
slowly as I had climbing up earlier that morning, fearful that if
one heel slipped on the loose pebbles I would careen down the
mountain. Gombu kept watch over me, pointing out a herd of
unkempt, runty animals in one pasture: the Chogyal's royal yaks.
We continued down through the rhododendron forest, past the
village where we had camped the first night, all the way to the
cabin outside which we had eaten our first trail lunch. By the
time we reached it, an hour behind the others, my knees were
twitching from the strain, and it was after sunset. I had trekked
for nine hours, nearly nonstop, at double-digit altitude.

Dinner was a quiet one. Afterward, I went directly into the
hostel. There was still one more day of hard downhill trekking.
My legs had turned to linguini. All I wanted to do was sleep. But
after Sarah came inside, she sat upright in her sleeping bag,
eyeing me. "Something happened today and I want to get it off
my chest," she said.

Good God! The last thing I needed was a replay of the day's
unfortunate events. Immobile, I lay in my bag while Sarah laced
into me, seconded by Leonard.

"I lost control up there," she admitted, "but I lost control because you were behaving like a child. I don't like to leave things
with the bad vibes I've been feeling." She charged that I had
taken a poor attitude from the start, had expected everything to
go my way, had not cared about the welfare of others. She
claimed that I had not kept pace because I hadn't wanted to.
Why had I come, when I obviously didn't enjoy it? Leonard
demanded. On and on they droned.

I concentrated on my own bruised ego and damaged expectations. Trekking had been a severe disappointment to me. Whose
fault was it? Partly my own, no doubt, but partly my companions'. Trekking on this journey was a very solitary, long, hard hiking experience. Not only was I unskilled at it; there wasn't
enough fun in the effort. I had expected to see the Himalayas

and instead saw a lot of little rocks and tree roots under my feet. It was a pity to learn this the hard way, half a globe from home.

Only much later did it occur to me how much fun it might have been, had the others, particularly Sarah, accommodated themselves one iota in my direction. If only she had not turned the trek into a macha competition! If only I could have declared, "Slow down or I'll refuse to take another step!" on the first day. After all, I was, in effect, the employer, she the employee. How did we let this adventure knot itself into a contest of wills?

Listening to Sarah and Leonard in the dark hostel, I wearily lit a cigarette. "I'm sorry you feel that way," I told them in a toneless voice. "But since Leonard and I are the two paying clients on this trip, Sarah, I thought you would take my wishes and my ability more into account. I didn't intend to hold you up. Why couldn't you slow down? I could have used the company. In any case, nothing I did was 'on purpose.' I tried as hard as I could and I resent being accused of loafing." Too tired to defend myself further, I stubbed out the cigarette. Sleep overcame me within seconds.

The final morning I wrapped Ace bandages around both my knees. They throbbed all the way down. It was a monotonous, depressing descent relieved here and there by bamboo bridges swaying high above the Kanchenjunga River. In early afternoon, the lovely green valley and thatched huts of Yoksum came into sight again. I was more relieved than glad to re-enter the hostel lodge. As an adventurer, I had been tested—and had been found wanting. *Okay,* said my inner voice, *it's over.* Let Peter Mathiessen find poetry inside a boot bloodied by his own trekking blisters. My poetry, my peace, my adventures would have to be sought elsewhere.

Sarah, her anger exorcised, was her spirited self from then on. During our last night in Yoksum, the porters danced wildly along with her as she spun like a dervish. She doled out their tips in regal fashion, with the staff lined up in front of her to bow in thanks, one by one, as each received his money. We made the long jeep ride back to Darj, with Gombu and Rita bid-

ding us gracious farewells. Leonard left for the States. Sarah and
I, once more on speaking terms, continued on to Nepal. There,
she demonstrated her ability to bargain fiercely for a rickshaw or
a carpet in Hindi and Nepali, to charm an airline official into
giving us seats on the lone plane from a small airport in the
Nepalese lowlands to Kathmandu, and to lecture like a professor
about each temple we saw in that capital city of Nepal. These
were variations of her performance before the Gangtok police
chief. But adept as she was in getting us good hotel rooms, buying gifts at the lowest prices or handling travel tickets, she did
not endear herself to me. Her behavior revealed the darker side
of machisma, the strutting and showing off to accomplish small
gains or to get an edge on people whom she felt were not her
equals. At bottom, she was a smart, calculating Yankee peddler.

To be fair, Sarah also displayed *joie de vivre* and insatiable
curiosity worthy of Workman and David-Neel. Perhaps that ac-
counted for her quick friendships in the East and her impulsive
plunge into the freezing stream at Ooblathong. In her Tibetan
dress, speaking encyclopedically about Buddhist customs, she
was a throwback to the likes of David-Neel. Scurrying up the
trekking trail, she carried on the tradition of Fanny Workman.
No one has written whether the Victorian explorers seemed to
care as little about the needs or feelings of their companions. But
if Sarah's energy and enthusiasm were not mine, whose fault was
it? I could continue to admire her as an adventurous symbol,
even when I could no longer endure her as a friend.

What chemistry there had been between us disintegrated in
Nepal. Her penny-pinching made me uncomfortable. My taste
for luxury made her irritated. Unable to clear the air of the hostility from the trek, I tried to kill my own psychological ills with
drugs from Kathmandu's no-prescription pharmacies. After a
month abroad, I went back to New York. Sarah stayed on. Five
months went by. One day, I picked up the telephone and heard
her familiar chuckle. She had just gotten back from months of

shuttling between Kathmandu and Hong Kong doing wholesale crafts trading.

She came to my apartment like a nomad, with a big vinyl shopping bag on wheels and a Tibetan rug rolled on top of that. She was wearing Chinese black slippers and a turquoise satin Chinese jacket. The big grin and the penetrating eyes were unchanged, although there were a few new lines in her sunweathered face. At thirty-three, her adventuring seemed to be taking its physical toll.

"I suffer real culture shock when I come back," she confessed. "I used to think the town my mother lives in, in Connecticut, was built up. Now, coming from Delhi, I think to myself, 'they could fit so many more people in there!'" She had shot tranquilizer darts into tigers with a zoologist at Tiger Tops game preserve before she left Nepal and had gone tubing down a Vermont river once she got home. She was, as always, the experience freak. She also obliquely acknowledged that, however bad I was at following a trek, she was not always good at leading one. She would still be adventuring, but for a bigger profit, in crafts. Sarah was truly a Yankee peddler at heart.

One of us briefly mentioned the fight on the mountain. We both laughed, a little too easily, and changed the subject.

8

THE BATTLEFIELD: WOMEN AND THE MILITARY

If there is a single activity most evocative of machismo, it is making war. The battlefield is the logical extension of the playing field upon which men are expected to demonstrate their macho style. It is the field from which women traditionally have been banned as participants. On a psychological level, pundits from Freud to Lyndon B. Johnson to Antoine de Saint-Exupéry have reinforced the idea that a rifle, a jet control stick or a jet airplane itself is an extension of the penis. The images and equipment of war are as potent symbols of machismo as we can find in civilized society. The connection carries over into related professions as well. In journalism, war correspondent is the job most boasted about by old-timers, most coveted among younger reporters and least populated by women.

Symbolism aside, the evidence of history and anthropology indicates that women have by tradition defended the home, the "nest" or the wounded while men have fought the battles. Two exceptions spring to mind: the Amazons and Joan of Arc. However, the latter was a religious mystic, perhaps a witch. She did not start or perpetuate a tradition of women warriors. The Amazons, too, stand alone. They were primarily creatures of mythology. A tribe of warlike women from somewhere in Asia Minor near the Urals (I picture them as Turks, or as oriental versions of Algerian women with their blood-curdling screams), their leader was a queen named Hippolyte. Some Amazon tribes reportedly singed the right breasts of their young girls, causing the breasts to wither so that the girls might shoot arrows or throw spears more efficiently. Theirs was a matriarchal society in which men were either scorned, employed cold-heartedly for procreation and then discarded, killed or enslaved. Boy children were either crippled for later use as slaves or killed. The Amazons were considered the original "man-haters" (the phrase Aeschylus used) who did not marry, did not nurse or rear their offspring, and were feared as killers. One story has Achilles slaying an Amazon queen, Penthesilea, in the Trojan War, then mourning over her body because she was so young and beautiful. He was, of course, a foolish romantic. Given what we know of the Amazons, they were not a tribe that contemporary women would choose to emulate. When they died out, no new Amazonian societies ever emerged to claim their bloody heritage.*

Margaret Mead, whose controversial views on women came under fire from, among others, Betty Friedan in *The Feminine Mystique,* once testified that there were very few cultures in which women were encouraged or allowed to deploy weapons. Studies showed that women were rarely asked to assist in any "overt aggressive activity." Either there was "some very deep biocultural objection," or records of female-warrior societies had never been unearthed, Mead said. In the animal kingdom, she added, females would fight in defense of their young more fiercely than males, but it was always the males who got the of-

* For a further discussion of the Amazons, see Chapter 12.

fense going. Mead's conclusion was that women, from the earliest times of acculturation, were trained to inhibit aggressive behavior, but once they were goaded into it, they heeded no bounds.

In defiance of such strong cultural prohibitions, there have been a good number of female warriors besides Joan of Arc. Molly Pitcher (a.k.a. Mary Ludwig Hays McCauley) supposedly took over her wounded husband's position as cannoneer against the British in the American Revolutionary War. In the same war, Deborah Sampson disguised herself as a man in order to fight. So did Lucy Brewer in the War of 1812 and Loreta Velasquez in the Civil War. An Army researcher also lists Boadicea, who led troops against the Roman invaders in Britain; Isabella of Spain, who, while pregnant, ordered appropriately designed suits of armor for herself; and General Juana Azurduy de Padilla of Bolivia, who led rebel troops in the Andes during the war of liberation against Spain.

In industrially advanced societies, the best-known cases of women at war were the Russian women who took the place of male soldiers on the front lines during World War II, when the Soviet army was decimated and the U.S.S.R. in danger of collapse, and the Israeli women who fought in the underground against the British and later, after independence, against the Arabs. However, the Russian women did not stay in action long. And the Israeli women actually "fought" far less than the popular myth would have us believe.

Israeli women did serve in convoys of the fighting arm of the Hagana during the 1947–48 War of Independence, according to one scholar. But while they knew how to fire guns, their role often was to hide them or to clean them. Lesley Hazleton wrote that very few women actually saw, or are likely to see, combat. Israel has compulsory conscription for women, yet those women are specifically forbidden to hold combat or combat-related jobs. When Israeli women were seen in photos of the 1973 Six Day War marching in uniforms with rifles, that was "generally the last time" they carried a gun in the army. "For Israel's army women are wearing paper khaki," wrote Hazleton. "They are the secretaries, the clerks, the telephonists, the teletypists, the nurses, the teachers and the social workers . . . filling all the service roles determined by the feminine stereotype."

Two jobs are reserved strictly for women in the Israeli army: typing and parachute folding. Worse, armed forces men sexually exploit female recruits, pressuring them into performing sexual favors, Hazleton contended. This practice is subtly encouraged by the Israeli military brass. (With the growing numbers of women in U.S. armed services have come growing accusations of sexual abuse and harassment.)

There is one war-related role to which women have had access for centuries—that of spy. In various guises, costumed or under misleading identities, women since Delilah have wormed their way into the confidence of generals, have coolly bedded down influential politicians, have carried secret messages across enemy lines and have operated entire spy networks. There might be a "feminine" quality to intrigue in itself. Much "spying" consists of gathering and transmitting information of dubious value, i.e., gossiping in wartime, and women supposedly have excelled in gossip in every age.

However, female intelligence agents in recent wars abjured such "female" pursuits as often as not. In both World War II and in Vietnam, women participated in daring air drops behind enemy lines, worked as saboteurs and couriers and transmitted coded radio signals. The British, according to some researchers, were far more wary of employing women in intelligence than the French or the Germans. They believed, in typically Anglo-sexist fashion, that women were emotionally not stable enough. Besides, as one writer put it, the British Secret Service was among the last great male preserves along with "the Stock Exchange and the Church of England." When it came down to fighting them on the beaches, though, the British expediently abandoned their clubbiness in order to send women alongside men on spy missions in which discovery meant death or consignment to concentration camps.

For better or worse, the female spy whose exploits continue to burn brightly in novels and plays, as well as to haunt nonfiction archives, was no stalwart Vanessa Redgrave type, leaping in darkness behind German lines with a radio secreted in her pack, but the most famous graduate of the courtesan school of spying. Her true name was Margaretha Geertruida Zelle Mac-Leod; her legend lives on as Mata Hari.

Wily and feminine though her spying was, Mata Hari nevertheless was quite a risk-taker, both before the first World War and during it. She was certainly the most exotic item the Dutch village of Leewarden in Friesland ever exported. Although she was executed by the French on charges of being a double agent, Leewarden erected a statue in her honor in 1976, the one hundredth anniversary of her birth. Her story deserves a brief recapitulation, since what she was and how she was able to spy were not that different from the circumstances of two other Parisian performers who did a bit of the same—Mistinguett in World War I, Josephine Baker in World War II. In addition, one story (more than likely apocryphal) links the alleged Java-born daughter of Mata Hari to espionage, betrayal and death in Korea, more than four decades after a French firing squad ended the mother's eventful forty-one years.

Mata Hari remains the ultimate female spy in history and fiction not for the importance of the material she brought her French or German sources, but for the drama, the artist's sense of timing, the sex appeal of her missions. Starting with nothing, the impoverished daughter of a Dutch burgher, she faced a future as bleak as the North Sea in November. But Margaretha Zelle invented herself over and over again. She married a career army officer, who spirited her off to Indonesia. Any other wife might have borne children, made the best of her boring days in the colonial outpost and died in obscurity. Not Margaretha. Lonely and perhaps abused by her alcoholic husband, she did bear at least two children, a boy and a girl. But she also consorted with the natives, learned Hindu dances and the Madya language of Java, and may have had an affair with a Javan man.

Nor was this adventure enough for the young Dutchwoman. She walked out on her husband, courageously returning to Holland in about 1903 to embark on her own pursuits. They were not the ones prescribed for a woman of her class in those unliberated times.

According to her most reliable biographer, she was accepted by the impresario Guimet in Paris around 1905 as an "exotic" dancer after months of tryouts, failures, and "private" performances—the kind that flourished in the glittering decadence of Paris at the turn of the century. There is no question that her act —"oriental" dances staged both partially clothed and nude, made up of undulating erotic movements borrowed from her Javanese observations—did catch the fancy of Parisian society. Calling herself Mata Hari, meaning "eye of the morning" in Madya, she was a short-lived sensation, briefly rivaling Isadora Duncan and Lola Montez in popularity. She was, as well, an eminently successful *cocotte*—a courtesan of the most expensive, refined variety. Her favors were bought by the highest public officials in Europe and paid for with country villas and diamonds. One measure of her fame was that the cigarette brand named for her became the best-selling smoke in France.

Why did she become a spy? Perhaps it seemed a logical, almost inconsequential extension of her liaisons with German and French officials. To carry a few letters, to pass along bits of conversation might have seemed trifling to her. She carried a Dutch passport, enabling her to cross borders with ease even after war broke out. Also, her star was waning as a dancer. She was growing older in the midst of a conflict that had dampened enthusiasm for her kind of entertainment. The City of Light was blacked out. Having worked hard to establish her new persona, Mata Hari may well have thought spying was the most interesting of a narrowing range of options open to her. No doubt it appealed to her risk-taking nature. It also paid well, and by the time the war was under way she was accustomed to wealth. Most historians do not credit her with espionage vital to either the French or German cause. When she was arrested by the

French in 1917, it was as much the result of intragovernmental power plays as it was an attempt to curb the flow of intelligence. Her trial and condemnation were used by the French as a *cause célèbre* to divert public attention from the war.

Mata Hari died before a firing squad in October, 1917. She protested her innocence every step of the way and never divulged any new secrets. Her romantic image was strong to the end. For years afterward, a story circulated that at the last minute, she had ripped open her fur coat to her executioners, so blinding them with her nudity that they missed their target and she escaped. (It is clear this never happened, but what entertainer could ask for a more spectacular closing number?) Whatever the details of her death, her contribution to espionage was almost irrelevant. What counts is that the woman willed herself toward adventure, followed its road unflinchingly and left a legend in her wake.

As if her own life were not great melodrama, the matter of her daughter remains to tantalize Mata Hari-ologists. E. H. Cookridge, a British popular historian, baldly stated that Margaretha left a daughter named Banda behind in Java. Before being executed, Mata Hari wrote Banda from prison, supposedly revealing to this girl (whom she had not seen in fifteen years) her fateful legacy. Banda was a teacher in Dakarta when it was occupied by the Japanese during World War II and was induced to spy on the Europeans there, betraying friends who were spies, according to the Cookridge account. Banda's lover, an Indonesian, was killed, giving her further incentive to spy both for the natives and for the Japanese. This fanciful tale has Banda still later in Saigon as a spy for the French against Ho Chi Minh, then in Korea, where she was unmasked in 1950 and machine-gunned to death at the age of forty-nine, in a muddy ditch. The story sounds like the work of a screenwriter in search of a sequel. But it does attest to the enduring power of the Mata Hari legend.

No subsequent female spy ever made headlines that would have cast Mata Hari in shadow. The adventuring trade of espionage may have lost its appeal to most women. The only female intelligence agents brought to light since World War II have been hopelessly lumpen Soviets in their GUM support hose and brown oxfords. There was a fleeting vogue for the fictional Modesty Blaise, a second-rate female knock-off of James Bond. But while the lady spy declined, her place was usurped by a more modern kind of female adventurer: the terrorist.

Spies are usually loners. The terrorists of the sixties and seventies were, in contrast, apostles of collectivism. Their ranks were filled with women and, in a few cases, dominated by them. Interestingly, opponents of women in military occupations have argued that females could destroy the male bonding so basic to combat, especially "in groups involving the control of interferences to social order" such as war, police work, the military and "elite units closely associated with a machismo image (such as airborne and ranger units or warships)," in the words of a Brookings Institution report. "The type of volunteer might change if women were introduced, perhaps disrupting group cohesion."

However, the report then questioned its own argument, citing "the mounting evidence of women's prominent role in terrorist and guerrilla groups" such as the Symbionese Liberation Army, the Palestinian Liberation Organization and the Baader-Meinhof gang.

The most prominent terrorists of recent years on this continent were the Weathermen. Among their leaders: Bernardine Dohrn, one of the FBI's most wanted fugitives, who surrendered in 1980 after ten years underground. Among their followers: Diana Oughton, who died in the act of assembling bombs in the basement of a Greenwich Village town house in 1970; and Susan Stern, who wrote a personal, nondidactic memoir about her radical years. These young women did not merely cancel out the notion that group combat was antithetical to females. Their words and deeds revealed them as a particularly virulent strain of contemporary daredevils who explored the bloodiest boundaries of machisma.

Dohrn stands as a classic symbol of the Weather Underground. Her frank stare, peering out from an attractive, unsmiling face on her "Wanted" poster, triggers memories of the Vietnam protests of the early sixties as they escalated from silent vigils to calamitous trials to pitched street-fighting. A compact woman, Dohrn stamped an indelible impression upon enemies and allies alike. "She was not so much beautiful as she was commanding," wrote Susan Stern. "There was something in the way she carried herself that exuded authority. She had large breasts, which were partially exposed because her blouse was half unbuttoned. She wore no makeup and her straight hair fell in wisps around her shoulders. Her eyes were clear and steady but not unfriendly." Stern was thrilled the first time she met Dohrn: "such self-assurance, such elegance. . . . Her presence seemed to dominate the room."

In the Weather Underground, Dohrn was a notable fanatic. It was she who authored diatribes issued after bombings, she who exhorted the Weatherwomen to carry chains and baseball bats, she who led troops into battle with phrases like "Vietcong women fight," she who openly admired the brutality of the Charles Manson gang.

In Stern's eyes, Dohrn was the incarnation of the New Age feminist revolutionary: "Wonder Woman" as Red Guard. Jailed in the same cell in Chicago after their "women's action" riot during the 1969 Days of Rage, Stern observed her idol as almost a "fashion model." Dohrn wore a black leather jacket, boots, "everything just so." Stern decided Dohrn "possessed a splendor all of her own. Like a queen, her nobility set her apart."

Although the Weathermen were torn asunder by ideological battles over the role of women, Dohrn began her career in the front ranks and remained there. If she underwent a wrenching psychological struggle to mold herself into the macha woman she became, we do not know of it. On the other hand, both Oughton and Stern *did* have to take lessons in toughness, and painfully suppressed their softer sides. They belonged to the generation of upper middle class women who carried the banners of the new feminist movement. In fact, Oughton's revolutionary politics grew out of the same experiences—civil rights work and the Peace Corps—that nurtured the early feminist radicals. But while those feminists clung to their original code of nonviolence, the Diana Oughtons abandoned it with a vengeance.

Oughton was the daughter of privilege, as were many of her terrorist and radical feminist contemporaries. Her father was vice-president of the family bank in a small town south of Chicago. Right up until her accidental death in the town house, she received trust-fund checks. She felt anguish at the disparity between her wealth and the poverty of others, her biographer, Thomas Powers, noted. It was one reason for going to Guatemala as a Peace Corps volunteer. But there, the first glimmer of her combative side showed. A local priest invited Diana and another volunteer to take target practice in the courtyard of a convent. Oughton, who had learned as a child to use a gun on family pheasant hunts, surprised her companions by hitting every target. The priest took to calling her Diana La Cazadora (Diana the Huntress). A few years later, she was hurling rocks at Chicago police alongside Dohrn and Stern during the Days of Rage. Two years after that, she was dead, identified by a piece of her pinky finger that matched her FBI fingerprint.

Stern, too, came from a well-to-do family. She made it obvious that her aggressiveness, her exhilaration at rioting and her love of guns were more the psychological rebelliousness of a neurotic Jewish American princess than the cogent actions of a revolutionary. Was this also true of other Weatherwomen? It could be. Conservative critics harped on peer pressure and adolescent rebellion as the roots of the defiance of the late sixties. Susan Stern affirmed this in her autobiography:

> Weathermen had swung a pendulum in me. The vogue was to be tough and macho, and I was as overzealously aggressive and abandoned as a Weatherman as I had been timid and frightened prior to it. I was intent on being as outrageous as possible.

At the same time, though, Stern articulated the connection between her personal rebellion and the increasingly violent spirit stirring in radical women. Recounting the 1969 riots in Seattle, she wrote that they had fostered "a heavy corps of street-fighting women." Their attitude was analogous to male bonding. The women were "full of electric energy," once repressed, now "suddenly and daringly un-damned." Nothing short of fighting would now satisfy them. "We were tasting the macho strength that characterized men, but we felt it as keenly as women. . . . It was a precious, dazzling moment."

With each taste, Stern's appetite for more violence intensified. Her desire went beyond purely ideological bounds. She was a "Macho Mama." Smashing windows was part of her "gut-check," which she defined as doing "something foolhardy just to make sure you weren't afraid of doing it." It was Susan Stern's dogmatic, Vietnam-era substitute for scaling Annapurna or for driving at one hundred and eighty miles an hour around the Indianapolis oval, for proving herself in ways similar to male macho rites of passage. She might have been the only Weatherwoman to set it down on paper, but surely she could not have been the only Weatherwoman for whom machisma and revolution were inexorably interwoven.

Stern died in 1976 of an apparent heart seizure. By that time the Weather Underground, jolted initially by the 1970 town house explosion, had long since ceased its terrorist activities. A comparatively tiny outfit, the Symbionese Liberation Army, had taken its place in the headlines, almost exclusively because Patty Hearst was under its spell. In Europe, meanwhile, terrorism had its counterparts in the Baader-Meinhof gang, named after a German male revolutionary and a female journalist who were its leaders. The significance of the Baader-Meinhof gang in terms of women was that it encouraged the growth of "second-generation" terrorist gangs that counted numerous young middle-class women among their bloodthirstiest members. The single most chilling act of the seventies wave of German terrorism was performed by a lawyer's daughter, twenty-six-year-old Susanne Albrecht. In 1977, she appeared at the front door of a friend's fa-

ther, who happened to be the chairman of an important bank
and an adviser to German Chancellor Helmut Schmidt. She was
carrying a bouquet of roses. The banker led her and two companions inside. When the man's wife heard sounds of a struggle,
she rushed downstairs to find Susanne gone. Her husband lay
dead on the floor, five bullets in his head and back.

Whether the setting was the United States or Germany,
whether the motives were political or psychological, terrorist
women in recent decades have blown to smithereens the idea
that warriors must be male.

The most serious female assault on male military bastions in recent years has been directly upon the U.S. armed forces. Inroads
by women have been remarkable, both toward the top of the
pyramid—officers in all branches of the service and officer-candidates at the service academies—and at the bottom, the recruits.
What made these inroads possible? It was *not* just the influence
of equal-opportunity employment, since feminist spokeswomen
have nearly all been in the pacifist camp. Instead, the impetus
came first from the Vietnam aftermath and the changeover from
conscription to a volunteer army, second from the growing number of women wage earners in general. As the Vietnam war
whimpered to a close, releasing thousands of veterans from the
armed forces, the services suddenly discovered they needed bodies. A whole crop of willing ones happened to be female.

At places like the Army's Fort McClellan, the Navy's Norfolk
naval base, the Marines' Camp Pendleton and the Air Force's
Williams Air Force Base, what had been a trickle of women was,
by the mid-seventies, turning into a tide. In 1968, the height of
the Vietnam buildup, women constituted 1 percent of military
personnel—about thirty-five thousand in all. What's more, there
was a legal ceiling, limiting their numbers to 2 percent. Ten
years later, female military personnel had soared to one hundred
and ten thousand, or 5.5 percent. By 1983, the estimated total
was to be 10 percent.

Not that there was anything new about American women in

uniform. In the course of World War II, some three hundred and fifty thousand women served the United States in military support positions. (The most dashing were Jacqueline Cochran's WASPs, mentioned in Chapter 5. A total of 38 WASPs were killed in the war, yet none was allowed a single veteran's benefit until a special law was passed by Congress in 1972.) Still, from the end of World War II through the Vietnam war, women who joined the military were confined almost exclusively to health care and administrative roles—nurses, typists, secretaries. Once the world war was over, the Pentagon imposed the 2 percent ceiling, refused to permit females under the age of eighteen to enlist (though males over seventeen could) and severely restricted the upward mobility of women who chose a military career.

By contrast, in the late seventies, with the draft ended and the percentage of male recruits dropping precipitously, the attitude of the military brass shifted. A full 80 percent of military jobs have been opened to women, including such controversial ones as jet pilot, drill instructor and able-bodied seaman. In 1976, one of every thirteen enlisted recruits was female. Over 40 percent of them have landed in nontraditional jobs: 15 percent in communications and intelligence, nearly 10 percent in service and supply handling, nearly 7 percent in electrical and mechanical equipment repair. The United States, by the decade's close, had a higher percentage of women in its armed forces than any other country—8 percent, or one hundred and fifty thousand women.

Such extreme changes could scarcely occur without resistance. Women were still prohibited by a 1948 law from serving on combat vessels or combat planes, and prohibited by an Army regulation from joining its infantry or armor combat units. There were still traditionalists like Lieutenant General A. P. Clark, a former Air Force Academy superintendent, who thundered that the idea of female combatants "offends the dignity of womanhood. . . . Fighting is a man's job and should remain so." Great minds like that of General William C. Westmoreland, the former Army chief of staff, drifted even further into absurdity by declaring that "maybe you could find one woman in 10,000 who could lead in combat, but she would be a freak. I don't believe women can carry a pack, live in a foxhole or go a week without taking a bath."

Skirting, for a moment, the relevancy of the general's opinion on bathing, there *are* substantive hurdles to be overcome, from separate washrooms aboard ships and the sizes of Army-issue boots, to the ability of women in forced marches and the philosophy of women as suitable warriors. Yet even as debates on these issues were being conducted, events were overtaking them. Women joined the astronaut space program in 1978, broke old taboos by integrating combat-support naval ship crews, took command of officer-candidate squadrons, flew combat-support planes and learned how to survive in a mythical enemy jungle by knifing wild rabbits for food.

At the same time, a retired Marine infantry major, writing in *Army Times,* complained that women recruits at Fort McClellan boot camp were still *not* getting equal training hours in such key elements as the M-16 rifle, defensive tactics, and marches and bivouacs. Thus, if they were to find themselves in a combat situation, they would be subjected to greater risks. Would he want his daughters to join that man's army? "Maybe," the former Marine concluded. But he felt that the training was "unfair" to female recruits. "My daughters might be in an active theater without having been trained in the basic tactical maneuvers [that] I consider essential for their survival."

No one knew more intimately how complex such a quandary could be than Lieutenant (j.g.) Sue "Mace the Ace" Mason, jet pilot, of VAQ-33, the Firebirds, based at Norfolk Naval Air Station, Virginia.

Sue Mason's tousled light brown hair was blowing in the Indian summer breeze as she leaned out of her Volkswagen to watch an A-4 jet streak over Chesapeake Bay. "Sure is easy to see why we call 'em 'Scooters,' isn't it?" she drawled in a voice that had an

Okie sense of humor built into its tone. "It just *looks* like a scooter," she nodded with finality. "Better ride than you'll ever get in an amusement park!"

I believed her. After all, she flew the A-4 for a living. She flew it fast and flew it well, piloting it to 20,000 feet above the clouds and through mock attacks a few hundred feet above aircraft carriers. Mason was as familiar with that attack plane, now climbing until it was a glint of steel disappearing in the distance, as Janet Guthrie was with her Lola Cosworth race car. For Sue Mason was one of fewer than a dozen female jet pilots in the U. S. Navy.

The irony was that this distinction, which put Mason in the front row of female adventurers, also placed her in a triple bind. First, she was expected to play the pioneer woman warrior to the hilt, to show "the right stuff" like other jet pilots, to live up to the cocky male "I-can-hack-it" code. Second, she had to do it without the superior jet training that her male counterparts received, because the pipeline through which women pilots were funneled after Naval Officers Candidate School was less thorough than that of male pilots. Third, she had to do it and still confront the one question her male colleagues never had to ask themselves: should she, or any woman, be a warrior at all? What made Sue Mason so impressive was the thoughtful cheeriness with which she faced these perplexing issues.

In the air, she was a natural. The mission of VAQ-33 was electronic warfare: Its pilots made believe they were enemy attackers in mock war games played with aircraft carriers somewhere out in the ocean, on various "exercises" during the year. Sue Mason was a featured character in this drama. She was a "bad guy" who nosed her A-4 jet toward a "boat," (naval pilot lingo for any kind of battleship) simulating a "bullet" (air-to-surface missile), while the navigator in her back seat tried to jam the radar aboard the carrier. The object of the game was to take over the radio frequency that the carrier used to guide its own "good guys" planes, fooling those planes by ordering them far away into the harmless blue yonder. The carrier's role was to detect

the "bad guys" (planes of an enemy nation), intercept their mis-
siles, stop the attempt to jam the radar, and keep its planes in
the sky nearby for a counterattack. For Mason, there was no better playground in the world than the skies over a big "boat,"
messing up its radar as if she were splattering a raw egg across
somebody's television screen. There was no better role than that
of a bad guy, vectoring some poor "good-guy" pilot way out into
left field with her skillful fly patterns. So what if a few fellow
"bad guys" flew so close that they were almost within shouting
distance, swarming like a bunch of steel-plated bees at nearly
the speed of sound in a small area where one wrong turn meant
a fiery collision? That was the game, too.*

Every few weeks, VAQ would prepare for one of these "de-
tachments." Gladly leaving her paperwork behind, Sue would
step into her tan, one-piece flight suit, slip over it her heavy life
vest and unique outer pants built to counter the pressure of
gravity forces, wriggle her head into her snug crash helmet, and
mount the stairs to the cockpit. It was so tight it was like crawling into a cocoon. She would attach her oxygen mask to the
plane's oxygen supply and hook her flight suit to the ejection
seat, adjust the clear plastic canopy, and then take off for a
ground station in Florida, California or Puerto Rico. Most of
VAQ-33 then regrouped for a briefing on the game plan. Mason
loved the sense of trust among the thirty or more pilots and non-
coms while on detachment, loved the soaring morale as everyone
anticipated two or three weeks of daily flying.

On Day 1, the "bad guy" planes, either singly or in formation,
flew out to a given spot in the sky. By radio, the planes (as many
as fifteen in a group) then got their "push" or attack times, and
headed toward the carrier. When they were within ten miles of
the ship, Mason could see little dots aiming for the carrier—the
other attack planes. Both A-4s like hers flying at four hundred

---

* Despite the warlike activity, VAQ-33 was classified as a combat-*support*
unit. Women were still not allowed in those categorized as actual combat
units.

and fifty miles an hour and some faster, they buzzed the ship or
orbited overhead. It was a time for her to have every nerve ending tingling, yet to remain poised and, above all, alert. Mason
had to make certain she stayed on her assigned altitude; if she
strayed, she could be in someone else's airspace in a fraction of a
second. It only took from five to fifteen minutes to make the actual run, but during those minutes her head would be swiveling
around watching for the others, and she would wish she had
eyes on four sides of her head. She knew that everyone else was
as capable a pilot as she. She also knew that to the air controller
in charge, the blips on the radar screen approximated mayhem.

After converging on the ship for the specified time, she and
the others headed back to the ground station. Some days they
would make one run, some days two. It was what she had joined
the Navy to do, what she yearned to do every day of her career.
(The rest of her time was spent in more mundane chores as a
line-officer, keeping planes in good condition and watching over
squadron personnel.) Just once had the flying been really hairy,
and that was back in training.

She had been flying a different jet, a T-28 transport, over
Santa Rosa island off Florida. She was in the sector reserved for
acrobatics, and she was leveling her wings after a barrel roll
when—Bingo! There was another plane dead center in her wind-
shield. It was there and gone in a second, but it had come so
near that if it had not been traveling so fast, she would have
been able to read the numbers on its tail! A few seconds passed.
Whew, that was close, she thought to herself. A few more seconds passed, and her knees began to shake. Pilot error. The two
words could spell death. She didn't like to think much about
those words in the air.

On the ground, Mason was one of the boys, one of the wise
guys. At the end of a routine exercise over the Pacific Ocean
once, Sue, in her front-zippered flight suit with "Firebirds" lettered on a diagonal red patch across one side of the chest and
"Mason" across the other, slipped into the A-4 cockpit's front
seat. She pulled the canopy down over her head, waiting for the

go-ahead hand signal from the line man standing on the runway ahead of her.

When he gave the signal, she saluted back . . . by flipping up a "Mr. Bill" hand puppet. The line men doubled over with laughter as Sue's A-4 taxied off and up toward home.

Ever since, at lunch in the officers' mess in Norfolk, Mason and her cronies would lapse into falsetto Mr. Bill "oh, no!" banter at the slightest provocation, to the confounded stares of diners at neighboring tables. "I don't know how many of these ladies you've met," a senior officer confided after a particularly hilarious lunch, "but Sue is special. She's the best." He paused for the highest compliment. "She's a *professional*."

Actually, Sue Mason became something special the first day her father sat her on his lap in his combine in the wheat fields of western Oklahoma. The second girl in a family of two daughters and two sons, Sue had an entirely unorthodox upbringing compared to her older sister. "She got stuck in the kitchen helping Mom," Sue explained, "and I got to run the tractor." By junior high school, little Sue's feet could reach the pedals, and she spent every summer doing custom-combine harvesting with her father, from Oklahoma clear north to the Dakotas. Other children might have grown up hating their summer chores. For Sue, jockeying the three-ton machine through acres of wheat from sunup to sundown was as much fun as any carnival ride. Entering Oklahoma State University with no particular career plans, she soon decided to move a giant step up the transport ladder by enrolling in her first flying course. And it was just as natural for her to love it. It wasn't so much the power she felt as she pushed a little Cessna through its paces, nor the sensation of freedom in the sky. It was just, well, *neat* tooling around up there. And there was so much more scenery to be viewed from the cockpit of a single-engine tail-dragger than from the cab of a combine.

She finally majored in social sciences, mostly because she had taken more anthropology and psychology courses than anything else. She also advanced to a commercial flying course and then to the job of flight instructor. Without stopping to ponder it, Sue had begun a full-fledged affair with airplanes, and she sought any means she could to spend more than the routine "two Sundays a month" in their company. Soon, she was asking herself how she could get her hands on bigger, faster planes. The answer, in 1976, after a year as a full-time flight instructor, was the Navy's Aviation Officer Candidate School.

Why the Navy? She did not have much choice: the Air Force was not yet training female aviators. Besides, "Sue-Bob" as friends kiddingly called her, was definitely a flatlander. "Having come from Heartland, U.S.A., anything that was on the coast was pretty exotic," she recalled, and that included the Navy. The five-foot-four-inch dynamo who thought nothing of putting a Cessna 150 through a loop-de-loop got flutters in her solar plexus when she saw a body of water that did not have trees on its horizon. Sure enough, that's what the Navy showed her. "Whoa! Where's terra firma?" she thought, her nerves a tad shaky, the first time she flew over the ocean. Then came survival training, which was not the most pleasant introduction to salt water. She was pushed off a boat with her parachute and flight gear still on, hitting the waves like a three-year-old dressed in fourteen snowsuits. "I mean, you're out there treading water, not that mobile, and you're trying to find that little toggle switch to inflate your life vest and you know it's down there somewhere. . . ." She shook her head wryly. "It's not like basking on a beach."

Her unfamiliarity with oceans did not stand in the way of her becoming an outstanding Navy pilot. The more of an adventure a job was, the more Mason enjoyed it. She was the kind of young woman who never thinks about competing against others; it was her own standard that was hardest to measure up to. Mechanically inclined, she was not insecure in the technical courses at the Pensacola, Florida Officers Candidate School, despite the fact that she and five other women in the forty-member class were the first of their sex to complete the course. Oh, there were a few weird moments. Like being issued a man's undershirt and wondering what to do with it besides fold it into the basic Navy-regulation four-inch by four-inch square. . . . And then wondering how to fold a brassiere into a four-inch by four-inch square. . . . And then working out with her squad at a very cold sea wall with the instructor commanding them to strip to their undershirts in order to slip on an extra sweatshirt. . . . And *then*, with all sorts of ships on the water viewing this striptease, realizing why it would be a good idea to wear the silly undershirt in the future. . . .

But that was minor weirdness. Major problems arose after the sixteen-week course when she was assigned to Whiting Field for four months of primary flight training. Male ensigns, following twelve to fifteen flights in primary prop planes, went directly into primary jet training. Sue and the other women, however, were forced to go through the whole prop "pipeline," both primary and advanced. Only after they received their wings and were named to a squadron did they get a chance to learn jets. As a result, Mason arrived at VAQ-33 with about seventy hours of jet experience, her male counterparts with two hundred hours. Regardless of her self-confidence, she was entering the main phase of her Navy career with a serious disadvantage compared to men. The Navy argued that since women were not allowed in combat, there was no need to "waste" expensive jet training on them. The women argued that if they were going to hold the same jobs as men, they should be equally prepared, but they were not. In addition, the cost of the extra jet training was miniscule in comparison with the million-dollar price tag on the very jets they were piloting. It was Catch-22, Navy style.

There was more involved than just hours. As we watched the jets take off on that balmy December day in Norfolk, Mason explained that switching from props to jets was almost akin to switching from a custom-combine to a Ferrari. "When you spend time in multiengine props, you're learning things that can work against you in jets. You're taught crew concept—here's your copilot, work out coordination between you—but what good does that do when not only is there no one in the right seat; there's not even a right seat to be in!" Or smoothness. A prop pilot strives for it. In a jet, "smooth" could mean "crash." Jets are high performance items that demand what Sue called "right now!" responses. "In a multiengine prop, you've got more time to think, get a cup of coffee, call out the altitudes, da-dee-da. In a single-engine jet, you've got one engine there to fail. If it flames out, honey, you better be trying to get a relight on the thing—right now!—because if it doesn't go, you're out of luck, out of cards, bottom of the deck," Sue declared with her Okie penchant for multiple metaphors. A safety valve? Naturally, there was always the yank on the yellow ejection-seat grip. But for Mason or anyone else, it was the last resort. "You're going to—phffffft!—blast yourself out into the cold air 30,000 feet above the ground, right? And hope that your parachute works?" She spoke as if she were describing what it was like to jump in front of a speeding subway train. "It's not a ride I'd buy a ticket to go on," she finished calmly.

Carnival rides . . . amusement park . . . scooters. Sue's metaphors illustrated the almost childlike, happy-go-lucky air with which she approached one of the world's most demanding jobs. But there was a serious side to this merry little mechanic with the Firebirds' thunderbolt-and-eagle insignia on her nameplate, a side evident from the books on her coffee table at home: Lorenz's *On Aggression*, Morris's *The Naked Ape*, Mary Gordon's *Final Payments*. It was the side that made her conscientious about keeping in touch with other female Navy pilots, whether they were based in the next hangar at Norfolk or way out in the California desert testing the latest prototypes from Lockheed. Right stuff or wrong, jet pilot though she was, Sue Mason was always aware she was a woman in a traditional male role. Her intellectual side kept striving to make sense out of the intensely "macho" occupation her mechanical knack had made her so attuned to.

The first time she sat in a jet simulator, its blacked-out canopy preventing her from seeing anything but the dials and switches and meters on the panel, she realized props had been a mere tickle compared to the kick she would get from a jet that could hit eighty knots an hour a second after she nudged the throttle. She felt hyperalert, totally alive. But inevitably, it made her think about what would happen if the rules were changed, if she were sent into combat.

Sipping a beer in her house in Norfolk, with Joni Mitchell singing about Amelia Earhart on the stereo, Sue slowed her naturally fast drawl, trying to put those thoughts into comprehensible sentences.

"With the training I've had, I know I'm more aggressive now than I was three or four years ago. I've *learned* that aggression. I've learned it's a valuable thing in certain situations. I *could* be put in a combat situation. I think I could go out and fight another airplane in the air and fight very, very well. That would be the *ultimate* challenge." She caught her breath and said even more slowly, "I think I could really *love* it . . ." she paused again, ". . . if I could jump right in, before I had time to sit and think, 'what would Margaret Mead say?'"

She laughed, but she was terribly serious, as if she were voicing aloud for the first time an internal argument that she had not dared to express before. "If I could stop those thoughts—yeah, I could do it. I could do it feeling it's him against me. Him or her, as the case may be, one on one. I think that would really get my blood going.

"But there's this *thinking* thing. This doesn't happen in a vacuum. What effect would it have on me afterward? So much of our society is based upon the idea of the *man* being the one who goes out and does whatever fighting there is to do. For sure, the female has the capability of staying home and defending the nest. But going out aggressively and seeking to do battle? If it gets to the point where women, as a matter of course, are going out and flying combat, the male-female relationship has got to change drastically."

Sue looked up over the rim of her glass and her eyes crinkled into a smile. "I have a hard time seeing myself with a little one on my knee, explaining to the little one how Mommy got all her war medals on her chest for shooting down the bad guys."

Was it any better for a man to boast to his children about combat victories? Mason wasn't sure. "It's a bit of an appalling picture, even to think of a *man* with a little person on his knee, explaining about shooting up other people. But that's the way the natural selection process has brought things about. It's more socially acceptable than for a female. Looking at it from an anthropological perspective, it just gets to be a can of worms."

Given the razzmatazz manner of most male pilots toward combat flying—"they think of it as something between an orgasm and a car crash," Sue said—it was hard to imagine men burrowing as deeply into the implications of war as this woman did. Nor did every female pilot poke around in so many anthropological corners. Lieutenant (j.g.) Nila Sandusky, a twenty-four-year-old Indianian who flew T-39 jet transports out of Norfolk as well as A-4s, took a more typical position. Aerial maneuvers, for her, were high-risk performances that gave great personal pleasure. She giggled about games she and others played over carriers: "We go up and do dogfights," she said, grinning from ear to ear. "You just dive at the deck and at the last minute you pull out. It's really scary. Maybe that's why I love it." She and Barbara Habedank, also a T-39 pilot, both got a terrific jolt out of one other antic. "You get going just a hundred or so feet off the ground," Nila said, "you fly level for a while, and then— whoosh!" She traced first a slow horizontal line with her arm, suddenly turning it into an almost vertical ascent. "Straight up! It's quite a feeling!"

"Power," Barbara Habedank emphasized. "It's the feeling of power."

Sue Mason loved flying as much as the other two women. Indeed, she felt women might have an advantage over men because touch and finesse, requirements in jet combat, supposedly came more naturally to women. But Mason would not admit to loving the power, as Habedank did. What Sue loved were the rolls and loops, "punching holes in the sky," acrobatics. Even as she flew right on the edge, Sue doubted that she could ever come to grips with the larger questions posed by her actions—the questions of men and women and combat. "Power" did not crop up often in her conversation. "Exhilaration" was as far as she would go in describing how it felt with a stick between your legs, a hand on the throttle and a jet warplane embracing you.

There was no question that female jet pilots were a breed apart from male ones. Their private cars were one example. Male pilots love to drive as much as they love to fly, and the Corvette is so common among them that it is known as the "ensign-mobile." Yet Sue Mason drove her old Volkswagen (nicknamed Bug-Bob), Nila Sandusky had a two-year-old Oldsmobile Fire-bird and Barbara Habedank a fourteen-year-old Ford Falcon. Humor came more easily to the women than the men, who pre-ferred to brag about how alert they could be in the air after par-tying all night. Sue Mason, however, poked fun at herself repeat-edly, telling of how she had gotten tangled up in her parachute, or how she once mistakenly inflated her life jacket while stand-ing on a runway.

The differences between male and female jet aviators might have been summed up best by a highly personal symbol: the hel-met. Each pilot decorates it any way he or she wants. A male pilot in VAQ-33 had so many purple lightning bolts painted on his that it could have belonged to a Hell's Angel. Sue Mason's helmet was white, with three decals: a rainbow, a sunflower and a butterfly. "The fellows were a little upset that I had a flower, so I put a bee decal on, for a while too," she said, smiling. "I told them it was a killer bee."

The majority of Americans—civilians as well as military person-nel, women as well as men—would rather *not* see women get "the right to fight," according to studies made in 1977 and 1980. Still, the outlook is for more and more women to enter military professions, whether they wind up learning to fire a weapon in combat or to provide support for the men who do. And as Sue Mason predicted, these women will undoubtedly alter the male military establishment as profoundly as they are altered by it.

Nowhere has this been more apparent than at the three major service academies.

At West Point, the most traditional of the three, the pioneering plebes who became the class of 1980 suffered the hardest knocks. By their third year, nearly half—47.9 percent—of the initial women plebes had dropped out. One-third of the women in the next group, class of 1981, had also left. (The comparable drop-out percentages for men were 38.2 percent in the class of 1980, 27.2 percent in the class of 1981, strongly suggesting that West Point is tough on *all* its cadets.)

The service academy women have already made an impact. More than half of the first female graduates of West Point were assigned, at their own request, to combat-related branches of the Army, including field artillery, air defense and aviation. Malicious hazing with a new co-ed twist also cropped up at West Point's field training course, Camp Buckner. The most squeamish of the female cadets reportedly were picked on and forced to commit such acts as killing chickens by biting their necks. A particular male cadet was taunted for dating a female cadet; the young man later said one of his male colleagues declared that he would rather shoot a female officer in the back than follow her into combat. The dating pair represented a new phenomenon at the academies. Women especially found it expedient to latch on to male cadets as steady companions, perhaps for self-protection in addition to other reasons.

At the Air Force Academy, adult female advisers, expected to be guidance counselors for the first female cadets, were gone after their initial year. The younger women preferred to comfort one another rather than confide in any officer, even if one was a woman. At least one Air Force Academy cadet resigned before her first year was over because she was pregnant, a medical problem never before seen by Academy doctors.

Male cadets at both academies came to believe that overall standards had been reduced to accommodate the "weaker" sex. In fact, separate, lower physical fitness standards *were* established for women (as they were at regular officer candidate schools and recruit boot camps). No women could meet all of the running, chinning and climbing requirements set for men, no matter how hard they tried. But in academic areas, the standards remained the same for both sexes. Women, who tended to enter the academies with higher verbal and English academic qualifications than the men, but lower mathematics and science scores, matched the men stride for stride once classes got underway.

The most fundamental impact upon the service academies has been psychological. If the Stock Exchange and the Secret Service had been Britain's most enduring male preserves, their counterparts in the United States included, until 1976, the academies. Imagine, then, how traumatic it was for male officers steeped in macho tradition to see *girls* lining up for induction at West Point, Annapolis and the Air Force Academy that bicentennial summer. Why, it bordered on the unnatural. . . .

The sun was peeking through the ponderosa pines in Jack's Valley when reveille sounded over the loudspeaker. "Come on, ladies, you're wasting time!" *A woman's voice, in "Beast!"* Lieutenant Rhoda Schweitzer was shouting into the tent that was temporary home for the fifteen young women of Invaders Squadron, Class of 1980, Air Force Academy.

Dressed in black baseball caps and ill-fitting khaki fatigues, they stumbled out of the tent, blinking, and lined up. "Present arms!" yelled an upperclassman. Their right hands swept up to their foreheads in salute. It was 6:15 A.M. on day 29 of Basic Cadet Training—Beast—a grueling six-week prelude to the next four years of study.

"Cain, Utley and Benjamin—latrine duty," barked Lieutenant Schweitzer. Three cadets trotted off to the large lavatory that served the women's tent encampment. The others began straightening their cots, fluffing up the sleeping bags, sweeping the floor and rolling up the side flaps. With their name tags sewn above their shirt pockets, and their dialectal babble, they looked and sounded like an all-female cast for *The Sands of Iwo Jima*.

Peggy Walker, seventeen years old, Bensonville, Ill.; Donna Smart, eighteen, Huntsville, Ala.; June Van Horn, twenty-one, Glidden, Iowa; Gail Benjamin, twenty, Laurelton, New York; Joyce Cain, eighteen, Ocean Springs, Miss. . . . Thirteen whites, two blacks, brought together in the foothills of the Rockies for the first phase of what they hoped would be a career in the military.

It was also the most punishing physical and emotional phase. Each day, they were being run through marching drills, obstacle courses, rifle practice, armed and unarmed fighting. They were being lectured on "the honor code" and "the morality of war." They were being shown motivational movies such as *Patton*. Math, political science, engineering—they would come later. Jack's Valley was designed as their first dose of combat skills. College? Hardly. This is the Air Force, Ms. Jones.

0630 hours. The women were hustled outside again. "Parade rest!" In unison, left feet took a single step sideways, hands were crossed at the small of each back. "Atten-HUT! Forward, MARCH!" Off they went through the trees to join the men of Invaders Squadron. One woman was on crutches; several others were in sneakers instead of black boots. Among the first differences to show up was the relative inability of female feet to take a constant pounding in boots shaped for a man. (Sue Mason had the same trouble; in training, she looked at her feet one day and realized that her toes had never touched the inside of her spacious boots.) In Jack's Valley, dozens of women had developed shin splints, stress fractures and blisters.

The Invaders filed through a mess tent for scrambled eggs, bread, meat, milk, juice and cereal—the start of seven thousand calories scheduled daily to keep their strength up. The food was gobbled in regulation, straight-backed silence.

The day before had been a strenuous and humiliating one for both sexes. They had to practice on the "assault course," a nasty series of gravel pits strung with barbed wire, followed by dirt-covered tunnels, log barricades and wood targets. The idea was to climb and crawl through the whole thing, rifles in hand, to get the feeling of jungle warfare. The upperclassmen who conducted assault training were regarded as the most sadistic in the Valley. Today, the assault performances would not just be repeated. They would be timed.

The girls were tired and scared as the squadron marched, double-time, to the first test of the day—the "confidence course." It was similar to the "ropes course" on Outward Bound, except that these women knew what was in store for them. "We're looking for sick squirrels, because they've told us that if we find one case of bubonic plague they'll move us out of here," said one Invader, only half-joking.

Beast was living up to its name for everyone, regardless of sex. Three of the new women and thirty-two men (out of one hundred and fifty-five women and fourteen hundred and fifty men, total) had quit already to return to civilian life. Most "basics" (first-year cadets) left because they simply did not like military discipline. Others could not take the competition. But the women who stayed had made an immediate impression on the academy superintendent. "Our goal was that we'd work for an equal level of effort in the physical activities, rather than an equal level of performance," said Lieutenant General James R. Allen. "Well, we're not getting equal effort from them. We're getting a greater effort."

"Come on, Patty, let's go! That's it. . . . Pull yourself!" The members of Patty Ryan's group, male and female, were bellowing encouragement as the eighteen-year-old with one finger in a splint struggled to shinny up a high rope that led to a bridge of widely spaced logs. She fell after reaching the first big knot in the rope, picked herself up, started again. An upperclassman gave her a little boost and she finally made it over the bridge. When she crossed and climbed down at the other end, her group broke into applause. "Never climbed a rope before!" she said proudly to a beefy upperclassman who hugged her. He was her brother, Mike. Patty was one of seven women whose brothers were currently attending or had attended the Academy.

"She was real busted up," Mike Ryan said later, referring to Patty's finger, "but she was good." Like everyone else, he pointed out that women were disadvantaged in the physical activities that put a premium on strength or height. The disadvantage was obvious at the "Slide for Life" section of the confidence course, where Gail, June and Peggy were nervously egging one another on up a ladder of logs that rose fifty feet high. From a platform at the top, they started edging down a rope that was angled toward the ground, hanging by their knees but also holding on with their upstretched arms. "I feel like Tarzan!" June shouted. "Gail, it ain't that bad," yelled Peggy. "Nah, it's fun!" came the reply. Their lesser upper-body strength nevertheless made them slower than the men. When I took a turn at the slide, the ladder logs were so widely spaced I could barely reach from one to another. My palms were wet as I inched onto the rope. I was frightened speechless, and a quarter of the way along I thought the muscles in my arms would snap. I was a sweating blob of jelly when I was low enough to drop to the ground. By then, June, Gail and Peggy were scrambling to the next obstacle. Tough? Courageous? These kids were in the Annapurna League, and I wouldn't have made a rookie team. "Don't help me!" screamed June when an upperclassman went to boost her over a parallel bar. "I want to do it myself!" The confidence course was living up to its name.

The next activity was an ethics lecture on war; then it was almost lunchtime. The Invaders lined up for premeal chin-ups on a crossbar. The women were permitted to hold themselves with heads above the bar, rather than raise and lower their bodies as the men did. Gail Benjamin, her face distorted into a frozen grimace, won cries of "all right!" when she lasted twenty long seconds. One of a total of four black female enrollees, Gail had spent a year working in the probation department of a New York City courthouse after dropping out of Vassar. She had come here in part because a younger brother was already enrolled, in part because she had decided she was "ready for a little discipline." She was getting plenty of the latter. So was Peggy Walker, who was being subjected to a nose-to-nose quiz from an upperclassman before being allowed to eat.

"Who was the leading American ace in World War II?" yelled the interrogator.

"Sir, I do not know." She was sent to the back of the line. When her turn came again, the question was the leading Canadian ace. She missed. French ace? She missed again. Finally, "Who was the leading all-around World War II ace?" Peggy's blue eyes widened. "Major Erich Hartmann with 352 kills, SIR!" she yelled. A top-ranked public school graduate who yearned to be an astronaut, Peggy at last got lunch.

With their meal quickly eaten, the Invaders were ordered double-time across a field to their moment of truth—the assault course.

First, they went through a panting set of calisthenics. "You make me sick, Basics!" sneered one older cadet as sweat ran in rivulets down the grime on their faces. When they were about to collapse, they were run to put on helmets, sling ten-pound rifles over their arms and begin crawling through the pits. An upperclassman had advised them earlier on how to handle the anguish of the assault course. "Just yell 'KILL!' all the time and you'll be all right." Whistles blew; "KILL!" became a steady chant. The air crackled with a ferocious rat-tat-tat-BOOM from a tape recorder. Simulated howitzer shells exploded and suddenly the course was filled with writhing, leaping bodies.

June Van Horn, already engaged to an Academy upperclassman, was scared to death. But there was no way she would let anyone know that. "KILL!" she shrieked as she bellied her way across the first pit; "KILL!" as she came through a tunnel; "KILL!" as she scrambled under a treacherous set of concertina barbed wire; "KILL!" as she jammed the rifle barrel into a target; "KILL KILL KILL!" as she dashed the final sprint past a timekeeper who yelled a number at her. She ran to an instructor with a scorecard. "14:15, Sir," she said, her teeth caked with spittle. "Hold your rifle up, Miss Van Horn!" he howled back. "Repeat!"

"FOURTEEN FIFTEEN KILL SIR!" she scurried to the lineup and joined in the "kill" chant until the entire cadet squadron was baying like a herd of deranged animals.

The afternoon was not half over.

Joyce Cain, like so many cadets the daughter of a military "lifer," had graduated with a 95 average from high school and, like so many cadets, had been quite athletic. But, she had been sick in the early days of Beast. Now, she was not in condition for the rigors she was about to face. It was time for armed fighting. Joyce was filled with dread. The cadets were paired off according to weight. Everyone had helmets and face masks. The women were given baseball chest protectors, the men, protective "diapers." Each was handed a rifle-length "pugil stick"—a board wrapped in thick padding—and ordered to start smacking one another until one of them dropped. Joyce found herself opposite June Van Horn. Awkwardly, the two began batting away, tripping over their own feet, an expression of sheer horror on what one could see of their faces through the masks. Here, the gap between girls' and boys' upbringing was most visible. The men, though tired, were immeasurably more adept and dangerous as they whacked at each other.

I was appalled—almost nauseated—by the sight of Joyce and June trying to bash each other's brains out. The scene convinced me that Margaret Mead was right—however much self-defense is a feminine trait, women do not enjoy an aggressive fight as some men do. In a sudden move, June caught Joyce on the side of the head and the Mississippian went down. June dropped her weapon and rushed to comfort Joyce, who was stunned and crying. It was hard to tell whether June's psychological pain hurt more than Joyce's physical pain. But there was no time for comforting words. The group marched off immediately to still another combat course, unarmed self-defense. The cadets were warmed up first with a chant: "Kill, Kill/Hate, Hate/Murder, Murder/Mutilate!"

After the ugliness of the pugil sticks, the judo that followed looked almost benign. The girls seemed to have fun practicing forearm chokeholds on the boys and vice versa. But each group of combative women has its own limits. Sue Mason and Barbara Habedank had to square off in judo in Officers Candidate School. They looked in one another's eyes and refused to move a finger, until an instructor threatened to fail them. Both pilots somberly recalled the ensuing fight as among the single worst moments of their own "Beast."

At Jack's Valley, everybody had a wonderful time at judo. Rolling around in the dust with a tight hold on a female Invader, one young man exclaimed, "First time I have my arm around a girl in four weeks, and I'm trying to strangle her!" It was the last major event before dinner on that exhausting twenty-ninth day. The Invaders were congratulated by their squadron leader. "What we saw today was a squadron that went out on that assault course and tore it up!" he shouted proudly. The cadets roared their approval. "How about a cheer?" someone asked. The group responded with one voice: "Invaders! Invaders! We've got the bionic plague!"

After dinner, several male Basics privately acknowledged that they respected the guts the girls showed in sticking through an experience that was hellish for everyone. "At first I thought, 'Girls? What good are they?'" said one. "But I've seen them do the same things I had to do. I've had a pretty hard time of it. I've got to have some respect for them now." An upperclassman remembered that during a lecture, he had kept calling his group "guys." He had stopped himself to apologize. "When I say 'guys,' I mean guys and girls," he had told his listeners, "I was brought up in another culture. I don't mean to insult anyone."

But a majority of the young men had started out with prejudice against female cadets and this attitude was strengthened, not softened, by "Beast." In the words of a subsequent report, "instead of perceiving that female cadets performed well beyond that of an average co-ed, [a significant number of] the men felt that women did more poorly than men. . . . Male cadets felt that women slowed the squadron or reduced its effectiveness and overall performance. . . . Men perceived that women's limits were less than theirs and/or that women were not trying as hard. . . . Both fourth class (plebe) and upperclass cadets felt that [Beast] was 'easier' or 'different' for women. . . . Since few women performed up to male standards they were perceived as having failed the 'rite of passage.'" Many were also jealous of the publicity the women received.

Were the women themselves satisfied with their performance? Yes and no. Said one: "You hate this place and you love it. There's no in between. You despise it, but you wouldn't leave for a minute. They haven't got me down yet!" If someone had interviewed Mason or Habedank midway through their basic training, they might have said essentially the same thing. The cadets who hung in at the Air Force Academy were not necessarily the strongest physical specimens, but those like Gail Benjamin, who shrugged off the absurdities because she was convinced a decent career was the light at the end of this tunnel. Joyce Cain, after a few more weeks of misery, saw no light. She turned around and walked out. Her psyche was still bruised a full year later from the insults and the "Kill!" chants. Worse, she felt she had let down her father, a retired master sergeant.

Among those who remained, every single one contemplated quitting at least once during that awful "doolie" (freshman) year. Gail Benjamin was at least able to reap positive feedback by representing her sister cadets on the *Today Show* and in national magazine profiles. Patty Ryan got her kicks by helping to lead the volleyball team. But each of the women had been heckled constantly, subjected to as much or more verbal abuse than the male doolies. Punishment for even minor infractions of regulations was severe. The young women had to endure confinement to quarters and forced marches. "Every time you turn around, you're breaking some regulation for something you've never heard about," complained Peggy Walker. Another Invader was sentenced to eight "tours" (a tour is one hour of marching with a rifle on one's shoulder) for failing to collect a book at the school commissary. "Spirit missions"—pranks that demonstrate class spirit—were encouraged. Yet when Patty

Ryan, among others, was caught one night as fifty cadets tried to "liberate" an F-104 fighter plane from its moorings on Academy grounds, she got demerits, marching tours and confinement. For a long while, it seemed to many of the women that there was nothing they could do without criticism.

June Van Horn, baited the second summer by the male cadets with her on survival training, met the challenge, literally head-on. Her cadre, representing soldiers evading detection while in enemy territory, killed a cow for food. The men dared her to sink her teeth into the cow's eye. She picked up the eyeball, sucked in a deep breath . . . and ate it. Unlike her West Point counterparts, the thought of reporting the incident as unfair hazing never entered June's mind.

9

THE CONSEQUENCES
OF DARING

By choosing a military, athletic, or otherwise physically adventurous career, women put their bodies and emotions through a wringer. Like Outward Bounders, they suspect the experience will be rough, but they have no sense of its enormity until they are up to their necks in it. Outward Bounders (or adventure vacationers) can be consoled by the knowledge that their stress is short-term. For military or athletic women it could be lifelong. It is relatively simple for Outward Bounders to quit when they can't take the pressure. Resignation is far more serious for a woman who has made her occupational commitment.

The majority of cadets, recruits and officer-candidates pull through, as do the seriously committed athletes and daredevils. They are not ordinary women. There are unmistakable boundary lines they will cross that even a reasonably "daring" amateur will not. Do these women begin with unique physiological or psychological qualities? And what happens when they do survive? Do they risk becoming hardened, masculine, leathery? Do the acts required in order to survive permanently alter their personalities? Could it be that women are *better* equipped to handle certain physically demanding roles than men are? Do women who enter groups that were once exclusively male accept the macho notions of those groups? Do the men whose fields they invade ever accept the women? By what standards do the men judge them?

Questions like these have been researched in recent years, especially at the service academies and by sports medicine experts. The questions have been raised constantly as well among the women themselves. The answers, so far, are incomplete and occasionally contradictory. Yet they provide compelling insights into the consequences of daring—of machisma in general—on the new breed of women.

An intriguing composite portrait of such women and their male counterparts has been drawn, as mentioned earlier, by a clinical psychologist, Marvin Zuckerman, and fellow researchers, who observed more than ten thousand "sensation-seekers." In constructing a test to measure a person's degree of sensation-seeking, Zuckerman created four subterms. *Thrill- and adventure-seeking* was judged in part on reactions to the statement "I'd like to try parachute jumping." *Experience-seeking* was summarized by the statement "I like to have new and exciting experiences and sensations even if they are a little frightening, unconventional or illegal." *Disinhibition* meant enjoying drugs, alcohol, sex, wild parties. *Boredom susceptibility* referred to dislike of routine work. Zuckerman's first data, in 1964, based on student interviews, "rather surprisingly" showed no differences between men and women in general. Subsequent studies did, however, continue to find men's average scores higher in sensation-seeking than women's, although tests were conducted over a period that embraced the blossoming of the women's movement, the fitness revolution and the "Me Decade."

Zuckerman was careful to call attention to considerable overlap: "Many women are higher than men and vice versa" in the degree to which they seek excitement. He was the first to acknowledge that not enough tests have been run on women as a separate group to make definitive pronouncements about them. As indicated in Chapter 5, Zuckerman did find that there were sex differences in sensation-seeking based on biological differences—the levels of sex hormones and the changing levels of the brain chemical MAO. (In men, the higher the level of the sex hormone testosterone, the higher the score was. In women a higher estrogen level corresponded to higher sensation-seeking.) Zuckerman's conclusion was that for both sexes, the motivation for such activities is based on an "appetite" for sensation-seeking that is in the nervous system. No wonder such adventurous women as Nancy Snell testified that "danger is a physical high."

In women, cultural background and family background were somewhat more influential than they were in men, where sensation-seeking was more related to sex and age. In the "experience-seeking" category, no sex differences turned up. Instead, this urge—the most generalized of the four—seemed to be a by-product of middle class, college-educated upbringing. "Thrill- and adventure-seeking" also appeared to be a particularly white, middle-class undertaking. Those who scored high in this category were drawn to risky sports (as were many women profiled here) but their interest in thrills declined continuously as they grew older. The women in this category were generally better educated than the men, and were brought up by better educated parents as well. Single and divorced women sought thrills and adventure more than did married women.

High sensation-seekers were not necessarily more intelligent than the rest of the population. "These people are clearly more creative and imaginative," Zuckerman said, but such traits only occasionally were reflected in their scholastic achievements. There seemed to be a distinct correlation between high sensation-seeking and certain professions, a correlation that diverged sharply along sex lines. The men were apt to be in "helping professions" such as psychologist, physician and social worker, plus one other clear-cut vocation, music. (Low male sensation-seekers were typically in business, accounting, purchasing, banking, pharmacies, mortuaries.) Among women the profession that stood out for sensation-seekers was that of lawyer. The same women rejected "conventional feminine" jobs such as housewife, elementary school teacher, home economics teacher and dietician.

The need for high sensation could be a factor in antisocial and delinquent behavior, while it had no relationship to one's order of birth. It could also be a factor in a person's sex life, especially among those who scored high in the "disinhibition" category. (This will be treated more fully in Chapter 11.) As a group, high sensation-seekers were "more alert and aroused" to novel stimuli; that is, they needed a lot of change to keep their interest level up. As personalities, they were impulsive and extroverted, with a "need for new and varied experience in many forms of sensation and arousal—sexual, gustatory, perceptual and cognitive."

In other words, the sensation-seeking scale provides as good a clinical "match" as one could hope for in describing characteristics so vividly exhibited by macha women, be they on Annapurna climbs or in Aspen boutiques, on the white water of the Southwest or in the sky above Monticello, competing in college basketball or in pro auto racing, training at the Air Force Academy or in the ocean off the Florida coast.

Studies of female physical fitness continue this composite portrait where the sensation-seeking scale leaves off. As one might have guessed, young women on the whole were *less* able to meet many standards set for the young men with whom they entered Army boot camp, a service academy or a college athletic program. Indeed, one controversial report on Army recruits at Fort McClellan concluded that "female trainees entering the Army from civilian life are in poor physical condition." The judgment seems sexist and unwarranted, when investigated closely. Of twenty performance tests, women failed significantly in only five —two speed marches, two long road marches, a "confidence course" (similar to "ropes" in Outward Bound and to the Air Force Academy confidence course) and a general "fitness" test with a heavy emphasis on strength. What it proved was something any physiologist could have told the Army beforehand: women are not as strong or as fast as men. Even the best female physical specimens cannot match the performance of average men on cross-country runs, chin-ups or other specific trials. But at both West Point and the Air Force Academy, as soon as the women's tests were modified to account for accepted female levels of strength and speed, women succeeded or failed at approximately the same rate as men.

In fact, on certain tests of trainees at Fort McClellan, women *did* slightly outscore or equal men, without a single adjustment having been made. These included the use of hand grenades; "fire and maneuver" (training in two-person movement techniques and placement of suppressive fire); the "defensive course" (being able to identify fields of fire, and so forth); basic marksmanship; and the seven-mile (intermediate) road march. Moreover, the women did that well despite boots that were too big for them.

High school girls who choose a service academy are apt to be exceptionally capable of handling physical stress. At West Point, women in the classes of '80, '81 and '82—the first three sex-integrated classes—averaged between fifteen and sixteen minutes for a two-mile run. That was a slower time than their male classmates, but more than respectable in comparison to female college students elsewhere. At the Air Force Academy, the physical condition and stamina of the female cadets increased "dramatically" after one year's training.

None of this is news to those who have been keeping records of women's advances in fitness. It is well established that until puberty, girls, on average, are as strong, fast, tall and broadshouldered as boys. From age eleven to fifteen, girls are actually broader-shouldered than boys. Therefore, in prepuberty competition—Little League baseball, for instance—girls have every anatomical opportunity to equal or surpass boys. After puberty, boys quickly outgrow their female playmates and become more muscular. But they *don't* have the edge in every trait that produces a better athlete. Postpuberty girls, according to one research team, tend to have wider knee joints, which probably gives them more stability in relation to their size. Girls also develop a lower center of gravity that provides naturally better balance, a key element in sports such as gymnastics and skiing. Women as a group develop a greater percentage of body fat, with its advantage of greater buoyancy in water and greater tolerance of heat, two factors in long-distance swimming or any hot weather activity. Women have been measured equal to men in their speed of reaction to a visual stimulus, as in driving—take that, Bobby Unser! Women also have greater manual dexterity than men.

Year after year there is proof that with training, women may be more naturally suited to extra-long endurance tests, such as marathon and ultra-marathon runs and swims. By the 1968 Olympics, women's times in both sprints and distance events, the longest of which was only 1,500 meters, had crept up to almost 90 percent of the men's times. By the 1976 Montreal Olympics women had inched forward again, with female performances in the 400-meter individual medley in swimming above 93 percent of the men's, while 200-meter and 400-meter freestyle swim times were above 92 percent. In order to make "a valid comparison" between athletes with similar training and coaching, a Temple University researcher pitted 1976 Olympic times for the phenomenal male and female East German swimmers opposite one another. Astonishingly, several of the best times for women came within 96 and 97 percent of those of their countrymen. Meanwhile, eight years earlier, women at the 1968 Olympics tolerated the 6,000-foot altitude of Mexico City better than men, although three out of seven of the women were menstruating at some point during the games. Since tolerance for high altitude is a necessity for mountain climbers, maybe we should expect Annapurna to be but the first of many extraordinary all-women climbs.

The towering imbalance between men and women, of course,

is in strength. Women average two-thirds of the muscle strength
of men. Even when adjustments are made for height differences,
women still have only 80 percent of men's strength. Still, at least
one research team, noting that female swimmers are already setting faster times than the men of twenty-five years ago, predict
further startling gains for women in various events, provided
they don't require "great strength or 'explosive' power."

In short, on a physiological level, there is nothing to stop rap-
idly advancing cadres of women from excelling in a slew of
sports once considered strictly macho—from horse racing to road
racing, from mountaineering to one-hundred-mile runs to solo
sails around the world (the latter was accomplished by a plucky
New Zealander, Naomi James). Accomplishing such a record of
success would be the point; putting women in strength contests
against men would be beside the point.

A word or two about menstruation. Many female athletes
don't feel at the top of their game at that time of the month.
Contrary to popular belief, however, it does not automatically
cost a female competitor precious seconds or turn her into an un-
stable harridan. The Army discovered, apparently to the surprise
of its Fort McClellan field instructors, that women did not
have to be excused from strenuous training while menstruating.
The marks set by a majority of track and field athletes during
their periods, in one study, were either as good or better than
their usual performances. (Interestingly, *best* performances most
often occurred in the days immediately preceding a woman's
period.)

There has been concern because up to 30 percent of female
athletes—especially long distance runners but including gym-
nasts, swimmers, ice skaters, distance skiers and ballet dancers—
experience "irregularity," either not menstruating for months on
end or less than once every forty days. Headlines about "disruption" of natural processes frighten parents about the future child-
bearing capability of their daughters. But it must be pointed out
that hard training, heavy travel schedules (such as those of
world-class tennis players) and plain preperformance anxiety

cause irregularity in numerous serious and weekend athletes
alike. As Dr. Mona Shangold, a marathoner and gynecologic en-
docrinology specialist, pointed out: "There are also many nonathletic women with irregular periods. Just because a woman
runs and is irregular, it doesn't mean that running is the cause."
A founding mother of female sports medicine, Dorothy V. Harris
of the Penn State Center for Women and Sport, declared that
there was no reason for alarm, since an athlete's normal period
resumes once she halts her training.

No one is sure what causes some athletes to become irregular.
The most widely discussed theory linked the exceedingly low
body fat ratios in skinny runners and ballet dancers to a temporary halt or slowdown in menstruation. A lot more scientific work
needs to be done on the entire subject. Then there are athletic
physicians such as Joan Ullyot, who viewed the situation from
another perspective. For serious runners, irregularity (technically
known as secondary amenorrhea) can be an excellent birth control device, she said. Besides, she asked, "has it ever struck you
how inconvenient it is to menstruate while you are training?"
Her own theory was that "when we were a nomadic species, no
women had periods, and it wasn't until we became sedentary
that we developed this abnormality of monthly menstruation. I
think we should look at these young, fit girls who are not having
periods as the way super healthy people should be."

Depending on your own leanings, Ullyot's theory is either
woefully inverted . . . or a superb argument for the sporting.
Take your pick.

Physically active, risk-taking women are unquestionably
stronger, leaner and aerobically more efficient than the female
population in general, as Drinkwater found among the Annapurna climbers. The second part of this one-two punch in the
nose of male traditionalists is this: *such women are psychologically stronger as well.*

It is a tribute to the women's movement that much of the
research in this field has been produced in the past twelve years.

The movement, in addition, has helped women gain this mental strength. Throughout western history, greater participation of women in physically demanding activities has gone hand in hand with increased feminist awareness. So it was that in ancient Sparta, as in the early twentieth century in the United States, there was a marked upsurge in women's running and fencing. The turn of this century also saw women's colleges engage in bicycling, tennis, boating, hockey and basketball competitions. The precipitous decline in society's acceptance of female athletes in the late forties and fifties coincided with "the feminine mystique" that relegated women to second-class status. With the onset of the American feminist wave in the late sixties, the curve turned upward again. There is a clear connection between a culture's encouragement of female competitiveness and an awakening of the desire to get involved in competition.

The issue is a thorny one. Whatever we mean by the word aggression ("an offensive action . . . especially an unprovoked attack" is the first definition in Webster's Third International Dictionary), there is considerable data suggesting that this trait is part of even the youngest male's nature. "The greater physical aggression typical of boys is thought to be at least partially due to gonadal endocrine factors, specifically, higher testosterone levels," according to one summary. On the other hand, there can be little debate that at certain points in history (such as the late forties and fifties) women were socially conditioned to reject aggressive tendencies, to hide any inclination toward competitive or assertive behavior. Bits and pieces of that message of submissiveness linger. As a result, wrote Carl E. Klafs and M. Joan Lyon, "overt aggressive behavior, competitiveness and leadership are accepted and even encouraged in boys, whereas there is pressure upon girls to control and sublimate their aggressive feelings. . . . Women are probably much more aggressive than most experimental studies reveal."

In spite of this cultural quicksand, female athletes who defy it display a strikingly positive set of personality traits. Both male and female athletes are similar in some attitudes: They are out-

going, bright, emotionally stable, self-assertive, happy-go-lucky,
high in conscience development, slightly distrustful and rather
tough-minded and self-sufficient, according to psychological
studies. Men in such tests are a little brighter and more outgoing
than nonathletes; the women are "much more venturesome and
bold, more experimental, lower in resting level of anxiety and
less tense," the Klafs and Lyon study said.

Less tense than whom? Their sedentary colleagues. Compared
to female nonathletes, collegiate female athletes show up as
more intelligent, tougher-minded, more reserved, assertive, stable and happy-go-lucky—as well as suspicious, casual and placid.
Vague and contradictory though some of these findings are, their
overall impression is upbeat. Given such attributes, who
wouldn't want to be classified as a female athlete? Maybe a
handful of dependent Barbie dolls. But surely a great many teenaged and adult American women would be proud to list most of
the above characteristics on her psychological résumé.

One trouble is that, like the rest of present-day American society, psychology is suffering from gender confusion. Many researchers have accepted as the umbrella word for such sets of
characteristics a loaded term—masculine. At best, some of the
traits come under the heading "neuter," but few are called feminine. Attempts to unscramble the definitions only seem more
confusing. For example, in devising her widely used "sex role inventory," Sandra L. Bem made it clear that the adjectives she
chose would reveal how someone "has internalized society's sex-
typed standards of desirable behavior." In effect, she blamed society for sexual stereotypes but then perpetuated them. The
"feminine" adjectives on her scale are: affectionate, cheerful,
childlike, compassionate, does-not-use-harsh-language, eager-to-
soothe-hurt-feelings, feminine, flatterable, gentle, gullible, loves-
children, loyal, sensitive-to-needs-of-others, shy, soft-spoken,
sympathetic, tender, understanding, warm, yielding.

Among the corresponding twenty masculine items on her scale
are: assertive, competitive and willing-to-take-risks.

It comes as no shock that young women at both West Point

and the Air Force Academy rated themselves high in traits such as dominance, assertiveness, self-confidence, self-reliance, intelligence, analytic ability, achievement, competitiveness, ambition, leadership ability and the drive for responsibility—all of which are identified as "masculine" by various psychological leadership test scales. Stripped of that loaded definition, one research team's description of the Air Force Academy Class of '80 (which could easily be applied to West Point women), was a complimentary one: "Self-confident, bright young adults who have met the challenge of academic work, peer-group relations and athletic competition."

What turmoil must healthy and self-confident adventurers, athletes and military candidates endure as they make their way through training that is geared to men, run largely by men, and identified with the very concept of maleness? The short answer is: a great deal of physical and psychological stress.

Fortunately, the extended answer is that this stress motivates them even more powerfully, strengthening their already excellent ability to cope, often in the face of male resistance. As one Marine lieutenant (female) remarked in the midst of maneuvers at Quantico, Virginia: "How you do [here] really depends on what kind of woman you are. You have got to be aggressive."

Neanderthal thinkers once believed that "the intensities of severe competition could result in unpleasant or harmful aftereffects to the female psyche." Klafs and Lyon responded, "this idée fixe simply does not hold true. Emotional control in stressful situations is usually stabilized through experience."

Indeed, each of these studies found that women tend to underrate their ability to cope, so that overcoming obstacles in adventure, sports or the military can become all the more energizing. Both Army recruits and the first Air Force Academy female cadets admitted that the demands made on them were greater than they had anticipated. Once they had met those demands, their self-esteem shot upward. A woman like Joan Ullyot discovered in running the extra boost that even she, always an achieving woman, needed to make important changes in her life. For a woman like Diana Nyad, each hurdle overcome was a reaffirmation; after one swim she declared, "I impressed myself."

Not everyone is stimulated by the actual *doing*. AFA female cadets saw themselves as "more anxious, stressed, depressed, fatigued" than male cadets both before and right after a combat-related stress program. (One explanation, suggested researchers, might be that women are more willing to admit their feelings.) Jet pilot Barbara Habedank, too, found her training a harrowing experience. She felt she and other women were "taxed to the ultimate of our physical and mental ability" in Officer Candidate School. "It was the ultimate challenge," she continued. "We had to think like men. I actually had a hormonal change." She had secondary amenorrhea, lost inches around her breasts and sprouted a little hair on her upper lip. "I finally went to a doctor and he put me on hormone pills. The mind will do amazing things to your body to adapt," she said. Yet her sister pilot, Nila Sandusky, did not see her experience in the same light. "I don't think I ever thought like a man. Of course, most of the time we were so hot and sweaty, nobody ever looked at us as 'girls,' either." She gained confidence from the training. The only thing she truly resented was being ordered to cut off most of her hair.

Research literature supports Nila Sandusky's overview. A majority of women emerge from such an experience with both renewed self-assurance and without any loss of their sense of femininity. On a biochemical level, this was shown in the "sensation-seekers," both male and female, who registered high amounts of both male and female sex hormones. On a psychological level, West Point and AFA test results showed female cadets retaining high "femininity" perceptions of themselves along with scoring high on the "masculinity" and "neuter" scales. This put them in the category referred to as "androgynous." Still another analysis, based on female distance runners, concluded that high-achieving women "are more likely to possess both masculine and feminine attributes than their male counterparts without suffering any deficit in their femininity." The female runners, also defined as "androgynous" (literally "both masculine and feminine"), were ranked highest of any group in self-esteem.

Sandra Bem herself, in creating her sex role inventory scale, voted for "androgynous" as a better measure of adjustment to American culture in the ideal. "Androgynous represents the equal endorsement of both masculine and feminine attributes," she wrote. "In a society where rigid sex role differentiation has already outlived its utility, perhaps the androgynous person will come to define a more human standard of psychological health."

Ah, but here's the rub. Women adventurers, athletes and soldiers usually enter their male-dominated areas over the objections of men, and those objections do not necessarily dissolve. Men may applaud their achievements while still clinging to their tired old traditional ideas of how women should behave.

At a bastion of maleness like a service academy, both upperclassmen and new male cadets retained a more old-fashioned opinion of a woman's place (in the home, far from combat, submissive) than their male equivalents in civilian colleges. After six months, those cadets in sex-integrated squadrons showed on tests that they were less hidebound, but not much less. After a year of training in an institution with a small group of nontraditional, physically fit, highly motivated women cadets and a large group of very traditional male cadets, the men showed a big decline in self-perceptions of their *own feminine* attributes. They were less likely to describe themselves as "warm, understanding of others, helpful, gentle, kind," etc. (Women, as mentioned before, showed no signs of decreasing femininity.) At the same time, the men judged the leadership potential of the female cadets directly in proportion to how well the women were able to keep up with the *physical* demands of the academy. Further, "male cadets resisted the leadership attempts of the appointed female cadet leaders," one study reported. Thus, for these military men, the worn, macho notion of masculinity as synonymous with physical ability extended to their opinion of leadership roles for female cadets.

At both service academies, women, like so many pioneers before them in other male-oriented fields, got a double message. Outwardly, society and the institutions themselves encouraged them to break the traditional barriers, to spread their wings, to become leaders. But inside, the men would rather see them get married, have children and resign from the military.

How do women react to this male feedback? It is easy to guess. As already mentioned, large numbers attached themselves to cadet-suitors, probably for protection as well as to escape the incongruity of the double message. Said an exasperated female cadet: "If you date, you're considered a whore. If you don't date, you're a lesbian." For close to 25 percent of the AFA women, the only solution was "going steady"—in eight cases out of ten with a male cadet or other military man. The other common female reaction? Quit the academy. As the dropout rate for women increased, a social scientist ruminated that it could be a case of "rising expectations." The women were "seduced by the Air Force propaganda. They go to the Academy expecting to be liked, and they're put in a bind when they discover it's not going to happen." The difference between West Point and the AFA, concluded the researcher grimly, was that at least at the former, women *knew* they were going to be hated.

The more male the bastion, the colder the reception a woman is likely to get there, regardless of whether she presents a high profile or low, tough image or sweetness-and-light. In her early days as a much-heralded basketball star on athletic scholarship at Old Dominion, Nancy Lieberman was resented so fiercely that the tires of her car were slashed. She later wrote off the incident. "It was an adjustment period." She didn't help matters by coming to the southern university with a schoolyard swagger. What she did not say was that no one slashed Kareem Abdul-Jabbar's tires when he arrived at U.C.L.A., a heralded star on an athletic scholarship. He was a ballplayer, and he was welcomed with open arms.

A high profile is no help to a woman in such circumstances, but a low one might be useless as well. One of the first female Coast Guard ship captains had her troubles with that particular male bastion, even though she was as low-key as Lieberman was high. Lieutenant [j.g.] Susan Moritz even took the precaution of marrying a Coast Guard commander before taking the helm of her ship, and she was treated decently enough by her all-male crew, to her face. Behind her back, though, crewmen made sexist jokes and gave her ship, the Cape Current, a scabrous nickname —the "Cape Cunt."

The resentment women encounter is not limited to male bastions where physicality is of prime importance. Being a visible female "token" in any organization, corporation, university or industrial plant dominated by men is a no-win situation.

Rosabeth Moss Kanter elaborated on this theme in exhaustive studies of what she labeled a "sex-skewed" group. Her definition of "skewed" was any group in which the minority (women) were less than 20 percent of the total. Using the sales department of an unnamed industrial corporation as her initial model, she watched the handful of saleswomen there get caught in a triple-bind of performance pressure, polarization, and role entrapment.

To begin with, because the saleswomen were visible whether they liked it or not—as are adventurous women generally—they were subjected to more careful scrutiny of their performance than the men in the department. "Their mistakes and their relationships were known as readily as any other information" and "symbolic consequences" were attached to their work. The token women had to work twice as hard to have their achievements recognized or to merely "prove their competence." They were warned that how they did would affect the prospects for any future women in the sales department. Their very bodies were scrutinized all the time. No "correct" behavior could extricate them. The women who worked twice as hard "evoked threats of retaliation"; those who tried the low-profile mode "limited recognition of their competence."

That was not the worst of it. The token women, simply by *being there*, polarized the sales staff. The reaction of the male

majority was to erect higher psychological walls to keep women
out of the "in" group. The men tended to dramatize their tales of
sexual conquest, their off-color jokes, their talk of work prowess
and sports. They put on "exaggerated displays of aggression and
potency" when the women were around.

Lastly, the men "assimilated" the token women by distorting
their sex roles. They forced the women into stereotypes as
mother-figures, seductresses or "pets." Some women countered
by trying to ingratiate themselves, by laughing at antifemale
jokes or by remaining silent. Nothing worked. Kanter concluded
that "even if tokens do well, they do so at a cost, overcoming social handicaps, expanding extra effort and facing [additional]
stresses."

For many women who pay the unwanted excise tax on to-
kenism—in adventure, sports, the military, business, academia,
the arts—the unfortunate result is a sense of isolation, less-than-
expected promotions, personal neuroses. The providential ones,
the strong women, gain a hard-earned feeling of self-worth that
is possibly more valuable for having come out of so basic a
conflict with the "stronger" sex. "Could it be that the sportswoman has, through the demands placed on her by the role
conflict in sport, become very secure and positive about herself
and her body?" a college physical education specialist asked.
Could it be that the same is true of daring women, whatever
their occupation or vocation? A woman who should know,
Dorothy V. Harris of Penn State, hailed athletics as "a laboratory for achievement orientation. . . . It's not by chance that
most of the women moving into executive and managerial positions have had sports experience," she remarked.

An excellent case can be made for youthful competitiveness as
a prerequisite for both men's and women's adult achievements. A
political scientist stated flatly once that most successful women
"in a wide range of endeavor" were tomboys as children.
"They were more independent, risk-taking, adventurous, strong,
achievement-oriented than their passive, conforming, dependent
sisters. We're beginning to find out that muscle development and

coordination go hand-in-hand with learning." A list of one hundred and twenty "notable American tomboys" published by *WomenSports* magazine contained three mayors of major cities, nine women in Congress, two female governors as well as dozens of writers, actresses, academicians and corporate executives.

If the one hundred and twenty notable tomboys were asked for their own list of men who tried to block their progress along the way, or who ostracized them as punishment for their success, a safe bet is that there would be at least two men for every tomboy. Adventurous women need the support of the men in their life, but that reward is not automatic, the way female support of adventurous men often is in American society. In certain macho roles, men get what a thoughtful Navy captain has labeled "positive maleness feedback." The typical jet pilot, this captain told a rapt audience of pilots' wives in Florida, gets the same masculine reinforcement by flying "at the edge of the envelope" that he gets driving a fast car or showing how he can hold his liquor. The reinforcement is addictive: "there is a quantity he's got to have and will get, almost no matter what." Without such feedback, according to the captain, the pilot feels a loss of control over his life and subsequently "punishes himself" by cheating on his wife, by involving himself in inappropriately risky sports such as motorcycle racing, and eventually by flying his airplane dangerously. The concept of "positive maleness feedback" seems applicable to adventurous men in a wide range of activities. Yet the only male feedback adventurous women too often receive are negative reactions from men who dislike their attachment to "masculine" endeavors. At the extreme, there was the attempt by Mary Kaknes's Greek father to prevent her from joining rough-and-tumble games in childhood, and the collective opposition of top male drivers to Janet Guthrie's racing career.

Luckily, such women do get impressive psychological support from other men who count in their lives—husbands, brothers, fathers. Guthrie's airline-pilot father encouraged her explorations.

Billie Jean King's father, a fireman, was her earliest ardent rooter and her husband followed suit. Irene Beardsley Miller learned mountaineering from her first husband. Mary Kaknes's late husband learned hang gliding alongside her. Naomi James, the solitary sailor, was introduced to the sailing world by her husband. Patty Ryan and Gail Benjamin could lean on their brothers at the AFA. Sue Mason's father gave her her first transport lessons and later shared ownership in a small plane with her.

As we shall see, the pattern of "Daddy's Little Girl" holds for risk-taking women well beyond the confines of the playing field, the airfield or the battlefield. Not every American girl has the opportunity to learn "male" behavior or discover "male" preoccupations because of an attentive father willing to share his enthusiasms. But Margaret Mead, for one, felt that fatherly indulgence was far more pervasive in this relatively young country, its population cut off from the very sexist child rearing practices of ancestral European cultures. As an anthropologist, Mead saw the style of American fatherhood as potentially confusing to little girls, compared with the rituals of simpler, tradition-bound societies.

In the United States, "the little girl is flattered and spoiled by an indulgent, non-disciplinary father, and emerges very sure of herself indeed," wrote Mead. Add to this the American prohibition against being a boy or girl "sissy," and the American girl winds up with a confounding set of values:

> She is told not to behave like a boy, not to be a tomboy. This admonition . . . so prevalent even two generations ago [Mead wrote in 1949], while it angered the active and especially gifted girl, was at least clear and simple. To be a tomboy meant to run wild, climb trees, steal apples from orchards, fight, play boys' games, rather than stay closer to home, keep one's hair ribbons on, play dolls and house, and sit quietly with legs crossed. . . . . Conversely, for the boys it was fairly simple to be told not to play with dolls, or . . . run away from open encounters with other boys. As long as each sex was asked to avoid the well-defined pattern of the other sex, a few members

of each sex suffered . . . but the majority were able to adjust. . . . . Women wept and fainted, men swore and stamped, but did not weep.

Egalitarianism and fatherly indulgence changed all that by midcentury, according to Mead. Boys and girls were being "brought up more and more alike." Was the scientist in Mead at odds here with the female-achiever side of her? For many tomboys growing up at the time she wrote *Male and Female*, the egalitarianism had not progressed far enough. For the Irene B. Millers, the Billie Jean Kings, Janet Guthries and Sue Masons, fathers who were the first, most influential teachers were indispensable to their ultimate success as self-reliant grown-ups.

To give Margaret Mead her due, she was well aware that the sometimes confusing pattern of fatherly indulgence could also bestow great freedom on daughters. In *Male and Female*, she argued that "cultures in which ideals are a blend" should allow a good deal of leeway in judging whether boys or girls fit in stereotyped sex roles. Thus, "the fact of sex can be used to classify together male rabbits and male lions and male deer, but would never be permitted to obscure for us their essential rabbit, lion or deer characteristics." In the same vein, a little girl who displayed mechanical talent would not automatically be pegged in a stereotyped way, "nor would any child have to pay with a loss of its sense of its sex membership for the special gifts" such as having "a delicate sense of touch" or the ability "to ride a horse with fierce sureness."

The bias against tomboys, in any event, has been in retreat for the past decade, having been routed by Title IX. This section of the Federal Education Amendments of 1972, which mandated equal treatment of women in school and collegiate sports programs, channeled hundreds of thousands of fresh dollars into female physical education departments, athletic scholarships and gym equipment. The availability of the money prompted a new emphasis in schools on girls' athletics even at the elementary grade level.

Moreover, in Mead's young-adult day the new jogging corps would undoubtedly have been put down as a group of late blooming tomboys. Today, the corps is too chic to care. Among professional athletes, Billie Jean King in the early seventies had to defend her femininity even as the boom in women's tennis was echoing from Wimbledon to Kooyang. But the champions who followed her were accepted much more easily. When Chris Evert Lloyd realized she was more muscular than other little girls her age, she didn't know whether she liked it. "I was different. But I never felt unfeminine. I thought, maybe I'm special." Chris could forget the "maybe." On the collegiate level, Nancy Lieberman, in her difficult freshman year at Old Dominion, learned that her teammates did not appreciate her ultra-competitiveness. "They got mad because they didn't know how to deal with a woman who wanted to win so badly. If I dove for a loose ball or threw an elbow by accident, I was a villain." By her sophomore year, the same teammates were cheering those not-so-accidental elbows. "Now it's a feather in my cap. It's hustling," she remarked during her senior year, pinpointing the new attitude.

The shift in favor of female muscularity can be witnessed in hundreds of "health clubs" and gyms where female athletes and active women work out regularly with weights. An anathema to most women of Mead's generation, weight-training (body building with either old-style barbells or scientific machines like the Nautilus) has become almost as chic as jogging. Margaret Court, considered the strongest female tennis player of the sixties and seventies, was among the first pros to lift weights in her off-season training. Diana Nyad incorporated Nautilus programs into her training regimen because maintenance of upper body strength—a woman's natural weakness—was so crucial to long distance swimming. A University of Arizona study showed that a six-month weight-training program could help female athletes improve their bench press strength by 15 to 44 percent, giving them a higher rating than untrained men of the same age. But the little lady straining under Nautilus steel pulleys these days is just as likely to be a rock singer, a police detective or a home-maker, since body building for fun and health has become commonplace.

Not every Nautilus enthusiast would want to be dubbed "macha." Nor, for that matter, would Chris Evert Lloyd. There are dozens of women among the "one hundred and twenty former tomboys" who are not in the same league with Nyad, King, Lieberman, the West Point cadets, Carolee Campbell or Nancy Snell when it comes to joyous risk-taking and/or showing off. The point is that in order for the idea of "machisma" to flower, the acceptance of tomboys, the collective parental approval of competition for girls, the national craze for fitness that includes weight-lifting all had to be nurtured first.

So, too, did the rise of the "self-indulgent" daddy. Perhaps the confusion and the threat that active women injected into bastions of "maleness" such as the armed forces were necessary; they acted as a goad. At the Marines' Camp Pendleton, a female lance corporal remarked, "It's a macho thing. There's a lot of resistance to us, but we can do more than some of the puny guys." Similarly, Janet Guthrie was goaded by the taunts of racing male chauvinists to push still further in her own racing career.

Finally, as Zuckerman's work on sensation-seeking demonstrates, the consequences of risk-taking can accommodate much more than physical activity. Just as sports can give women the confidence to pursue wider, nonathletic goals, so the psychological leap of daring can be a prelude to risk-taking in business, the arts, family relationships and arenas still further afield. The next chapters explore women in those realms, women for whom a botanic term a full 180 degrees away from "shrinking violet" needs to be coined. They are the varieties of the species that feminism's most profound philosopher, Simone de Beauvoir, must have had in mind when she wrote: "Let her swim, climb mountain peaks, pilot an airplane, battle against the elements, take risks, go out for adventure, and she will not feel timid before the world."

RISK

Part Two

RISK

Part Two

10

THE WORKSHOP: BUSINESS

She knew about all the tricks in *The Woman's Dress for Success Book* before it was published. She recognizes aspects of herself in old Katharine Hepburn and new Faye Dunaway movies. She is the new breed of businesswoman, macha variety, for whom climbing an organization's ladder of success is only one criterion of satisfaction. She's a climber, to be sure, but unlike the majority of businesswomen/achievers, she climbs with flair. She has a style in which the put-down and the put-on are among the leading components. She is a deadly competitor. But for her, competing is grand fun.

Machismo has always been accepted in the business world. As with sports, that world is increasingly open to women—and to displays of adventurism as well. The difference between the risk-taking woman in the executive suite and her female associate, the "managerial woman," is that the latter has played the corporate game according to men's rules. Many of these associates also followed their fathers into business or were accompanied by their husbands. A recent survey by *Fortune* of the top ten women in big business showed seven out of the ten entered business ranks via familial associations. More often than not, they carried inflated titles, such as vice-president, without the corresponding high six-figure salaries that their male counterparts had. In addition, they tended to be fairly low-key in terms of dress and deportment. A perfect example is Kay Graham, former chief executive officer of the Washington *Post* conglomerate, once considered the most powerful businesswoman in the country, whose father *and* husband preceded her in running the family publishing empire. (Her title was assuredly not inflated.) Women in the Kay Graham mold do not necessarily seek business success, nor do they flaunt it when it flows to them.

The motto of the new breed of women in business could be, "Kay Graham doesn't live here anymore." These businesswomen, most of whom are not yet vice-presidents, are self-made and self-promoting. The one word never used to describe them is the adjective so commonly applied to Kay Graham: shy.

Since the seventies, corporate America has allowed many more female executives into its ranks. The new breed of women tends to be younger, hungrier and more openly aggressive than Olive Ann Beech, chairman of the board of Beech Aircraft, or Marion Sandler, vice-chairman of Golden West Financial Corporation, both of whom were on *Fortune*'s top-ten list. A more appropriate role model for the macha women might be Mary Wells Lawrence. The chief executive officer of Wells, Rich, Green Inc., Mrs. Lawrence broke away from a male-dominated company to form her own successful advertising agency some years ago. She snatched Braniff as one of her first big accounts and then married the airline's president.

The new women are still clustered in industries relatively hospitable to women, such as cosmetics, advertising, entertainment and retailing. But again, the incentives provided in the seventies for job-seekers with economics degrees have spread them throughout international trade, heavy industry, journalism and finance, as well as law and medicine. The emergence of assertive

young women in the professional world is acknowledged throughout current prime-time television, a good barometer of popular
acceptance. For instance, in a situation comedy about a law firm,
The Associates, two of the firm's three newcomers were women.
One was typically sweet, dependent, supportive—the vulnerable-
but-competent type. The other was a ballsy gorgeous blond
woman who immediately claimed the only available private office
and just as cuttingly short-circuited the amorous advances of an
office boy—Ms. Macha, L.L.B. In the dramatic series about a Los
Angeles newspaper, *Lou Grant,* a hotshot female reporter went
after as many tough assignments as her rival, the hotshot male
reporter.

Nor are the new working women bull-in-the-china-shop, offen-
sively ruthless executives. As shown by Rosabeth Moss Kanter,
many women in business still must carry the burden of being a
"token," part of which means being judged on personal and professional performance more closely and more harshly than men.
Loudmouths or unnecessarily free-swingers undoubtedly try to
climb the slippery corporate success ladder all the time, but antisocial behavior is not shrugged off or tolerated in executive
women the way it is excused in abrasive executive men. Macha
businesswomen are likely to have poise and femininity in as rich
abundance as Graham, Beech or Sandler. How they cannily use
these attributes to further their careers without compromising
themselves is quite another story. The point is, given inflation,
periodic recession, shrinking corporate expectations and the
ever-narrowing pyramid that leaves room at the top for so few,
the women who do business with a flair may be gaining an advantage over the quieter managerial women who still abide by
men's old precepts.

Such a flair certainly has not hurt Bettina Parker, Jill Steiger,
Marcy Sigler or Hazel Jacobs, for example.

The year was 1966. Leonid Brezhnev was strolling through an
international trade exhibit in Moscow. An attractive woman with
cornsilk hair swept back into a bun was in charge of one booth

representing an American communications equipment company. She instinctively knew this was her golden opportunity. "I walked up to him and I introduced myself," Bettina Parker recalled. "I had spent a lot of time putting this show together and I was not going to let the biggest dignitary in the country pass me by. Would you?"

She didn't. Brezhnev stopped for a while at the booth. "He was a very strong and handsome looking man then," Parker added. "He tried out the equipment." He also asked if she was married and when she explained she was a widow, he said he would have to do something about that. "The rest of the exhibitors were flabbergasted! It was really one of the high points of my life." So, in her own personal version of Richard Nixon's Soviet "kitchen debate," Parker made a name for herself among firms seeking business ties with the U.S.S.R.

Within six years, she had set up her separate international consulting firm, Parker Associates, to help clients sell everything from infant formula to business machines to amusement parks in Communist bloc countries. When we met a few years later, Parker was running her high-powered but personalized operation out of offices in New York's United Nations Plaza and in Moscow, with a staff of seven.

Born in Holland forty-odd years ago, Bettina Parker had been mistaken for Liv Ullman so many times that she was ready to sign autographs in Norwegian. She presided over a regal apartment in the Sovereign, a flashy East Side Manhattan building, which she shared with a dashing, dark young man and, occasionally, with her two almost-grown children. More than three-quarters of her year was spent on the road, around the world, in pursuit of new business. Her friends and associates invariably described her as "dynamic," "a dynamo," "a dynamite lady."

I sensed that kind of personality the minute John, her housemate, answered the doorbell at home. (Parker was late at the office.) The living room was spacious, with bold, black-and-beige octagon pattern carpeting. There were two elegant sitting areas, one dominated by a mammoth sectional couch, the other by a set of mirrored-aluminum chairs. On the wall was a Russian painting. A floor-to-ceiling glass door led onto the terrace, bedecked with plants. If there was such a thing as "the power look," this was it.

When Parker arrived home, a Russian fox hat was jauntily perched on her carefully combed hair. She settled into an aluminum chair, chased away Misha, her Doberman, and accepted vodka in a tall iced glass that John had ready for her. The drink reminded her at once of her first voyage to the United States.

She came to New York when she was eighteen. It was her one successful departure from Holland, although she had tried to run away from her father, a fishbroker, from the time she was nine. ("I used to dig tunnels under the fence of our house," she said.) Her vehicle to the States was a transatlantic ship, where she managed to get a job working in the first-class bar even though all she knew about drinking then was rum and Coke.

From the moment she got off the ship, determined to make her way across country to California, young Bettina was not an ordinary immigrant. "The first thing I saw was a Coke machine. I got so excited." She had never seen the machine before. She put a dime in right away, and when the bottle refused to swing free, she searched until she found someone who could give her her dime back. She had one thing uppermost in her mind: "Money. Money, which meant freedom." After spending the night huddled in Grand Central Station, she hopped a train for the West, getting off in St. Louis for a look around. A department store she entered there overwhelmed her. "Who ever heard of more than one Sunday outfit!" she thought to herself. Learning her English from news magazines and a dictionary ("I quickly advanced to *From Here to Eternity*"), and her pronunciation from the radio, she journeyed to Stanford University. There, she shared a foreign students' house with seven girls for a bit. She worked her way through college as a switchboard operator, cocktail waitress and model. "I didn't have the credits [to enroll in a degree program] but I had the guts," she said of the school. She remained two years, majoring in business administration.

In 1952, she met an American army officer while skiing. They married, and she moved with him to Alaska for nine years. She had a small son and was pregnant with her second child when her husband died. After the birth of her daughter, Bettina returned to California, holding down a succession of jobs in order to raise her family in comfort. A good job opportunity led her to Chicago doing exhibits, including the 1966 exhibit in Moscow. After spending some years at her parents' home in Holland to care for sick relatives, she came back to the United States for good in 1972. Parker's ability to make contacts overseas, and her obvious charm combined with a smart head for marketing brought her rapid recognition. But now it was no longer the drive for money or freedom that propelled her. It was the kick that she got out of her deals. "I can get things done that no one else can. I can sell anything. I like 'firsts.' I have sold a hell of a lot of amusement equipment in the Soviet Union, and nobody's ever done that, and it's still working beautifully," she said with pride, flashing an incandescent smile, her voice touched with the barest hint of an accent.

What was evident in Parker was a strong, nearly arrogant sense of self, softened by humor and by that genuine personality that captured Brezhnev. She knew precisely who she was and she enjoyed being herself. Asked if she preferred to be addressed as Miss, Mrs. or Ms., she shrugged. "Take your pick. I'm all three," she replied. "Plus, I have been called many other things!" In a moment of self-analysis, the first quality she highlighted, without apology, was her lack of patience. She was a woman who never waited for stoplights, who couldn't stand drawn-out business lunches, who used her endless flying hours (always in a first-class seat) to catch up on her endless business reading. Both a perfectionist and a risk-taker, she had her own system for doing nearly everything—and heaven help the man, or woman, who interrupted her. Although she did go out to lunch occasionally, she preferred breakfast meetings. She would ask clients, "What's a good time, 7 or 7:30?" They would worry about dinner running long and missing a late train home to the suburbs.

"No," Bettina would say, "A.M." She laughed telling the story: "That throws them off. You bet your ass it does!"

Every once in a while, even in the first-class cabin, a gentleman on a plane would make the mistake of trying to win her attention away from her homework. "One time, it was on a ride to Hong Kong—a $3,400 ride," she recalled. "A guy asked me, 'can I buy you a drink?' So I said, 'only if you can buy my ticket, too!'"

Bettina Parker was, in short, one tough cookie. Did she mind the appellation, as Janet Guthrie did? "No, I laugh," she said, tossing her head. "Listen, I'm in a tough business. What do you want?"

Still, she claimed that as she got older, she had toned down the tough instincts that might prove to be liabilities. She learned to appear to be more patient, not inside, but on the outside, on the surface she showed the world. She believed that women could be far more ruthless than men, and recognized occasional flashes of ruthlessness in herself, especially when she got angry at a business rival. "I turn anger into determination. Then, I see nothing. I'm blind. I just want to go after it."

The "it" was usually a new client or a new territory, such as Bulgaria. She was about to jet off to that country to set up new markets for four different companies. It was a challenge, and she had thrown herself into the preparations. The way she described her methods, they sounded not so much ruthless as determined. She did not cheat or lie. She simply did her homework better than anyone else, going after a contract with a single-mindedness that bordered on tunnel vision. It was not unlike the way many male entrepreneurs operated.

"I'm opportunistic," she offered. "When a project comes, I can see it all in my head. It's almost freaky." She would work alone, preferably, sometimes staying awake three days running in order to "play out" meetings or deals in her mind. She called the process "windmilling," a system akin to what athletes call "visualization," imagining a perfect golf swing or a point in tennis before actually doing it. The striking thing was that Parker was not merely self-reliant and self-confident. She accepted these traits, reveled in them, used them as strategic weapons. "Wielding power," by her definition, was getting a job done "the right way," with excellence and "without behaving like a real shit." She could accomplish this because she brought to her business an acknowledged "presence."

Could she describe it? "I guess it's pretty strong," she began tentatively. "It's always been that way. I have been told I walk very erect. I definitely am an athletic type. And I always look like I'm in a hurry."

Employing this self-confidence in dealings with men, Parker never felt that her femininity was at stake if she came on *too* strong. Did men ever feel uncomfortable or threatened in dealing with her? Well, that was their fault. She was not going to make adjustments for male insecurity. "I think when a man who is competent meets a woman who is competent, there is respect for each other. Men will ask you many more questions than they would another man. That doesn't faze me. All I care about is what I want to get done. Besides, most men who have a hard time with women in business have deep-seated psychological problems," she declared, dismissing chauvinism with one sentence.

Fine and good. But what if the man with problems happened to be a powerful executive whose business she wanted? "If it is very important, I'll get it anyhow, because he'll need me more than I need him. Or I'll go to the competition," she responded, sipping her vodka with supreme self-assurance.

Observing Bettina Parker in action in her office was like watching Twyla Tharp dance. Parker was the best interpreter of her own idiosyncratic business style, just as the choreographer was the most satisfying performer of her own ballets. Parker's private office had a commanding view of the East River and midtown Manhattan's skyscrapers, but she worked with her back to it, swiveling in a chair facing a Parsons work table, with her shoulder cradling a phone by her ear. A simple couch and coffee table were near the window for informal conferences.

"Yes, I agree." She was completing a long distance talk with a client. "It's going to work out very well. I stopped in Moscow on my way home from Bulgaria last week to make sure. *Chorosho* . . . *dos veydanya.*" With hardly a pause to say hello to a visitor, she rose and marched out the door to see Pam Perkins, one of two principal assistants. She explained what she wanted done as a result of the call. Calmly, yet in an unmistakably impatient tone, she wanted to know why her next overseas call had not yet gone through.

"Telephones and Telexes—they drive you crazy," she said, not really meaning it. "As you see, we are a morning company because we must catch the Europeans at their desks before their day is over." The phone rang; it was long distance. Parker took it in her own office, closing the door while I got a guided tour of the rest of the suite from Pam. There was nothing extraordinary to see: a desk for a secretary, another for a bookkeeper, boxes of brochures, a Telex, an automatic typewriter. Still, Pam, a veteran of two years at Parker Associates, said, "it's not your average run-of-the-mill place." Bettina kept her two associates hopping, sending streams of international messages each day. Every desk was littered with the pink Telex copies. Pam admired her boss's savvy in foreign trade. "It takes a lot of diplomacy, and she's very good at reading between the lines." Moreover, Parker had taught Pam that at the outset, being an attractive woman (as they both were) was a plus. If you knew your stuff, good looks would throw a new client off when he finally met the woman personally. "It gives you an edge," Parker counseled. Thus, she had willingly delegated authority to Pam, who was already making her own trips to Moscow on behalf of Parker Associates while her friends who had graduated college three years earlier were still in "entry-level" typing pools.

Pam was also learning how Bettina treated visiting clients once they were on her home ground. The boss liked to entertain in a few carefully chosen restaurants or jazz clubs, where the clients would be made to feel quite special. No matter where they were, Parker, when the time came, would consciously "sell herself." Or, as Vladimir Egger, her male associate, put it, "she'll trumpet her accomplishments. She dominates the conversation at a business dinner. The fact that she's bright and that she's a woman makes it work. Company presidents tend to listen more closely to her. They figure any woman who's been through hell to get where she is has got to be real good."

Vladimir compared the small shop's atmosphere to that of the old *I Love Lucy* television shows, where Lucy would get a brainstorm, everybody around her would tell her the deed could not possibly get done, and Lucy would prove them wrong by "going at it 150 percent." It was an interesting comparison, since in conversation Parker had singled out Lucille Ball as a woman she respected, for her comic skills, of course, but primarily for her business acumen in managing the Desilu Production studio.

Parker's youthful team of associates was impressive, as was the easy rapport among the three of them. Vladimir and Pam made it clear that Bettina called the shots, although she still gave them each enough leeway to run her plays at maximum efficiency. But Parker could not control everything in her life, however she may have liked to. Her offices were uncomfortably overheated and numerous complaints by her to the building superintendent had been unavailing. "It's like menopause in this place. We get hot and cold flashes," sighed Bettina Parker. How perfect! Parker was such a securely feminine tough cookie that instead of the locker room phrases men spouted ("calling the shots," "ballpark figure") she used an analogy only a woman would dream of.

Jill Steiger* would probably never think of that analogy. At thirty-five, she was considerably younger than Bettina Parker, for one thing. Moreover, she was representative of a second variety of macha businesswoman: sassy on the outside, insecure on the inside. Behind her polished veneer lay a woman who was Jell-o at her core. She trusted her brains, her business instincts and her social skills, but did not quite trust her ability to show them off

* A pseudonym to protect her privacy.

to men. Had she not told me this, however, I never would have guessed . . . given her Polo Lounge performance.

The year was 1977. The place: a table at the Beverly Hills Hotel's celebrated bar, complete with a plug-in telephone. Jill had flown out for a convention. She was employed by one of the television production companies to develop miniseries and movies-of-the-week. Here, in between glasses of white wine, she was entertaining a veritable procession of eager male producers. They arrived at appointed half-hour intervals, one by one. Jill effervescently waved each onto the banquette next to her, kissed the air in the vicinity of his after-shave, and proceeded to grill him guilefully about the most promising shows being produced in his shop. The drinks were put on her tab, which ran to three figures in the space of three hours. The conversation was spiced with gossip of the television business, but Jill did more than talk; she reigned. She might as well have been a very eligible princess interviewing possible consorts.

The table was, in effect, a public extension of Jill's desk. Nor was this a social occasion. It was a workday afternoon in the glamor industry. Nonetheless, the two of us giggled like schoolgirls in between guests, whispering about Warren Beatty, who sat in a corner. To make matters better, Jill had instructed that her calls be put through. At appropriate moments, a waiter would glide through the lounge, calling out "Jill Steiger, telephone!" and she would signal him to ring our table.

"Don't you just love this?" she asked conspiratorially. "It's so schlocky, but it's so much fun." An engaging smile spread over her slender, nearly taut yet beautiful face. She was in her element and she basked in it. After rising swiftly in the industry through her early thirties, she could have taken a bored or jaded attitude toward her job. She chose instead to enjoy it as it came. She maintained exactly enough distance to see its inherent silliness. "Tell me what you're up to. . . . Think NBC's going to get it off the ground. . . . I heard something about that back in New York from Fred, can you fill me in on the real story. . . ." There was an ease, an enthusiasm for each fellow, even a glimmer of sexual intimacy, as she elicited trade news from each person. I had known Jill as a weekend athlete and a smart business head. At the Polo Lounge, I saw her for the first time as a star, with nothing more to her stage costume than her lustrous long russet hair, a silk blouse and a well-tailored, clinging midlength skirt. Manipulative yet pleasant, authoritative yet accessible, she was a woman with her hands on the controls.

She was not born to power. Jill was the daughter of Midwestern schoolteachers. She had grown up feeling somewhat underfinanced amid her friends' ostentatious wealth. As she was a bright student and a reader, it seemed natural after graduating from one of the best state universities to go into the magazine field. Following a decade of gestation, during which she married a physician and then left him, edited some good articles without feeling an author's glow, she was drawn into television. A network gave her more room to wheel and deal than magazines did. It was gaudy, and so was she. At the production company her superiors, she believed, were more willing to give women a chance, less hidebound by tradition and by gentlemanly paternalism than magazine publishing was. She started as a story editor. In a few years, she moved up to the title of executive producer. As an executive, she was courted by other big television companies. Outside work, she was wooed by attractive, powerful men. The surface Jill was the kind of woman who might have stepped out of the pages of *Vogue*—the New York woman on the go, on the escalator of success.

Yet in the privacy of her Soho living room, Steiger put herself down for her lack of self-assurance and assertiveness.

"It *looks* like I do a lot more than it *feels* like I do," she insisted one evening, curled up in an authentic Art Deco chair. "I appear to be in control and to have strong opinions and to be tough. Often I make the right decisions, but I don't feel good about them." She had struggled with a lifelong ambivalence about power. She was never sure whether she wanted to be boss or a trusted assistant. She wound up being frustrated when she was either.

None of this jibed with the Jill I had seen in Beverly Hills. There, she had been holding court and she had been wonderful in the role. She nodded. "I loved that. I do it a lot. I'm very good at it, and I feel comfortable." The times she was uncomfortable were those spent sitting around a conference table in a glass-box office building with a bunch of male executives. She was insecure if she had to offer opinions or make decisions. It was hard for her to differ with her actual boss, a younger man more experienced in television production.

It was difficult to understand the contradiction. How could she act with such confidence at a cocktail meeting but not in an office?

Jill curled deeper into the chair, pulling her knees up to her chin and staring at her latest acquisition, a pair of red high-glitz Ralph Lauren cowboy boots. "That's a terrific question. Socially, I can meet the King of England and charm him and not feel unequal. I've always felt socially at ease. I was well brought up. I have the manners and all that jazz. And I'm confident about the way I look, about my charm. That's what has been rewarded." Because the *setting* at the Polo Lounge meetings was social, though the transactions were business, she could bring this know-how into play. In the office, on the other hand, the setting was completely professional, and she reverted to being an assistant, serving her boss. Of her off-duty, social behavior, she said, "I haven't yet translated that skill to the office. It's partly because I don't want to threaten my boss"—a copout since her boss was obviously not easy to intimidate—"and it's partly because I don't realize that I've got as much power as I have." The latter was more on target. I suggested, in jest, that Jill have tablecloths, drinks and waiters hovering over her at future business meetings, to make the transition simpler. But Steiger was pointing up a common theme voiced among the new breed of outwardly aggressive businesswomen. Swept ashore in the land of corporate achievement with help from the feminist tide, they have a sense of being beached in a foreign country. They have mastered the social skills, the egalitarian spirit between men and women of equal business rank. But once they walk through the boardroom doors, they sense rightly that they are in an alien environment defined by men. Its upper reaches, indeed, are occupied mostly by men. The brave new businesswoman may cover up her feeling of being an unwelcome newcomer, a novice—but it gnaws at her. The men, as Rosabeth Moss Kanter noted, do everything but make her feel more welcome.

This does not prevent women like Steiger from being effective. Quite the contrary, a number of them, Jill included, have stormed the beach despite their queasiness. Like her, they may deliberately deploy bravura and charm to help gloss over their inexperience with the male-dominated culture, projecting themselves as dynamic executives even though, underneath, this image of themselves is profoundly disquieting. It has a great deal in common with Sarah Larrabee's superficial forcefulness as a trek leader, and her underlying fury, and with Sue Mason's Okie good-ole-gal surface that covered her thoughtful intellectual side.

In her own life, Jill Steiger identified this alienation as a fear of showing her own personal authority. Being an assistant and pushing her boss to take greater risks in program planning was her way of masking that authority. It was less complicated to be an ensign than to be a captain, anyway. Higher executives saw only the facade and accepted Jill as a cheeky, tough ensign. But in her own mind Steiger was failing by not thrusting her own ideas forward as much as she thought she could. This was still a far cry from the "managerial women" of Henning and Jardim's book. Those female executives, an older generation, knew they were assistants regardless of title and were content to leave things that way. They have made comfortable niches for themselves in the male business world by acting as trusted aides to important men throughout their careers. Whatever early conflicts they had about their role, they resolved them. Brave new businesswomen like Jill Steiger have not.

Her alienation manifested itself whenever Steiger attended an important conference. Instead of seeing her colleagues as men and women, she saw them as "skirts and suits." Every time she spoke up, she felt her stomach contract with a case of the flutters. She convinced herself that she, not the television business or the game of business meetings in general, was "infantile."

At one meeting, she arrived early to find herself alone in the conference room with three men. As if following a Kanter script on the polarization of a token woman, the men began cracking jokes, most of them relating to sex. When Jill sat down and slipped off her blazer, the men took elaborate notice. "I'm the single 'skirt,' you see," Steiger angrily recalled. "I feel like a four-year-old! Now, how is a four-year-old going to talk in a meeting with forty-year-olds?" Jill was so flabbergasted that she did not know how to deflect the attention. Yet, in another business dealing, a man who did not take Steiger seriously enough was figuratively karate-chopped by this same woman who sometimes saw herself as a four-year-old.

They were developing an idea for a television series. They had had an affair years before, but now theirs was a strictly business relationship, or so Jill thought. The man was a divorced father, a pleasant fellow but an alcoholic. He seemed to like women, although underneath Jill sensed enormous hostility toward her species of bright, aggressive female executive. Because she threatened his masculinity, he paid heed solely to her "feminine" side. Interpreting his thoughts, Steiger reasoned that upon first seeing her, he thought to himself, "pretty young girl, smart, sweet, nice." Steiger had her own word for this opinion of her: patronizing. "It's easy to patronize a smart twenty-five-year-old; it's not so easy to patronize a smart thirty-five-year-old," she commented.

For their projected series, he was supposed to supply her with letters from experts on a certain disease. After much badgering, he came up with unacceptable ones. She badgered him again. Another month passed, and she called him up. "Where are the letters?" she demanded. "The letters are coming, and the script is coming in next week, and it's all wonderful," he said, trying to humor her.

She replied, in an even tone, "Hey, it's not wonderful. Where are the fucking letters?" He tried to stall further. It was time for the karate chop.

"No!" Steiger's voice took a sharp turn toward annoyance. "The idea is going to the lawyers, and without the letters we're not going to get approval. Do you want to make this series or not?" He was hurt. She was firm. In such situations, she had to "seize 'em and throw 'em against the wall." The exchange ended their business relationship, but not before she got the letters. Later, she fired a good friend who wrote what Steiger determined was a poor script for the same series. "I make a lot of enemies in my job," she said, neither gloating nor showing remorse.

Unlike the managerial woman, who would never have an affair with a man she might later be doing business with, Jill let her social life cross paths with her company life. She also knew the right time to turn on businesslike anger, a calculated emotion the managerial woman was loath to use. Steiger understood the men's game, and played it by their rules when the situation called for it, employing their techniques. But both she and Parker preferred to play by their own rules. Even if such a risky strategy caused an insecure executive like Steiger anxiety, it was effective, and that was what counted. Neither woman was afraid of success, as many of their older forerunners were said to be. Neither was just a talented player who had gotten to first base on a fluke hit. They were both nervy competitors who made the most in business of their personal dynamism.

Marcy Sigler combined Bettina Parker's entrepreneurial acumen and Jill Steiger's bent for adventure. She sought her thrills from eclipse-chasing. It was also her business.

With her husband as part-time partner, Marcy Sigler invented the highly publicized *Voyage to Darkness* expeditions. Since 1972, the Siglers have searched out the best area—be it a Montana wheatfield or the middle of the Atlantic Ocean—to view the most spectacular of astronomical events, the total eclipse of the sun. A vivacious thirty-nine-year-old former schoolteacher,

Marcy made eclipse-chasing profitable enough to install Phil and herself in a Fifth Avenue apartment with a magnificent view of the canopy of stars over Central Park. In the process, she grew from an immigrant grocer's daughter into a sparkling, ambitious New Yorker.

Her maiden name was Mercina Pedas and her Greek parents were as traditional as they come. Marcy was the classic rebel from the first time she ran away at the age of seven (she got as far as the railroad tracks in her small western Pennsylvania hometown) to the numerous times she defied her father's attempts at arranging a typical Greek marriage for her, to the time when she broke temporarily with her family by attending college in Ohio, to her supreme moment of rebellion when she married a Jewish sociology teacher. She climbed trees as a child, hid contraband Charles Atlas body-building books in the attic, and sometimes wished she were a boy, since her brothers were permitted so much more freedom.

Once Marcy burst through the barriers of Greek male domination, however, not even Charles Atlas could stop her from striving for new horizons. She was egged on quietly and persistently by Phil Sigler, the sociology teacher who recognized her potential and fell in love with her. He helped her move to Youngstown State University, where she got a bachelor's degree in philosophy while holding down a job at the telephone company. She, in turn, coaxed him into widening his professorial ambitions.

They married in 1964. Marcy, working as a public schoolteacher, followed Phil to Boston, then New York, where he was a professor at the City University. The two of them followed Marcy's brother, a planetarium education specialist, to Canada in 1963 to watch their first total eclipse. It changed their lives.

Marcy expected to be uninterested; she came away a convert. "It sent chills up my spine," she later recalled. "There's no comparison between a partial eclipse and totality. It gets darker and darker, you feel cold, you see the birds go to sleep. You can't imagine the color of darkness. And you find yourself thinking, 'I hope the sun comes back!' Now I know why wars were started and people beheaded during a totality."

Another total eclipse visible from the United States was coming up in 1970. Marcy, whose zest for new experiences was matched by her delight in sharing them with others, schemed with Phil to hold a rock festival that day in Eclipse, Virginia. The town fathers demurred, so the novice entrepreneurs next approached officials on Nantucket Island. There, too, they were rejected. On the ferry back to mainland Massachusetts, Marcy joked about renting the ferry for their eclipse party. The Siglers watched the 1970 eclipse on television, but directly afterward, Marcy started approaching steamship lines about an educational cruise in July, 1972 to the mid-Atlantic off Nova Scotia to view and photograph the next total eclipse.

She bargained, wheedled and plotted nonstop for two years. The Hayden Planetarium, looking down its official nose, refused to help sponsor it. The Cunard Line thought she was crazy. But rebuffs only strengthened her resolve. "It was the challenge, the utter gall of doing something no one else had ever done," she said in retrospect. Finally, she convinced the financially ailing Greek Line to let her charter the *Olympia* for her kooky eclipse chase. She and Phil gambled their life savings on advertisements in astronomy magazines, then his paycheck, then hers.

The Siglers were as startled as the shipping company when deposits poured in. The very first ones set the tone: a check for a party of three—two old women and their cat. Within a month, the entire ship was booked and there was a waiting list. Marcy did have her problems dealing with the macho Greek Line hierarchy, but at least it was a familiar adversary. At strategic moments she could argue at the top of her lungs in Greek.

In July, 1972, the *Olympia* sailed with Scott Carpenter, the former astronaut, and other specialists aboard to give lectures. A meteorologist plotted the ship's course to maximize its maneuverability and minimize chances of a "cloud-out" during the precious one hundred and fifteen seconds of totality for which clients had paid up to $1,500.

The meticulous planning paid off; despite anxious hours of zigzagging through the waves, the eight hundred passengers on the *Olympia* were the largest group in the world to see that eclipse, which was clouded out nearly everywhere.

Before 1972 was over, the Siglers were spending frantic weekends to arrange their next *Voyage to Darkness*. The 1973 eclipse would be the longest in modern history, the longest for 177 more years. With Marcy now a full-time organizer, they hit the financial and adventuring jackpot. So many "eclipse freaks" signed up that they sent two ships, one to the Caribbean, the other off the coast of Senegal, with such luminaries on board as Carpenter, moon-walker Neil Armstrong, writer Isaac Asimov, and New York *Times* science correspondent Walter Sullivan. Hundreds of scientists clambered aboard as well, loaded with a million dollars worth of telescopes and cameras. The desk of the ship *Canberra* was dubbed "Tripod National Forest" and Sullivan's account of the eclipse made page one of the *Times*.

Phil continued to teach sociology; Marcy enrolled in graduate business courses at Columbia University to learn what she was doing right. She was proving herself to be the Sol Hurok of eclipses, "the brains and the business sense" of the family, in Phil's proud words. Each eclipse, meanwhile, provided its own suspense. The two ships on their 1977 *Voyage to Darkness*, one with Margaret Mead among the lecturers, had to suddenly turn in their tracks and back away from a storm. For their 1979 land-based eclipse watch, they raced in buses to a clear opening among clouds in Roundup, Montana, guided by Carpenter's directions radioed from a small plane. By 1980, Marcy was preparing a true extravaganza for June, 1981, when a total eclipse would be visible from a number of locations. "I'm going to be a modern Helen of Troy," she proclaimed. "I want to launch a *fleet* of ships this time!"

The Siglers are as affectionate with one another as if they were about to go on their own honeymoon cruise. They intend to celebrate the April 8, 2024 eclipse for the special reason that it will pass over the Ohio church in which they were wed. Marcy, still with a bit of the Greek grocer's daughter in her, insists she could not have left her father's house, much less accomplished the rest, if it had not been for the calm prodding of Phil: "There are few males who are confident enough to encourage a woman. He found goals for me I never would have dreamed of."

One evening at dinner in their Fifth Avenue apartment, Marcy turned to Phil inquiringly. "Do you think I would have been successful if you hadn't been my husband?"

"You were already there," he said softly. "I just happened to go along."

Macha styles in business can be as diversified as the businesses themselves. Hazel Jacobs was as cool as Marcy Sigler was warm. Seeing her in person, I might mistake her for an ordinary business executive or a schoolteacher. Indeed, she was both. But her physical ability was awesome, her hands were lethal weapons, and the fashionable blazer she liked to wear often concealed a revolver. Like James Bond, she was licensed to kill.

Like Marcy Sigler, however, she was also an imaginative entrepreneur who created a business out of her private obsession. At the age of twenty-seven, she was president of her own all-female bodyguard/escort service, a subsidiary of the largest personal protection outfit in New York.

On a typical case not long ago, Jacobs, in blazer, skirt and stylish leather boots, stood behind a table in the conference room of a midtown Manhattan hotel, graciously showing potential buyers the rare coins enclosed in the glass case in front of her.* Beside her was her client, Harold Manning, an actual coin dealer from Baltimore. The case contained some of his best items, old and foreign coins valued up to $50,000 each. He was there for a show, the kind at which dealers like himself periodically congregate from across the United States to exchange merchandise. No one questioned Jacobs' presence; the other dealers assumed that she was Manning's secretary or assistant. Numerous men in the

* Minor details of the case were changed at Jacobs' request.

room also brought their secretaries, wives or girl friends on trips.

As the afternoon's showing drew to a close, Manning locked his coins in a carrying case he would not let out of his sight for the rest of the day. After accompanying the case and the client to Manning's hotel room, Jacobs took a cab home to change into a fancier dinner outfit. The gun, as usual, was a bit of a problem. A bulkier woman could hide it almost anywhere on her body. Jacobs, five feet six inches and slender, needed roomier attire. She took the .38 police special out of her shoulder holster, and exchanged the blazer and skirt for an outfit with harem-style pants. Fitting the gun in a calf holster under the ballooning pants, she returned to the hotel and picked up Manning at his door. They joined some dealers for a sumptuous dinner at La Côte Basque. Hazel was not terribly talkative, but her eyes never ceased scanning the restaurant. She savored the classic French cuisine; being able to dine like this was a great fringe benefit of the job. (She did regret passing up the wine.) The coin case rested on the banquette between Jacobs and Manning. No one would have noticed anything unusual about the evening, unless one wondered why, when they left the restaurant, Harold was so ungentlemanly as to let Hazel push through the door first, without his holding it open for her. It was a precaution against ambush.

Reaching home later, Jacobs was satisfied that another job had been accomplished without incident. In the bodyguard business, there was always the possibility of trouble, but the finest body-guarding was the most uneventful. She strived to plan a day smoothly enough to avoid confrontations. (For instance, she discouraged clients from getting into crowds like those at Madison Square Garden.) In her year as a professional, Jacobs had never had to use her black-belt karate chops. Tonight there was a slight welt on her leg from the gun. One small price she had to pay for her work, she reflected, was feeling clumsy in elegant evening wear.

Coin-dealer escort jobs, in which she was hired to make sure the dealer was not accidentally mugged or deliberately robbed of his precious carrying case, were fun. So were the jobs in which wealthy Italian and South American businessmen brought their wives on business trips to New York and hired Hazel to play wife-sitter. While the husband spent the day in meetings, Jacobs accompanied the wife, via limousine, to Bloomingdale's, Tiffany, Cartier. She did not leave the wife's side until the husband returned to the hotel suite. These men worried about kidnapping, especially since their wives advertised their wealth by wearing jewels on shopping sorties. But the men disliked handsome, muscular male bodyguards escorting their wives. Hazel was the perfect solution. From her point of view, such assignments were easy because she controlled the woman's wandering, often enjoyed the stores and had to be concerned mainly about keeping the woman's valuable shopping bags positioned between the two of them when they were exposed to public view.

Jacobs was in the bodyguarding business in part because the idea of "control" obsessed her. "I like to think of myself as a capable person, who has input into the way my life goes," she said. "I like to think I have a lot of control. I don't like feeling intimidated by other people's neuroses. I can't believe that there are men walking around who, if somebody came up to them, or wanted to harm their children, would not know how to protect them effectively."

As a child, she was just another nice Jewish girl from the Bronx, a tomboy who loved basketball and punchball. Her mother was a bookkeeper, her father an accountant, her older sister an art teacher. Young Hazel was not given to fighting, although she did get into one scrape after someone called her a "dirty Jew." Yet she always wanted to study karate. She was attracted by its blend of "pizzazz and efficiency." She got her chance as an art major at City College, where karate was a course in physical education. By her junior year, she was competing in tournaments for the college karate team. The first few times she came back from a tournament, her nervous mother would ask, "Is your body still in one piece?" But gradually, the family got used to Hazel's hobby. Within five years it was a consuming interest. She qualified for the black belt, but gave little thought to making karate a full-time career. She taught art in a public school, and karate in colleges and private schools.

Jacobs rejected both the military and the police as careers; neither offered her the freedom or control that her personality demanded. But in 1978, she hit upon an idea. She called up John C. Mandel, head of the security agency, and said, "I have an interesting business proposition for you." She outlined it at a meeting with him: She would assemble fifty women, herself included, trained in the martial arts, who would be on call for female "security escort" duty. Mandel readily made a deal—he had been getting more requests for women guards than he could accommodate. Hazel "auditioned" every woman before putting her on call. Some were dancers, others housewives, moonlighting teachers or actresses.

Jacobs turned down assignments that she felt were uncontrollable. One woman, for instance, was involved in a custody battle with her estranged, violence-prone husband and wanted Jacobs to guard her children. Hazel said no. Otherwise, the arrangement with Mandel was quite fulfilling. Jacobs, a devotee of self-improvement, had spare time for her speech classes (a Bronx accent did not fit with her taste for elegant clothes and restaurants), her jazz dance lessons and her continuing karate study. Above all else, Jacobs loved being active.

"Monday—I know that's the day to let my body explode with physical being," she said between spoonfuls of mousse at lunch one afternoon. "You know, just work out, pour out all the garbage." She was in better physical shape than most people, including her boyfriend, a physician. Nevertheless, she did not equate being active with being violent. Quite the opposite.

"Violence is what you try to avoid at all costs. You know who you are; you don't have to prove it," she said. Men might kid her about an arm-wrestling challenge, but the only ones who felt threatened by her, she reasoned, were those with inferiority complexes. "The competent man, the one who feels good about himself, he has no feeling of apprehension about what I do."

She relished keeping her karate moves sharp through frequent sparring sessions. But Hazel experienced no discontinuity from being a woman in a male-dominated business that was so intimate with violence. When she first took up the martial arts, hitting someone, even her instructor, was the hardest thing for her to learn. She could feel soft and feminine despite the fact that she was also potentially deadly. "If I told you that I liked hitting people, what kind of a human being would I be?" she asked. "I like to think of myself as not just normal-average, but normal-special.

"The ultimate woman," she concluded, "that's me!"

It is not happenstance that Parker, Sigler and Jacobs are, in effect, self-employed. Women rising to the top in a large corporation quickly discover, as Kanter pointed out, that men have strewn their path with emotional and psychological tacks. Jill Steiger had stepped on a few of them. A prime example of the new male-female corporate duel in recent years was fought at the highest level of the National Broadcasting Company among two of the highest-paid personalities in television: Fred Silverman and Jane Cahill Pfeiffer. Pfeiffer lost the battle, but not without a bloody public fight that might be symptomatic of corporate machisma in the future.

Before Jane Pfeiffer stepped on enough tacks to cripple her standing at NBC, she was earning more than $400,000 a year as its chairman of the board. Although she reportedly was the highest paid woman in a publicly held corporation, her position was unusual—she actually took orders from Fred Silverman, the network president, whom *she* had recruited while still a consultant to the parent corporation, RCA. She had been appointed chairman of NBC at the age of forty-five after a steady climb up the business ladder of International Business Machines to the position of vice-president. She left IBM when she married another senior official there, who was said to have a better shot at the presidency of the conglomerate.

But her orthodox movement as a businesswoman ended almost

as soon as she reached the level of power at NBC where real power lay. Nasty nicknames—St. Jane, Attila the Nun—were bandied about the network. They referred to her short stint in a convent as well as to her unflinching investigation of white-collar swindling among NBC personnel and her firing of important men inherited from a previous administration.

Pfeiffer, who rarely took outspoken stances at IBM, did not let the gossip at NBC go unanswered. In her first appearance at a convention of NBC affiliated station representatives, she attempted a light approach.

"I of course wanted to make a dramatic entrance," she told the gathering, "so I considered flying in on a hang glider. [The audience had just screened a sports film that included hang gliding.] Can't you imagine the headline?—'Attila the Flying Nun!'" The convention roared with laughter.

A year later, Pfeiffer was no longer in a punning frame of mind. NBC had its troubles; it was still number three among the three major networks, although Silverman had vowed to change that. The rumor mill was grinding out more frequent reports that Pfeiffer was about to be asked to quit, or else suffer the humiliation of being ousted. It was also said that the RCA boss, Edgar H. Griffiths, was upset by Pfeiffer's fervor in delving into the swindling problem.

At last, the word came that Pfeiffer had, indeed, been asked to resign by Silverman, perhaps acting as messenger boy for Griffiths. But Jane Pfeiffer, whose IBM mentor, Thomas Watson, had once described her as "tenacious and dead outspoken," was bitter about the way this corporate end-game was being played. Reacting to rumors in the newspapers, she issued a statement, not through a source, but under her own signature. "There are some who are trying to use the media to get me to quit. I try to be direct and open, and I'll try to be direct and open about this. I won't quit."

Imagine! A lady executive maneuvering like that! How unladylike! Two hours later, the network issued its own statement

under Silverman's name: "I have today relieved her of all responsibilities."

Pfeiffer still refused to roll over and play dead, or even play
by these men's rules. She fired a parting, bitter, public salvo. Silverman, she charged, had told her one of them had to go. "He
did not ask for my resignation then or ever. He simply stated
that the RCA people play hardball and that he would probably
follow me out the door in six months." Her statement dripping
with irony, the chairman of one of the country's three most
important media conglomerates concluded, "this afternoon, I
learned through the media that he [Silverman] had relieved me
of my duties." What she did not say was that if she hadn't
learned it before, she now knew the fundamental tactics of corporate "hardball."

Almost as fascinating as watching the power struggle reach its
climax in "prime time," as it were, was the interest the sacking of
the most famous corporate woman in America generated among
other executives, male and female, in every kind of business. According to the *Wall Street Journal,* "few events in recent corporate history" garnered more talk. There were no false tears for
Pfeiffer, but almost every management consultant, executive and
business school professor interviewed by the *Journal* faulted RCA
for its "messy" tactics. Men tended to view Pfeiffer's dismissal as
impersonal; women zeroed in on the implications of her powerlessness, despite her lofty title. But the last word, from a
male professor of business, encapsulated Rosabeth Moss Kanter's
theory of the "sex-skewed" boardroom. "Being a woman at that
level makes you unusual, a freak," said Warren Bennis of the
University of Southern California. "Every error and victory is
more marked, pronounced, and dramatized. The real issue will
be whether she gets hired very quickly by some other big organization. Top men executives usually are. If she isn't, it may be a
case of sexism rearing its ugly head again."

More and more executive women, certainly, understood before
the Pfeiffer incident that they had better become skilled at business "hardball." The reality was that, as one observer suggested,

"in a woman, success is considered deviant behavior." There were women similar to Jill Steiger, who had the talent for toughness but still needed to feel competent inside. There were those inherently macha, in the style of Bettina Parker, who nevertheless thought they needed lessons in maximizing that quality. In response to such women, a rash of how-to books and seminars spread like measles from Wall Street to Studio City.

The expanding market for "how-to-succeed-in-business-if-you're-a-woman" guides could be attributed to factors already mentioned—heightened career expectations and the paradoxically narrow space at the top of the executive pyramid. Throughout the seventies, women were still treading a hard road in quest of business parity with men.

A 1978 survey by *Fortune* yielded only ten women scattered in thirteen hundred major companies who could be considered "at the top." (The magazine's criterion was the salary of each company's three highest paid officers, or any director earning more than $40,000.) *Fortune* called that a "measly" 0.16 percent, and one woman fewer than it had located in a survey five years earlier. As mentioned, the ten included seven who were married to the head of their companies.

The picture was not much brighter among the younger generation of female managers. A Harvard professor's survey of men and women who had graduated from Harvard Business School in the first half of the seventies showed a median monthly salary range for women of $1,500 to $2,000 in 1976. That compared with $2,000 to $3,000 for men. The men were twice as likely to hold upper level managerial positions. In addition, a look at the class of 1976 indicated that a higher proportion of the men were earning above $24,000 a year.*

Conventional wisdom held that the younger female M.B.A.s streaming out of business schools (which had only recently

---

* See Chapter 13 for a statistical overview of present and future horizons for working women at various levels.

begun accepting members of their sex) were, if anything, more competitive about money and position than their male colleagues. And yet they needed more than competitiveness to reach parity. Understandably, some women sought help from the latest how-to books. While their mothers, older sisters or less ambitious friends might read about the Pritikin program or how to flatten one's stomach, these women read about managerial women and dressing for success. Some books came out of serious research, others were as sleazy as their dietetic cousins. The women who bought them apparently did not object to how the information was packaged, as long as it was practical. The first of the female business how-to books, *The Managerial Woman,* was a surprise entry on best-seller charts for four months of 1977. By mid-1979, there were 102,000 hardcover and 400,000 paperback copies of it in print. The expensive paperback edition of *The Woman's Dress for Success Book,* by John T. Molloy, was also a best-seller, with more than 350,000 copies in print. (Molloy's first book, the men's *Dress for Success,* did even better, with 800,000 mass-market paperbacks in print; it was also $1.00 cheaper than the women's book, lending credence to Molloy's point that the retail clothing field showed its bias against women by charging them for services men received free—such as hemming.) Another widely circulated item was Betty Lehan Harragan's *Games Mother Never Taught You: Corporate Gamesmanship for Women* (302,000 paperbacks in print). Besides these, there followed several "I-clawed-my-way-up-and-so-can-you" autobiographies by leading businesswomen and men, packed with inspiration and advice.

One irony of such unfettered careerism was that the women's movement in its early years rejected the idea of a competitive, capitalist female job market. Radicals with collectivist roots had called for replacing careerism with something better, some other model based on an equal share of parenting and home care as well as an equal paycheck and perhaps his-and-hers executive suites. As the movement moved toward a more centrist course, neither Bettina Parker nor Jill Steiger, nor presumably millions more like them, all considering themselves feminists, saw a contradiction. They did see barriers, and they want a leg up in hurdling them.

The Managerial Woman depicted an older group that had hurdled some of the barriers, although not always the salary differentials. Its executives had been "daddy's girls." They had been encouraged to be achievers, had deferred marriage and children in order to pursue careers, and often had male mentors at critical career junctures. More importantly, the book's how-to "message" was that to attain such heights, readers would have to tune in to male business attitudes, shedding their traditionally female ones.

What attitudes? For one thing, said the authors, women waited passively to be chosen for promotion; they should learn to make active choices, whether they involve jumping from one company to another, learning a specialized field or taking more initiatives within their companies. For another, women took criticism from within the system personally; they should learn to analyze criticism and put up better defenses, as men did. Women tended to play a safe game; they should learn to subject themselves to the unknown, to be risk-takers in attempting to make long gains. Women did not grow up with the team sports that formed the basis for male bonding in adult life; they should learn, even internalize, the lessons and terminology of those games. Women were often conflicted about long-range goals that might interfere with family life; they should learn to set such goals the way men did.

Couched in scholarly language, *The Managerial Woman* certainly put its finger on the problems of a generation of female executives and offered many constructive solutions. But much of its message was akin to that of other how-to manuals—"You, too, can get ahead by becoming a faithful watcher of Monday Night Football." The new businesswomen probably didn't need the advice, or watched Monday Night Football because they enjoyed it.

Slightly more subversive were the autobiographies, which took a more aggressive tack. Jane Trahey, the advertising executive, explained a host of ploys that a sneaky-ambitious woman could adapt to ease her career route upward. Trahey did not pass judgment on these ploys, perhaps because she used most of them herself. A good many were commonsense suggestions, repackaged in Trahey's zippy, headline-exclamation point prose. (A section on why a woman should spend her own money for a separate hotel suite on a business trip, rather than sharing a room with another woman, is captioned, "Playing Out of Town Poker.") Other ploys bordered on the dangerous. In one case, Trahey recounted how she did not wait to be appointed to a superior's job after that person was fired. She just moved her belongings, her secretary and herself into the superior's office the very afternoon the boss left, on the grounds that "possession is nine-tenths of the law."

Lurking behind such gutsy examples, however, was basically the message of *The Managerial Woman* or Jo Foxworth's *Boss Lady*—play the game by outfoxing the men, using their rules. This did not mean "imitate men in business," which could be disastrous. (Male behavior prohibited for women included getting drunk with the boys and using four-letter words.) What it did mean was that men establish the rules of business both for themselves and for women. If men decreed it all right for executive women to stake a claim to a departed boss's office, they could do it—but in ladylike fashion, without swear words or liquor on the breath.

Trahey, Foxworth and others did not rule out instances of macha behavior that equaled that of macho men. Some of the deeds described in their books (like taking over the ex-boss's office) were macha in the extreme. Elizabeth Arden, according to Trahey, surrounded herself with sycophantic male assistants, making her executive suite "a flashback to the court of Elizabeth and Essex." Though she put down Arden, she did not knock the idea of women enhancing their corporate image through the judicious employment of handsome men, the way men burnish their images with gorgeous secretaries.

The difficulty with such illustrations was that, as in the Arden case, they were also examples of reverse sexism, which is a consequence of playing by male rules. Arden might not have been imitating men consciously—the cosmetic industry puts a premium on beauty in anyone connected with it, even male secretaries—but her "harem" concept amounted to that kind of imitation. If Kanter was right, sexist or gutsy on-the-job aggressiveness that turns the tables on man-made rules would do nothing more than earn the woman the title of "bitch" or "Queen Bee." Token women can be made to seem wrong no matter what they do; the moves that Trahey and Foxworth promoted would hasten the day those nicknames are permanently affixed to a female executive. More impressive are the women like Parker and Steiger who struggle to invent their own rules. Parker curses, but somehow it sounds benign. Steiger hangs out with the boys but draws the line at fraternization where it suits her.

The lucky female executives are able to deal with men on a human-to-human level. There is nothing wrong with having an attractive secretary; but it *is* sexist to hire a secretary on the basis of his or her sexual allure. The issue might be trivial, except that too many women have been victims of actual sexual harassment on the job. Equality would be perverted by the idea of male victims. (The fact is, there are already cases of men being sexually harassed. A UCLA psychologist reported that of 178 men interviewed, almost 31 percent said they had been ogled, touched or propositioned by female supervisors or co-workers. The figure for women was just 2 percentage points higher.)

The most detailed of the how-to-act-like-a-macho-businessman books were also the most offensive. Purporting to be educational manuals, they demeaned the intelligence of readers by cataloging the obvious. In promising economic liberation—high-paying executive jobs—they insidiously preached a conformism which, they said, businesswomen ignore at their peril. At worst, these books sold the fraudulent notion that anyone could succeed if she learned how to manipulate herself and others properly. In this category were *Games Mother Never Taught You, The Woman's Dress For Success Book,* and two male-oriented books with sections for women, Michael Korda's *Success!* and *Power!*

They would be funny if they were not so popular and were not taken so seriously. *Games* was a snappy sequel to *The Managerial Woman,* combined with the Korda/Molloy brand of advice: carpet your office in "power gray" and wear only brown three-piece suits to match your genuine leather briefcase and you'll be promoted to account supervisor in no time, honey. The authors might have been cynical about knocking off these books but their buyers were not. Patricia Carbine, editor and publisher of *Ms. Magazine,* had a youthful acquaintance who bought the Molloy book "as if it were a ticket to middle management."

The author of *Games* was so intent upon teaching poor housebound women "the game" that the book was loaded (pun intended) with hilarious locker-room and military clichés. In the chapter, "Women Players Upset the Men," under the subheading, "Grab the ball and run!" Harragan declared that executive women

> must take advantage of the agitation on the field to discomfort experienced pros and keep them off balance so they can't mobilize against her. Women have an arsenal of tricks at their command. . . . Come on, come on! You're not 'playing house.' You're in a ball game. . . .

My, my. Shades of Vince Lombardi. Is this macha? Yes, ma'am. It is also asinine. Rah! Rah! Get out there and mix those metaphors!

What this and the other books failed to confront was the unquestionable, central barrier blocking women's progress in the workplace: sex discrimination. The writers took for granted that Title VII (The Federal statute that forbids sex discrimination in employment), the Equal Employment Opportunities Commission and state antibias statutes had rendered discrimination against women in the corporate hierarchies obsolete. Only a dose of know-how, they implied, was needed to catapult women into the seats of power. It was simply not so. "The notion that women aren't successful in the workplace because we didn't play football when we were twelve has a hidden 'blame the victim' message. It's not that we don't know how to play on teams. It's just very hard to play on a team that doesn't want you on it," said Rosabeth Moss Kanter.

Let us assume that there were women who did want to play men's games and were willing to try any deception necessary to crack the starting lineup at a company (cliché intended). Waiting for them in the locker room were Messrs. Molloy and Korda. Molloy called his advice "wardrobe engineering." (His secretary was undoubtedly called an "administrative assistant" and his maid a "domestic contractor.") His job was to make sure women select the correct "uniform"—his word—for the ballgame. His lone virtue might be that he was upfront about it. "The term *manipulate* may strike you as sinister," he wrote. "It's not. Wardrobe engineering, like all sciences, is really amoral." The uniform was the three-piece skirted suit, usually in gray or dark blue, with complementary blouses selected according to Molloy's test-marketed color chart. Not a single aspect in a woman's outfit was overlooked, right down to her pantyhose and the pattern on her silk scarf. Every item was chosen to appeal to the *men* who dominate business, regardless of what women might think. "It is not sexism," he wrote disingenuously, "it is realism."

Korda was both better and worse. Better, in that he not-so-secretly admired gutsy, smart women who outflanked would-be chauvinists, thus beating the men at their own game. For example, in *Power!* he described a certain editor who, being petite herself, had her office furniture cut down to her size. This gave "any man over 5-feet 2-inches the hallucinating feeling of being out of scale." Nor did the woman have orthodox male office desk and chairs; she had a rattan-and-glass table and delicate chairs made of bamboo and covered in velvet, "on which most men sit gingerly, afraid of breaking them." In another case, when a male executive retreated from an argument with a female executive by ducking into a men's room, the lady followed him inside! These special people aside, Korda built both his books on a set of rigid business premises that sounded almost fascistic. His route to the top, for men and women alike, was carpeted in "power gray" and led to a high-floor corner office in which even the choice of potted plants was dictated to achieve the "power look."

How wonderful it would be if books like these, or seminars on assertiveness, or a wardrobe engineering computer printout, produced hundreds of women like Bettina Parker or Mary Wells Lawrence. More than likely, taken together, they would spawn automatons. If Chase Manhattan Plaza in New York is an indication, the books may be a bit responsible for the many young women marching together at 9 A.M. in a mass of brown or mauve tweed knitsuits.

It would be definite progress, too, if "experts" like Jane Trahey gave the Jill Steigers more confidence in their own personalized flair for business. Unfortunately, women who need an elementary education on how to act or dress are a long way from the boardroom. Women closer to it, like Steiger, made it without a Trahey autobiography under their arms. It would *not* be progress to see eager beavers make the female secretarial pool as outdated as slide rules, only to transform themselves into skirted carbon copies of the Man in the Gray Flannel Suit. He went out of fashion a quarter of a century ago.

For these reasons—and because such action did ignore institutionalized sex discrimination—it is discomforting to see the corporate WACs of the World Trade Center on the elevators to their morning shape-up in skirted suits with gold-embossed attaché cases tethered to their hands. How far does their orthodoxy get them before they threaten enough men to be pushed back into their inferior slots? Individualistic women like Bettina Parker can be more successful and happier, too. (She happens to prefer not skirted suits but dresses. "When men start wearing skirts, I'll wear pants," she joked.) Furthermore, won't the women who copy male patterns of business behavior suffer the same consequences, such as ulcers, alcoholism and familial discontent? Do women want to become susceptible to the ills that turn nice guys in business into manipulative monsters?

An enlightened trend among businesswomen did reflect some male models, but altered them to suit female needs. In making alterations, women improved on the original models. One trend was "networking." An "old girl network" sprang up in many professions as women went through graduate schools together, or were united as executives by their trade, their collective status or their common goals. Formally or informally, at regular luncheons and clubs, they sought out their counterparts to exchange information. Whether it was "Women Who Win" in Los Angeles, a multi-industry executive group in Dallas, or a political action caucus in Washington, these female networks served to build links for a new chain. Knitted into such groups, women might begin by mimicking male groups—cocktail hour, luncheon, guest speaker. But it was not long before they swapped ideas, styles of work, clothing tips, wisdom about the new breed's aggressive work ethic. Thus, they loosened their total reliance on male-imposed systems.

Given the chance, and given the security of being among one's own kind, women invariably begin to conduct themselves according to their own standards. Before meetings, men often drink whiskey; women, white wine. Men loosen their neckties; women kick off their shoes. Men talk about sexual activities; women talk about their children *and* their sexual activities.

Growing to maturity together, out of a ghettoized "we're-all-in-the-same-boat" state of mind, women also tend to cooperate more among themselves in business almost as much as the women of the Lindbergh watch cooperated on the Outward Bound trip. It may be an illusion, but women at business meetings seem more willing to trade contacts and employment gossip, provided none of it gives a competitor a crucial edge. "Networking," like the consciousness-raising of a decade ago, encourages women to be themselves by assuring them they are not alone.

Soon, the typical businesswoman will not have to worry about fighting over the luncheon check with a male client. She'll have taken him to *her* club, she will tell him sweetly, "your money is no good here," and she will murmur to the waiter, with the smallest flourish, "put it on my account."

11

THE STAGE:
PERFORMING ARTS

Is that your sword, or are you
just pleased to see me?

MAE WEST

I am the sword/the wound/the
stain

PATTI SMITH

Mae West was born in 1893, Patti Smith more than a half-century later. They spanned a period in the performing arts in which women have marched to the center stage of popular culture. They had remarkably few precedents in earlier centuries. Now, the theater, film and music are full of women of stunning bravado who communicate not as spirits, nor sexual receptors, nor victims, but as conquerors. The sword is a classic masculine metaphor; this is the story of swashbuckling contemporary female artists who dared to brandish it.

In *A Room of One's Own,* Virginia Woolf, discussing why women were absent from the active creation of culture, asked her audience to imagine "what would have happened had Shakespeare had a wonderfully gifted sister." Woolf imagined a life for this sister that was as tragic as Shakespeare's was successful. The young Shakespeare ran off at an early age, wormed his way into the theater by taking the most menial job, became an actor and playwright and soon was the toast of London. His sister, Woolf speculated, might have been "as adventurous, as imaginative, as agog to see the world as he was." But she would have been kept at home, prevented from attending school, betrothed against her will. At seventeen, she might have become desperate enough to run away to London. However keen *her* interest in the theater, though, she would have been laughed at and humiliated in her desire to write or act. The one actor-manager who would take pity on her would leave her pregnant. Shakespeare's sister would see no alternative but to kill herself one winter's night, to be buried anonymously "at some crossroads where the omnibuses now stop." In short, the female creative genius of the sixteenth century would have been a runaway, a loose woman who went mad because of the contempt to which members of her sex were subjected.

The suppression of women artists—even actresses—lasted several hundred years more. The adventurous life ascribed to men of various professions, the kind Woolf and others believed necessary for the widening of artistic perspectives, was denied all but a tiny fraction of women. In classical music, playwriting, novels and poetry, women were often the inspiration, rarely the source. Marguerite de Navarre in the sixteenth century and George Sand in the early nineteenth century, both Frenchwomen, were notable exceptions. As Simone de Beauvoir showed in *The Second Sex,* the great ladies whose salons flourished in the seventeenth and eighteenth centuries were practically the only women who made an impression on "high" culture. The female novelists of the nineteenth century were far more cloistered than their male counterparts. It was left to "low" culture, to entertainers, to breach the walls of sexism in the arts. Actresses and dancers did become liberated, both on stage and in the conduct of their personal lives, relatively early—by the end of the nineteenth century —in part because their status was on a par with that of circus clowns and harlots. Not surprisingly, several of the outstanding female adventurers of our own century came from their ranks.

Mae West and Katharine Hepburn were at the top of the list of twentieth-century conquering heroines. They also illustrated distinct macha types. Among the century's younger actresses, Jane Fonda and Faye Dunaway carried on their line, in separate ways.

While actresses were the earliest female performers to be liberated, female rock musicians soon exerted greater influence than movie stars. Paradoxically, the musicians first had to break through a thoroughly misogynist barrier to assert themselves, even though they rose to fame in what otherwise was a more egalitarian time. Janis Joplin and Grace Slick in the sixties and Bonnie Raitt in the seventies were among the small number who projected a veneer of machisma in this male field.

Along with these actors and rockers were a pair of poets— Anne Waldman and Patti Smith. They personified a fusion and a breakthrough. They were avant-garde crossovers from the passive printed page to the active status of performers. Their passage could foreshadow the future.

How independent, really, were any of these women? Was each performer who exhibited a macha stance actually imitating the machismo of male performers, or were new qualities on display? Mae West does not equal Douglas Fairbanks, nor does Katharine Hepburn equal John Wayne. Or do they? And what about Janis Joplin and Jim Morrison? Or Anne Waldman and Gregory Corso?

Leading ladies of the theater and movies were pivotal in changing the mores of twentieth-century Americans. Not only did they bring to life new fictional heroines; by the nature of their celebrity, they also had a hand in setting new standards of conduct.

Mae West, more than any other actress of her day, extended

the boundaries for bawdy behavior by women. She was justly famous for delivering lines like the one about the sword, mentioned above, and for risqué repartee. ("How tall are you, son?" "Ma'am, I'm six feet, seven inches." "Let's forget the six feet and talk about the seven inches.") She was less well known as the author of those lines. Mae West was her own best scriptwriter, writing dialogue no man would have put in a woman's mouth on the "legitimate" stage. With all her vulgarity, and despite her theatrical persona (a campy parody of the sexy woman), Mae West was truly funny. She had a fine sense of humor about her image, understanding full well how it offended straitlaced members of her own sex. What else could a woman do but laugh when her name entered the dictionary as a synonym for "life-vest?"

She was born in Brooklyn in 1893, appeared on Brooklyn vaudeville stages before she entered her teens, and debuted on Broadway at the age of eighteen. In 1926, she starred in the first show she had written herself. The title, appropriately, was *Sex*. No New York newspaper would run its ads. After forty-one boffo weeks, the play was accused by puritans of being licentious. West refused to close it. She was fined $500 and sent to jail for corrupting the morals of youth! Her second play, *The Drag*, a homosexual story, never opened on Broadway because of objections from city fathers. While she was appearing in her most successful comedy, *Diamond Lil*, another play written by her, *Pleasure Man*, featuring a chorus line of female impersonators, opened two blocks away. The latter was raided by the police twice before being forced to shut down. Long before she reached Hollywood, Mae West was ahead of her times.

She gloried in her notoriety. "I was Diamond Lil offstage and on," she claimed. In an autobiography as brazen as her characters, she detailed a love life of multiple affairs that began sometime after puberty and, if we take her word for it, lasted until she was past seventy. She might have liked a man "what takes his time," but she didn't turn down quickies, either. In one case, she managed to carry on a torrid "hit-and-run" romance in every conceivable hiding place including self-service elevators. (Her autobiographical prose had about as much subtlety as adolescent soft-core porn: "Djingo had bedroom eyes, the body of a duelist and the charm of a French ambassador. . . . I wanted to muss his thick black wavy hair. . . . I was like a schoolgirl let loose in a regiment of guardsmen. . . .")

By the time she landed in Hollywood, West was nearly forty. Age, however, had not cowed her, nor was the motion picture business prepared for her onslaught. "So. This is the place a leaf falls up some canyon and they tell you it's winter," she said upon arrival in Pasadena, in that Brooklynese voice with its implicit smirk. "I'm here to make talkies. I hope the film can take the temperature."

Her movies were smash hits, like her stage plays, and caused the same gasps among the prudes. *Night After Night* (with one of her trademark lines, "goodness had nothing to do with it") came first. Next was the screen version of *Diamond Lil,* retitled *She Done Him Wrong* (with another trademark, "come up and see me sometime"). Mae drew her script material from her own life; off camera she amply demonstrated her flip attitude toward men. During the casting of *She Done Him Wrong,* West took one glance at a young fellow named Cary Grant and penciled him in at once as her leading man. Told he had not even done a screen test, she replied, "if he can talk, I'll take him." She was openly obsessed by sex. She preferred being surrounded by musclemen, not just late in her career as a Las Vegas cabaret performer, but as a youngster. She was briefly married at seventeen, but hardly lived with her husband before leaving him, vowing never to marry again. (He turned up twenty-five years later to sue her for alimony.) She boasted about marathons in bed, yet insisted on *sleeping* alone. If there were a female equivalent for a swordsman, it was Mae West. But not the Douglas Fairbanks kind; West had loftier aspirations. In her supreme egotism, she once labeled John Barrymore "the male Mae West."

On the screen, in early talkies, West was an original, cracking suggestive jokes about her boudoir, delivering songs rife with double entendres, parading her outsized hourglass figure like a stripper on a runway. It did not take long for self-appointed censors—the Hearst press and the Catholic Church in particular—to get on her case, each demanding that she tone down her act. She eventually did, under pressure from the Hayes Office, the official movie "watchdog," sacrificing the bite of her wit in the process. It took talkies a good thirty-five years to catch up again. What remains fresh about *She Done Him Wrong* and other pictures is that she made them work with innuendo, not with four-letter words or nudity. Mae West's movies were good, clean, dirty fun.

And yet . . . there was an element in her act that made contemporary women uncomfortable. Mae West believed she was a paradigm of sexual freedom. In fact, she was machisma in the extreme. She was so close to being grotesque, as a female critic pointed out, that no man in his right mind would accept her characters as real women, nor would any woman fantasize about becoming Mae West. She was, someone said, the ultimate female impersonator. As a woman, she mocked the conventions of femininity. Toward men, she was more than crude; she was sexist and manipulative. West enjoyed male, rather than female, friendship. She felt distant from, and occasionally contemptuous of, other women. It goes almost without saying that her tales of seducing (at the age of fifty-one) a twenty-year-old male virgin, and being infatuated with musclemen (half-naked, half her age) became as ludicrous as a drooling septuagenarian man who pants after a nubile prepubescent Brooke Shields.

West deserved credit for smashing taboos the way she did—with a wisecrack and a well-placed bump of her hips. She was a pioneering playwright. She was also a woman who never saw a risk she didn't like. The most ecstatic moment of her career came when, as a circus performer in *I'm No Angel,* she stepped into a cageful of lions who had just attacked a trainer. West subdued them with cracks of her whip. She was fulfilling a Coney Island childhood dream, a wild fantasy, without a tremor of fear. She described the incident in sexual terms: "I could feel the lions surrendering to my will, as they stared at me with their great, beautiful, dangerous eyes, fascinating me . . . Excitement began to take hold of me . . . I could see nothing, hear nothing, feel nothing but an overpowering sense of increasing mastery that mounted higher and higher until it gratified every atom of the obsession that had driven me. . . ."

Katharine Hepburn, fourteen years West's junior, revolutionized moviegoers' concepts of how the all-American girl (as opposed to foreigners such as Dietrich and Garbo) should be portrayed. Both professionally, in unconventional film roles, and as a movie star who lived exactly as she pleased, Hepburn showed a skeptical public that it was possible to break the rules of male domination and survive. Nor did she merely break them. She flaunted her unconventionality, carrying it off with a stylishness that reduced any argument about it to jealousy. Her admirers believed that if Kate Hepburn did something, no matter how strange (she once tried to silence gossip columnists by announcing she had three children, only two of whom were white) she was automatically right. In a career lasting over five decades, the boldness and continuity of her vision was astonishing. More than any other popular performing artist, Hepburn *acted*, rather than let herself be acted upon. In doing so, she filled in the contours that had been sketched by the suffragists, the jazz-age flappers and the others who helped conceive the "new" woman. Yankee spunk, brains, beauty and a self-esteem that almost made Emerson sound wishy-washy—Katharine Hepburn was to popular culture what Amelia Earhart was to daredevil sports.

It did not hurt to start out rich and well-bred. Hepburn, born in 1907, had a prominent physician for a father and a feminist crusader for a mother. She did not learn in the streets, as Mae West did, but at Bryn Mawr. In any case, she learned from her parents that values such as equality, fairness and standing up for one's rights were the foundations upon which character was built. Hepburn came to the theater equipped with the necessary qualities of an actress, plus a streak of iron.

The story goes that when she was eighteen, she told her father she was leaving Bryn Mawr to break into the theater. Although he thought her foolish, he gave her $50. If she could not support herself after it ran out, she was to come home. Whereupon, she stormed into the office of a Baltimore producer of stock shows and demanded a part—in anything. She got one.

To Hepburn, poise and outrageousness were not mutually exclusive. During the run of a Broadway show in the twenties, she bicycled to work in pants each day. During another, called upon as an understudy to take over the lead on a moment's notice, she developed an instant psychosomatic rash on her buttocks, impelling her to drop her drawers in the wings and hand them to the stage manager just before her first cue. She went to Hollywood with her reputation as an eccentric preceding her.

Still, no obstacle seemed too high for Hepburn to vault over. She endured the disapprobation of moguls who felt her angular handsomeness was not sexy, the cattiness of the press (to whom she was often rude), the misapprehension that brains were box-office poison. Hepburn was lucky to land in films when gutsy women were in fashion. While West was making the most of her lowdown jokes on one sound stage, Hepburn was preparing to make her mark as the classiest of the new comediennes.

What set Hepburn apart was her range. She was the perfect model of the active educated lady, in drama and comedy alike. Her most celebrated early role, Tracy Lord, in The Philadelphia Story, was that of a willful society girl. Yet other roles of the thirties formed a catalog of multidimensioned, nonvictimized characters. In Christopher Strong, she was a dashing aviator. In Little Women and in Spitfire, she was the brave tomboy Jo and the daring tomboy Trigger Hicks, respectively. In Break of Hearts, she was a composer. In Sylvia Scarlett, she was a girl masquerading as a boy thief. In Mary of Scotland, she was a queen. In A Woman Rebels, she became a crusading journalist. In Bringing Up Baby, she was a screwball heiress, and in Holiday she was an unstuffy romantic in a wealthy household of upper-class stiffs.

The free-spirited young Hepburn matured into an even more striking woman of achievement. (There was rarely a question of casting her as "the little lady" of a household.) She became an oriental guerrilla fighter in *Dragon Seed*, pianist Clara Schumann in *Song of Love*, a missionary in *The African Queen* and Eleanor of Aquitaine in *The Lion of Winter*. But it was in the trilogy of comedies costarring Spencer Tracy that Hepburn's characters presciently embraced liberation, although the scripts by Garson Kanin and Ruth Gordon were written before the new feminist resurgence. Each picture featured a pitched battle for dominance between Tracy and Hepburn. The format allowed Hepburn to run rampant over Tracy until the two agreed to peace with honor in the final reel.

The three films—*Woman of the Year* (1942), *Adam's Rib* (1949) and *Pat and Mike* (1952)—were revelations. Such was their timeless charm that a quarter of a century after their release, they almost convince us that dukes-up marriages of true minds might work in real life.

Woman of the Year was based on Dorothy Thompson, a powerful newspaper columnist and radio commentator. Her foil was a tough-guy sportswriter modeled after Jimmy Cannon. That an actual romance between them would have been impossible to imagine did not stop the writers from producing a script in which the hard-boiled pretensions of both personalities are crushed in order to bring the pair together. (The unfortunate ending, with Hepburn slaving domestically over a hot stove to serve her man breakfast, was rather incidental.) Ironically, upon completion of this, their first picture together, Tracy demanded his usual top billing. Asked if he had not heard of "ladies first," Tracy replied, "this is a movie, not a lifeboat!"

Pat and Mike was the most easy-going of the three films. This time, Hepburn was a physical education teacher with a gift for golf and tennis, and Tracy was a sports promoter who brought out her hidden potential. The writers were inspired by watching Hepburn take a tennis lesson from the great Bill Tilden. (Babe Didrikson, who played a golfer in the film, was also an obvious source.) The film's point was consistent—Kate became a champion only when she rejected her fiancé, who insisted she be "the little lady," in favor of Tracy, who held out the promise of a fifty-fifty partnership. The graceful ending had Kate winning a championship and agreeing to marry Spencer. They shook on both deals—fifty-fifty.

In *Adam's Rib*, a complex examination of two dominant personalities within a marriage, Hepburn's machisma was conscious, political and brutal. It gave the movie a cutting edge, with Kate's defense lawyer coming out less likeable than her athletic Pat. The plot involved Hepburn defending a desperate Judy Holliday, who had attempted to murder her husband. Tracy, Hepburn's husband, also happened to be the prosecutor on the case. At the outset, Hepburn beguilingly seemed to take Holliday's case purely to promote the cause of equal rights for women. It was just too bad that her husband had to be on the opposing side. Midway, however, it was clear that Hepburn was a lawyerly egotist who had taken the case both because of its publicity value *and* the challenge of besting her husband. There was no doubt of the kick Hepburn got in embarrassing Tracy in court when, to illustrate that women were the equal of men, she called a stuntwoman as a witness. At Hepburn's direction, the stuntwoman proved her strength by lifting up Tracy and displaying him to the judge as if he was a prized poodle in a dog show. This was the final straw. He walked out on her, exclaiming, "You've outsmarted me, outsmarted yourself—us—everything. Just what sort of a blow you've struck . . . for women's rights I don't know, but you've certainly fouled *us* up . . . I want a wife —NOT A COMPETITOR, COMPETITOR! COMPETITOR!" (Script emphasis) The point was driven home when Kate won a "not guilty" verdict, yet realized it was hollow because the cost was her husband's pride. The audience must side with Tracy, who was made the fool. But would audiences be as sympathetic toward Hepburn if their positions had been reversed and she had been made to look foolish? Probably not—and that was another point the script wanted to make.

It is difficult to escape the feeling that Hepburn-the-lawyer deliberately went too far in putting her mate down. It was also exceedingly realistic. As macha as she came across, that might have been a glimpse of the real Hepburn. According to biographer Charles Higham, the scriptwriters (close friends of the actress) designed *Adam's Rib* to "mirror every detail of the Kate-Spencer relationship. The public had the delicious feeling of seeing a love affair acted out in front of their eyes, with all of the tensions, the divisions of opinion, the intense intellectual give-and-take. . . ."

Katharine Hepburn's life and art were of a piece. She was eccentric without being dotty, gutsy yet regal, aware of the grand gesture in all things, prepared for any worthy risk. What she said about Eleanor of Aquitaine makes a fine freeze-frame: "Eleanor must have been tough as nails to have lived to be 82 years old and full of beans. Both she and Henry were probably big time operators who played for whole countries. I like big time operators."

Among Hepburn's contemporaries, Bette Davis and Barbara Stanwyck deserve more than a passing nod. If a single gesture could exemplify machisma in motion pictures, it was Bette Davis dragging on a cigarette. As her fingers pulled it from her lips, its glowing tip pointed skyward, her chin jutted out and her hand inscribed an arc of defiance that warned of a bumpy night, indeed, should anyone rub this woman the wrong way. Davis was not as insouciant a rebel as Hepburn against stereotyped roles. But she submitted to suspensions rather than play stupid parts. She was serious about her craft and professional about her career before these attitudes were the norm for most film actresses. In the thirties and forties, with the curl of her lip and the toss of her head, Davis triumphed in "women's pictures." Neither too beautiful, too naughty, nor too high falutin', she was a woman from whom other women could take courage. Barbara Stanwyck held the same credibility, but not quite the sympathy, among the female movie fans. In an era of tough cookies, she was the quintessential one and remained so, right through her television western series, *The Big Valley.* Stanwyck adored Western women. In her Western and her moll roles, she turned the symbolism of the gun around, making a masculine object into a feminine one, an extension of her hand, a trademark—just as Davis had done with the cigarette.

These actresses, whether shown to their best advantage as dramatic players or comics, as well-born ladies or as sleazy broads, contributed to a valuable composite picture of macha women in the years before, during and directly after World War II. The characters themselves—defiant, humorous, stylish, self-reliant, skeptical, ambitious, occasionally overbearing, sometimes evil— were role models for female moviegoers of Betty Friedan's and Pauline Kael's age.

The postwar reaction to these women, as critics have noted, went hand in hand with American society's regression from feminism. In the fifties and sixties, it fostered submissiveness and sexual objectification of female screen stars. Women were told to accept the image of Marilyn Monroe or Doris Day as their vision of fulfillment. Those who did not ran the risk of being boxed into a corner with Philip Wylie's domineering "mom." But the female fans who loved Hepburn, Davis, Stanwyck, and others refused to forget them. Finally, in the sixties, the original fans and their adolescent sons and daughters rediscovered the old gals on latenight television or in film revival houses. By that time, there were also new heroines visible to an audience much vaster than movies had ever enjoyed—women like Mary Tyler Moore, Maude, Rhoda, Edith Bunker, Charlie's Angels. However moronic the situations these television characters might find themselves in, their viewers could not write them off as pure sex objects or nasty "moms."

Eventually, a film actress matured into a star who could carry on the Hepburn-Davis tradition. With undeniable charisma, a famous last name, and a political bent, Jane Fonda almost single-handedly brought back the dynamic female characters who had been missing in action in the movies for too long.

Fonda's screen metamorphosis from Barbarella to Lillian Hellman evolved from both her personal and professional commitment. The appeal of her mature roles stemmed, in great measure, from the audience's knowledge of how far the actress and the women she played had traveled to reach independence. In *His Girl Friday*, we never saw Rosalind Russell's Hildy Johnson as a lowly copygirl or secretary, who would have had to prove she could write as well as type. The movie opens instead with Hildy as the hottest reporter in a hot newspaper town. In *The China Syndrome*, on the other hand, Fonda's ever-smiling television "reporter" began as a soft-news pretty face who then fought to cover a serious story, which ordinarily would have been assigned to a man. Even in a Western, Fonda showed a progression that Barbara Stanwyck did not. Stanwyck, as the ranch boss in *Forty Guns*, was in complete control of her loyal posse. Fonda, as a rancher in *Comes a Horseman*, was a transparently nervous cattlehand at the start of the movie, unsure of herself despite a tough, grim surface. The tough facade faded as she grew more confident of her ranching ability. Many of the wives played by Hepburn, such as the lawyer in *Adam's Rib*, began by being uncontrollably dominant until softened by Spencer and circumstance. In contrast, Fonda as the military wife in *Coming Home* underwent changes in her hair style, her politics, her sex life and her inner feelings during the course of the film.

Fonda, born in 1937, relived the changing consciousness of her generational sisters. Like Davis and Stanwyck, she had the range to cut across class and occupational lines, from the prostitute in *Klute* to the playwright in *Julia* to the suburban housewife-thief in *Fun With Dick and Jane*. Like Hepburn, she could exude intelligence and dignity. Like the contemporary women from whom she took her cues, Fonda was always reinventing herself, breaking through, taking risks. She projected health (and opened a health spa in Los Angeles), mental and physical. She played women with neuroses, but strove to overcome them. And heaven help anyone who would stand in her way.

The characters played by Faye Dunaway, about the same age as Fonda, were just as dominating, but many shades darker. Dunaway's women were often adventurous, but, in addition, they were in the grip of neuroticism. In *The Eyes of Laura Mars,* her fashion photographer was supposed to appear to the world as successful, stylish and sexually fulfilled. The film then revealed that her former husband was crazy, her new lover was a psychotic killer and Laura herself was a psychic who made her reputation by making photographs of violence perpetrated on women. In *Network,* Dunaway was also cast as the ugly version of a female achiever, Joan Crawford running amok in television's halls of power. It is difficult to imagine any of Dunaway's women as having once been young and innocent. Her first major role was the insinuating, sexually rapacious Bonnie in *Bonnie and Clyde,* who posed for photos with a cigar in her teeth and a gun at her hip, and who wrote doggerel about the gang's misdeeds for local newspapers. Bonnie was exceptionally adventurous in an exceptionally destructive fashion.

Dunaway's most affecting role, the mysterious centerpiece in *Chinatown,* was an adventurous woman for whom innocence was impossible. (The Dunaway character had a daughter who was the product of incestuous sexual abuse by Dunaway's father.) Just as Fonda's women usually wound up being optimistic about their personal growth, Dunaway's usually were left with a profound pessimism. Fonda perceived her freedom as a gift. Dunaway saw it as a burden.

What contemporary film and stage actresses discovered anew was that their profession gave them a license to hunt in daring places, to take risks emotionally on behalf of the rest of us. Elizabeth Ashley put it this way:

> Because I'm a performer I can justify and sometimes sell the things about me that offend and shock the conventional world. I need to live life in the fast lane. I need to do things to excess. I

need to go over the edge. I have an obligation to experience the things most people can't experience. The taboos. The things you're not supposed to know or do. That's part of my job. That's why I do it. I would probably do it anyway.

Ashley's justification might just as well have been written by Diana Nyad, Sarah Larrabee, Mata Hari, Mary Kaknes, Amelia Earhart, Bettina Parker, or some other female adventurer who seeks sensations as a means toward living life to its fullest. The quotation could probably be mistakenly ascribed as well to Mick Jagger or Janis Joplin. Rock musicians inhabited the most deliberately daring zone in the performing arts—by tradition and choice. Since the rock music business was also downright contemptuous in the treatment of women as song subjects, groupies or singers, it did not come as a shock that the most exhibitionistic female performers in the entertainment world should be pop singers: Joplin, Grace Slick, Millie Jackson, LaBelle, Tina Turner and Patti Smith. It takes a lot of excess to out-macho the Rolling Stones.

The earliest women bold enough to strut their stuff in popular music were black blues singers. The outlaw circumstances of blues gave a woman like Bessie Smith a permissive venue for her material. Its established lyrical language was frank enough for her to express raw desire rather than imply it. Bessie Smith, the greatest blues singer of her day, built a repertory of songs replete with unblushing demands for "that thing," "sugar in my bowl," "meat" and "hump." Her songs sound as raunchy now as they did in the twenties. Their lyrics warned that if a man was not forthcoming with his favors, his woman wouldn't waste any time finding them elsewhere. Nor were women's blues limited to sexual lyrics. In one song, Bessie demanded a "pigfoot" and some beer, meaning nothing more than that. Such songs were delivered, on stage or in primitive recording studios, with little coquettishness or averted eyes. Voices like Bessie Smith's were full-bodied, growly, insistent, rarely sweet. They belted out a message as irrefutable as a flung gauntlet or a Mae

West joke. No matter how many references were made to loss of pride, a listener understood that the singer was not a traditional, helpless-female victim. If she was any kind of a victim, it was because of a temporary situation or a cosmic one.

In the case of Bessie Smith, the singer was more often the victimizer in her personal affairs than the victim. She was a physically imposing, proudly dark-skinned woman, born in 1894 in Chattanooga, Tennessee under conditions of such rural southern black poverty they made Loretta Lynn's humble white southern origins look almost bourgeois. In spite of every obstacle—lack of education, lack of money, racism—Bessie Smith climbed to the pinnacle of the entertainment business, on her own terms. To have dubbed her "queen of the blues" would have been an insult; she was referred to as "The Empress." And she could act like one if she felt like it, donning her ermine coat and buying her man a brand-new Cadillac off the showroom floor with cash.

She could also act like an alley cat. Her principal biographer, Chris Albertson, wrote, "Bessie had a fiery temper . . . she would engage man or woman, regardless of size, in physical combat at the drop of the wrong word . . . she had periods when she drank up a storm." She was also known for prodigious sexual appetites involving men and women. She brawled with rivals over lovers, in public. She stunned white society on at least one occasion by rejecting the innocent hug of a rich white female admirer at a party by spitting "fuck!" to her face and knocking her hostess to the floor.

As the blues became less dominant in popular music, she refused to rest on her laurels. "Rather than sit back and observe" the new forms like swing, Albertson wrote, "Bessie Smith was prepared to break new ground." From every angle, she was as daring, as risk-taking an artist as this country ever produced.

Women were accepted as "girl singers" throughout the jazz and big band eras, but as the "feminine mystique" began to take hold, their songs "whitened." The lyrics and the voices grew refined, sentimental, subtle. The message changed from a demand to a plea. Bessie Smith sang "You've Got to Give Me

Some"; Helen Morgan sang "Don't Ever Leave Me." Sometimes, the girl singer's cry was heartrending: "Why Was I Born?" Or she totally abdicated control: She would love her man "Come Rain or Come Shine." Blues songs gave way to love songs, which celebrated the angst and imprisonment of love, as much as they did the joy. The "jelly roll" of the blues got mushier as the thirties and forties receded, and the mopey fifties shuffled into view. In the vacuum of 1955, Teresa Brewer's "Let Me Go, Lover," was typical of hits made by weepy women.

At about that time, rock and roll rescued pop music by bringing back the hard black edge of reality. Nevertheless, it was largely a male phenomenon. "Girl groups" did soar to the top of the charts with pulsating adolescent longings ("Will You Still Love Me Tomorrow?") and throbbing defenses of their boyfriends ("He's So Fine," "Leader of the Pack," "Don't Say Nothin' Bad About My Baby"). The music grew overtly sexual once again. But the macho man—Elvis Presley—was king, to be followed by fake macho wimps such as Rick Nelson and Frankie Avalon. White female musicians did not exist except as behind-the-scenes Brill Building songwriters or the rare solo star like Connie Francis, until the folk music movement in the sixties gave them an outlet.

Folk music as it was written by a Bob Dylan could be macho and powerful at the same time. Despite antiwar, antiestablishment, antipretension themes, a song like "With God On Our Side" or "Masters of War" contained a righteous defiance that belied the pacifism of the poetry. The folk material by white women, though lovely, was often traditional, sexless ballads or narratives of "pure" love. By definition, the folk music of the sixties was a protest against the fraudulent sexual and social posturing that came before it. It was music for the thinking man or woman, not the shitkicker or the redneck.

The sixties, however, were such rich years musically that there was room for more than rock and roll and folk music. There was room for soul. Aretha Franklin and Tina Turner belted out love songs about how to get respect and how to get laid, not just about how rotten their men could be toward them. Meanwhile, Smoky Robinson and the Miracles could croon sweetly about tenderness without sounding limp.

Most importantly, there was room for electric hard rock. Sweeping generalizations about rock and machismo are impossible, since there was an explosion of material. For every Rolling Stones anthem about "stupid girls" one could cite a tender Beatles ballad about "Michelle" or "Jude." The freedom allowed by rock to every kind of singer, player or composer lent strength to women with urges like those of Bessie Smith.

In concert and on record, Janis Joplin made the most indelible impression. Stamping her feet, whipping her hair and beaded costumes into a frenzy of motion, Joplin carried her needs to her audience, milking her sensuality and charisma for all they were worth. The act worked—she was as mesmerizing a white female singer as ever fronted a rock band. But what was she really singing about? "Ball and Chain," "Piece of My Heart," "I Need a Man to Love" and many of her finest performance songs were *not* about being tough, self-reliant or stylish. They were gropes for love and help. For all her stage boogieing, Janis Joplin sang victim, not victor, blues. Her macha fury as a live performer was at odds with the naked, "please-love-me" message of her songs. The blend of these two elements was precisely what made her unforgettable. Her off-stage antics—the drinking, drugs, nonstop partying, compulsive sex—confirmed the image of a woman who, in an uncontrollable gamble for everything, lost everything.

At first, Grace Slick gave every indication of being stronger. "Somebody To Love," which she wrote as well as performed, was an angry song. Though the lyrics, which asked, don't you want somebody to love? Won't you need somebody to love?—had question marks after them, Slick's driving alto voice put an exclamation point in their place. With "White Rabbit," she invaded another male province, that of drugs. It was a song that, in 1967, forced first-time listeners to do a mental double-take: Is she saying what I think she is? "White Rabbit," its elaborate flamenco guitar riffs building to the same musical climax as Slick's voice, celebrated mind-altering drugs nearly a decade before casual references to Valiums, Rorer 714 or Percs were in every Las Vegas comedy routine. To hear Grace Slick, not the usual male voice-of-experience rock star, exhorting audiences to "feed your head" was electrifying. It was audacious for a female rocker.

Slick was a very visible proponent in the late sixties of the Finch College of Advanced Hip. She might not have been terribly appealing in her reaction against upper middle class inanity, yet she was colorful. Who could help but cheer her attempt to brighten the White House by trying to bring a load of LSD and Abbie Hoffman as her date to Tricia Nixon's Finch alumnae party? Unfortunately, as happened in the case of Jim Morrison, the excesses of this talented performer lapsed into the banal. Slick, too, succumbed for a time to alcoholism and drug dependency. Tearing open her blouse at a big rock concert was not a political nor social statement, it was an embarrassing intrusion, an absurd gesture with neither humor nor irony, and certainly without a sense of liberation. In earlier years, when Grace Slick strode across a concert stage in high boots as the Jefferson Airplane played behind her, glaring into the darkness of a wildly clapping audience, she communicated a smart bitchiness that warned, "don't mess with me." How astonishing a stance it was in comparison to most white "girl singers," even in comparison to Joplin's "please-love-me" vulnerability! Slick did not set herself at a distance, as did female folkies. She put out a call, on the eve of the women's movement, that was as direct as it was erotic —she wanted somebody to love her *on her own terms*. Apparently, the demand went sour for too long. As time passed, Slick became mired in personal problems, and her voice lost its hard luster while her stage manner grew slovenly. Few rock stars approached the age of forty with dignity. Slick, a white woman refugee from the culture of the young, plummeted toward it on a path strewn with ugly public fights, smashed cars, empty bottles. She did attempt to halt the slide after leaving the band, and at forty made her very first solo album. Still, her machisma, for the best part of her career, was negative energy.

Was positive energy possible? Yes, if the career of Bonnie
Raitt, another adventuring woman from a good home who dared
the trip into the male rock realm, is an indication. Less defiant
on the surface than Slick, but more level-headed, Raitt could
have entered show business by the front door. Her father, John
Raitt, was a leading man in Broadway musicals. Instead, she
went 'round the back, serving an apprenticeship to traditional
black blues artists like Son House, Mississippi Fred McDowell,
Howlin' Wolf and an inspirational old woman who was a contemporary of Bessie Smith, Sippie Wallace.

Raitt's blues education had no gender. When she was ready to
display the skills she had learned, she used the black man's
idiom as much as the black woman's. She excelled in bottleneck
and slide guitars, a feat in itself for a woman. Her vocals,
whether infectiously female as on Wallace's "You Got To Know
How," or borrowed from the men as on "Big Road" and "Walking Blues," were faithful to the blues spirit but not slavishly imitative. Her first album, recorded in 1971 with blues musicians
like Junior Wells, was among the most inventively derivative de-
buts by a "rock" artist. There was never a question of her being
a white girl trying to "sing black," an accusation leveled against
others. She remained, then and later, Bonnie Raitt incorporating
her understanding of black music, courteously.

As a woman, Raitt was nervy to try this amalgamation, offering it to unschooled listeners for whom Mick Jagger's inter-
pretations of Muddy Waters was more palatable than the real
Muddy Waters. And it was touchingly gritty for Raitt to toss in
cliché asides—"play it, Junior!" "All right, boys!"—and sound
goll-darned sincere. She took her risks a step further. A major
segment of her repertory managed to be about and appeal to
strong women. It included earthy songs such as "You Got To
Know How," defiant ones ("Ain't Gonna Be Your Sugar Mama"),
rueful ones ("Women Be Wise"). The most innovative were
songs that presumed an equality between man and woman rarely
heard in rock.

The men that I've been seein' baby
Got their soul upon my shelf
You know they could never love me
When they can't even love themselves
But I need someone to love me
Someone who really understands
Who won't put himself above me
Who'll just love me like a man

Another song declared "pleasin' each other can't be wrong." Still another asked who was "good enough" for whom—the answer being that the equation had to be equal.

Raitt certainly recorded her share of "victim" ballads, such as the beautiful "Love Has No Pride." But the body of her work (written almost entirely by others) was strikingly the product of a grown-up, an independent yet not hardened woman who could take care of herself and did not want to coddle anyone.

Coupled with this stance was an on-stage patter and off-stage carousing that established Raitt for a while as Ms. Macha of the post-Joplin era. On one road trip, she did a show in Nashville, stayed up until near dawn afterwards drinking and jamming with other musicians, and could hardly recall later the exact sequence of events. "I think I got married to the bartender," she muttered the next day. That afternoon, joking during a sound check with singer Tom Waits about a song called "High Blood Pressure," she laughed as Waits complained she was preparing him for a drug fix. "How about if I just wrap his dick around his arm," Raitt shot back. In front of an audience another evening, she plugged her latest album by saying, "we had a lot of fun making it. I always have a lot of fun making it." She added, sotto voce, "oh, she's so witty, that darn Bon!"

Rough talk from a Quaker 'Cliffie! Obviously, Bonnie Raitt did not fit into any one-dimensional definition. She grew up in southern California, but contended that her strict Quaker upbringing kept her from being the normal surfer girl. Besides, she was red-headed, did not tan, lived in a canyon, "and couldn't get to the beach." Arriving in the East to attend a Quaker prep school, then Radcliffe, she was by her own reckoning an insipient beatnik and blues freak. Affected emotionally by the civil rights and peace movements, she landed on the scene too late to take an active part in either. Her concepts of equality found their place in her devotion to black blues, especially after she was introduced to the music of seventy-year-old Sippie Wallace. Sippie became her putative grandmother, occasionally appearing in concerts with Bonnie. After she left Radcliffe to pursue a singing career full time, Raitt insisted that traditional blues artists open each show for her.

Each of her albums since 1971 has featured blues along with contemporary material. In concert and in the recording studio, Raitt steadfastly downplayed pure commercialism in favor of an eclectic unorthodoxy. On tour, many female lead singers kept their distance from their band members or chose one as a partner. Raitt, however, was "one of the boys," a role that came naturally to a young woman who had long played "pal" with her brothers and their friends. "I was the only girl and I probably started to make off-color jokes as a way to get in with the guys," she explained. "I really like cracking up with my friends and fooling around with the guys. It's a release of tension. But I have to learn to curb it," she added, "because if I'm going to be a model, I should be a model."

As she approached her mid-thirties, Bonnie Raitt, unlike her hard-living predecessors, seemed en route to preserving her talent and her hoydenish independence. Her fidelity to political causes showed in her leadership of the musicians' antinuclear energy movement. She cut down her drinking. Aside from inherent good sense, she changed apparently because she accepted the fact that she *was* a role model, a member of a tiny minority.

"I feel a special obligation to the women in my audiences," she said, "like I'm kind of a spokeswoman for them, that it's good for them to see me get up there and be ballsy or whatever the female equivalent of that is. I feel real good and I can express both the pain and the foxiness of being a woman on stage.

And I think it's great that women who aren't sexpots can become successful now. Women can look at us performing and not be jealous." She hoped that before long women would be welcomed into the leading ranks of instrumental musicians, too. "This is still a sexist business," she added. "If a woman wants to get a Telecaster [electric guitar] for Christmas, it's thought of as not feminine. Women musicians have never been taken seriously." Raitt, wisecracks and all, might be responsible for hastening the decline of that discrimination.

"Jesus died for somebody's sins/but not mine." The first lyrics of Patti Smith's debut album presaged a voyage to the farthermost, venturesome shores of rock by a woman. Here was an underground poet, a member of the New York Soho avant-garde, who was also a New Jersey naïf obsessed with Rimbaud and Bob Dylan. Pop music had not seen the like of Patti Smith before. Scarecrow skinny, boyish in her stringy hair and white man-tailored shirt with a thin tie draped across her neck hanging between nearly nonexistent breasts, she exuded manic, maniacal energy. Smith also possessed a burning desire to be rock idol alongside her own idols, all of whom were male. Her poetry had been half punk (before the phrase "punk rock" came into the language, and "punk" still meant low class), half-surreal, circling around multiple visions of Christ and Rimbaud and back-alley sex.

At the heart of her poetry was the concept of breaking through, of smashing "false" gods of reason in the name of artistic freedom, insane ecstasy. Smith was the first female rocker to entwine poetic excess with the chaotic impulses of electrified music. From "Notice," the opening poem in her book *Babel*, she put her readers on the alert:

> heroine: the artist. the premier mistress writhing in a garden graced w/highly polished blades of grass . . . release (ethiopium) is the drug . . . an animal howl says it all . . . notes pour into the caste of freedom . . . the freedom to be intense . . . to

defy social order and break the slow kill monotony of censorship.
to break from the long bonds of servitude-ruthless adoration of
the celestial shepherd. . . .

. . . witness the birth of eve—she is rising she was sleeping . . .
in the eye of the arena she blends in half in service—the anarchy
that exudes from the pores of her guitar are the cries of the people wailing in the rushes . . . a riot of ray/dios . . .

For Patti Smith, "the music is visceral"—more visceral than poetry without accompaniment. So, the forces urging her past reason led to her fusion of poetry with the madness that was her vision of rock.

Although the fusion was not always successful, it was spectacularly stageworthy. Smith the poet transmogrified herself to
the pulse of electronic guitars and drums onstage into a whirl-
ing Jersey dervish, a frenzied Jaggeroid with a throbbing,
throaty song delivery. She was spellbinding, as she had always
longed to be. What's more, it took explosive chutzpah for this
small, not terribly coordinated person to pound her audience
into belief. She wanted to be seen as the illegitimate offspring of
Rimbaud, Dylan and the Devil, and it was amazing how con-
vincingly she carried it off. Like Joplin, she out-machoed male
rockers, but in a more calculated way. Unfortunately, Smith soon
made good on the threat of violence integral to her music. In
1977, less than two years after her first album had won hosannas
from critics, she plunged off a stage in Tampa and broke her
neck. Her career was sidelined for more than a year. New York
Times critic John Rockwell argued that Patti "always walked the
line between genius and eccentricity . . . between art and insan-
ity." In Tampa, she leaped over the line. Her blazing intensity
assumed a dangerous air, as if she had gone as far as she could
on the sensation-seeking scale, and then found the edge too
tempting to resist. "I was hallucinogenic all my life," she said.

Her best-selling album after the accident also pointed to at
least a temporary resolution of her love/hate mating dance with

religion. In early poems, Smith, who was raised as a Jehovah's Witness, appeared to be attracted to Jesus as a mystic but compelled to reject him on the egocentric grounds that he was artistic competition. Her album *Easter* suggested that she solved the problem by enrolling Jesus as her ally. Her lyrics wove religious images into the fabric of a mighty, heated mosaic of love as torture. If it sounded both pretentious and warped, that was Patti's way.

On stage after the accident, Smith made no compromises. Her lyrics were belted out yet buried under the weight of her band's music, and her chants were howled above the roar of the crowd. She was, as reviewers pointed out, a shaman. She reinforced her perception of that role by including an American Indian chant into one of her clearly religious songs, "We Shall Live Again." A shaman, a sword, a singer. . . . Patti Smith now declared herself to be, in addition, a Catholic. Resurrection was not only for Jesus, she said, it was for all of us, and most of all, for her.

Was this the bluster of a consummate poseur? It was hard to tell. Love lyrics and poems by Smith showed that, at bottom, she too was a victim. She was a slave to her excesses and a man junkie whose macha stance hid her dependence on men for love and acceptance. Nevertheless, any student of rock music or poetry who enjoyed seeing a bold woman flaunt herself with style could not ignore Patti Smith, no matter what her true feelings were.

Another poet more solidly grounded in words, but even more committed to shamanism, was Anne Waldman. It was in Waldman's work that there was a synthesis—the fruit of magic lyrics combined with driving, daring performance.

A child of Greenwich Village who grew up on MacDougall Street, Anne Waldman came from an unusual family. Her mother, a translator of Greek poetry, was once married to the son of a well-known Greek poet and had lived a romantic life. Her tales helped her daughter understand as a youngster that being female was no barrier to adventure. While Anne was in high school, her mother was already taking her to poetry readings by Robert Lowell and others. Her father, a rapid-reading expert, taught journalism and reading at a New York college. Words were as central to Waldman's growing-up years as football was to a typical American boy.

Her "bohemian" background was reinforced first at the Friends Quaker School, later at Bennington College. While her father worried about her poetic bent, her mother encouraged it. "She was going to be upset if I just went and got married," Anne recalled. At the height of the New York coffee house poetry-reading renaissance, Waldman took an apartment in the East Village and quickly became a fixture in evening readings. She then developed the St. Mark's Church poetry workshop, which became an important part of the New York poetry scene. As her own writing matured, Waldman felt impelled to widen her horizons with travel.

Her childhood ambition had been to become a foreign ambassador, so she could see the world. Now, as an adult, she was drawn to the "funkier" locales of Latin America and India. Waldman's wandering spirit put her in touch with two themes that rooted themselves in her poetry: Buddhism and shamanism. Both involved chanting, a technique that she refined during years of poetry readings. Although she started as a conventional "writing" poet and remained one in the sense that she continued to publish her poems in books, Waldman grew more and more experimental in exploring what happened when a poem was recited aloud. On a South American jaunt, she learned about a famous female shaman of the Mazatec Indians, a woman in her eighties named Maria Sabina, who initiated young women into shamanistic practices during all-night ceremonies. Hearing a recording of this woman, Anne formed her own chant, one she described as a "completely oral experience" compared with a written one. The inspiration she drew from Maria Sabina and "so-called primitive places" in Latin America found its voice in "Fast Speaking Woman," a chanted poem that brought Waldman considerably more attention than the small following a modern poet expects.

In content as well as performance, "Fast Speaking Woman" is a revolutionary work of art. Some of it had to be transcribed from tape recordings because in reciting it Waldman often came up with new lines spontaneously. She explained that the poem was "an experience," not just somebody getting up and doing a song or a poem that she had memorized. "It's an actual thing that happens, in the moment."

Thirty years old at the time "Fast Speaking Woman" was published in 1975, Waldman absorbed much of her poetic inspiration from the "beats." She was closely associated with William Burroughs and Allen Ginsberg, and she conducted workshops with them at the Naropa Institute in Boulder, Colorado. Thus, repetition, dream images and oral dynamics were incorporated in most of her poems. "Fast Speaking Woman," which, as Anne pointed out, sounds like an Indian name, was a breakthrough for her. "I was feeling my confidence more as a female, as a person who could get up there and speak," she said.

Dozens of images in the poem radiate a sense of activism, a positive view of the female condition, a flow that is uniquely the product of a woman's mind. It begins with a thesis:

> because I don't have spit
> because I don't have rubbish
> because I don't have dust
> because I don't have that which is in air
> because I am air
> let me try you with my magic power

Then, the chant commences:

> I'm a shouting woman
> I'm a speech woman
> I'm an atmosphere woman
> I'm an airtight woman
> I'm a flesh woman
> I'm a flexible woman . . .

And on it gallops, each picture emerging organically, onomat-
opoeically from the previous one, the pace rescued from monotony at crucial moments by a refrain with a different scan. Waldman was not shy about her intentions as a shaman in this poem.
"I was really trying to take on the consciousness of all women
and write a poem that could cover it. In fact, it still goes on. I
have more lines to it that aren't in the book," she noted. At one
outdoor reading, she was reciting this poem when she saw
policemen advance toward the crowd, apparently to investigate
whether she had a permit for the appearance. As they came
closer, Waldman saw they were police*women*. She improvised:
"I'm a blue cop woman/ I'm the woman with the stick/ I'm going
to close down this poetry-reading woman." The policewomen,
flustered, stopped and smiled.

The variety of women in Waldman's poem was extraordinary
without the "blue cop" women. There was "the architect
woman" and "the trout woman," the "woman deracinated, the
woman destroyed" and "the detonating woman, the demon
woman." In language as soft as "doe-eyed," as coarse as "red
meat," the chant accomplished precisely what the poet wanted—
it breathed exuberant life into a multiple, sweeping panorama of
women's strength and power.

But the printed word was only part of the panorama. The synthesis was achieved in Waldman's shamanistic performance. On
stage, she was the nonmelodic counterpart of Patti Smith's New
Wave rock singer. High-stepping from the wings of a theater in
one of her usual thrift-shop chic outfits (a mulberry-colored
jacket perhaps, draped with a spangled silver scarf, black slacks
covered by four-inch heeled boots, a wide-brim red hat with
satin black band) Waldman assumed an aikido position, one boot
thrust forward, her knees bent, her lips nearly touching the mi-
crophone. As she tapped a toe to the rhythm of her lines, she in-
fused the chant with a hypnotic energy only hinted at on the
printed page. In newer poems, she even changed her vocal pitch.
In "Skin, Meat, Bones," each of those opening three words was
recited nearly an octave lower than the previous one. The record

album of Waldman chanting her poems is as important as her books.

It was no accident that Patti Smith and Anne Waldman were friends, that they "double-dated" with William Burroughs and Bryan Gossen. With their "primitive" shamanistic energy, with their awareness of the synergy produced by performance and poetry, they chanted a song of female conquest with a refreshing candor that would have lifted Virginia Woolf—and Shakespeare's sister—out of their seats, cheering.

12

THE ULTIMATE
PLAYING FIELD:
SEX

The ultimate playing field for adventurers is, naturally, the bed-room. The sexual component of machismo, especially among Latin men, has been documented as a sociological factor in some parts of the world for centuries. Sex and its relationship to power and honor is at the heart of macho behavior. Now, sex is a component of many a modern woman's game as well as a man's.

In *Scruples*, one of the most widely read novels of the recent years, Judith Krantz described the archetypal female player, a powerful Hollywood television journalist:

> She was a belt-notcher. What became important to her was not whether the sex had been good, bad or indifferent, but the fact that she, Maggie MacGregor, had had sex with famous men, men whose names were household words. Fame turned her on.

Maggie MacGregor is a contemporary variation of a classic type, the star-fucker. What makes her a member of the new breed is that she was noteworthy in her own right, not a mere groupie. She, like other lusty women, kept score—an act considered a male aberration in earlier times. It is not unusual for such women to casually spice a conversation with references to the number of men they have bedded recently, their relative sizes, the quantity of the women's orgasms. A friend of mine scrupulously updates the list of lovers she has had and shares it with her pals. Some years ago, men at the Massachusetts Institute of Technology discovered, to their discomfort, how observant women could be when female students issued a "consumer guide" to MIT men. Two new self-help paperback books, supposedly conceived by women, clinically discuss what makes men "g.i.b."—good in bed—and vice versa. Mae West said she kept no records: "The score never interested me—only the game." However sophomoric keeping score might seem at first blush, the game itself *is* instructive, as it gives clues about what women are doing to draw even in the battle of the sexes.

Make no mistake; in numerous cultures a battle it surely is. Machismo in its most virulent form is terribly destructive, its ideology the excuse for rape, beatings, and murder. As Susan Brownmiller pointed out, "sexual aggression," that is, violent and hostile acts against women, is implicit in the usual definition of the word "machismo." Aggression is condoned as a way for a macho male to assert what he believes is his rightful dominance over women, be they in his own household (often a Latin, Greek or simply working-class one) or outside of it. In this territory, the battle of the sexes is a never-ceasing war in which women are the losers, over and over, from generation to generation.

In Greece, as of the late seventies, the state civil code still recognized the practice of placing a price on a woman's body—a dowry—as an inducement by her family to get a man to marry her. Feminists tried with little success to change the laws. Crimes of "honor"—macho attacks concerning the inadequacy of a dowry—were reported as "not uncommon" in rural Greek towns. One authority on Greek criminology, while not defending such attacks, declared that "the crime of honor is not only Greek

but a generally Mediterranean and Latin American phenomenon, the offended person even resorting to murder to avenge an
insult against a sister, mother or daughter or to settle a dispute
over property." The authority, Professor Constantine Gardikas,
added that under certain conditions in rural Greece "cold-
blooded murder becomes an honor." The courts, taking this into
account, routinely were lenient toward such confessed murderers.

A prototypic macho murder occurred in an unusually urbane
setting in Brazil on December 30, 1976. A forty-five-year-old
playboy killed the woman for whom he had left his wife and
children by firing four bullets at point blank range in her face.
Her crime had been to flirt with a few men in the cosmopolitan
resort town where they were living. Five years before, a female
friend of the slain woman had been killed by her husband as the
result of sexual taunts. Both that husband and the 1976 killer,
Doca Street, claimed in their trials that they acted "in defense of
honor." Both men were found not guilty and set free.

The trial of Doca Street captivated the Brazilian media because machismo itself was alleged as the real culprit. Street was
a well-known, accepted ladies' man from São Paulo. He had
failed at business but succeeded in marrying one of the city's
wealthiest women. Then, he took up with Angela Diniz, a rich
woman of thirty-two dubbed "the panther" in gossip columns for
her supposedly predatory nature. Diniz, Street's victim, was pil-
loried after her death. When the prosecutor attempted to por-
tray Street as a good-for-nothing living off the millions of "a las-
civious Venus," booing erupted in the courtroom. Street was met
outside court each day by friendly mobs carrying signs supporting him. Street's lawyer, the F. Lee Bailey of Brazil, built his defense around the power of jealousy, calling it understandable
and eternal, arguing that it was entirely separate from such
heinous "moralities" as "decadence, immorality and libertinage."

After Street's acquittal, nine out of ten respondents in one
radio poll said they would have returned the same verdict.

It was noted at the time that numerous crimes of passion had
taken place ever since the Portuguese colonized Brazil. A cultural

historian branded the treatment of women in that country during
the nineteenth century as comparable to "Arab isolation." The
Street acquittal proved little had changed. Said one leading lawyer afterward, "You could say that with this verdict Latin American machismo was judged and absolved." An American correspondent there, Warren Hoge, concurred.

"Male possessiveness and its attendant violence runs through
all the strata," Hoge said. "There is almost daily a murder involving a laborer killing some girl friend who wanted to break
off the relationship." Anticipating Latin machismo, the correspondent nevertheless was startled in Brazil at "how rigidly
women are controlled." Hoge knew "perfectly literate, cosmopolitan, educated, otherwise fair-minded men" who would not
let their wives be seen in public without them, not even with female friends. "A woman acquaintance of mine drove home alone
one recent night from a woman friend's house at 1:30 A.M. in
Rio, a city where kidnappings, rapes and robberies of drivers are
commonplace at night, all because she was worried that her husband, in Brasilia for a day, would call and not find her home," he
continued. On another occasion, the correspondent invited his
assistant, a married woman whose husband was also a friend, to
accept an extra ticket to the opera that night. Although she
adored opera, she refused. Later, she explained that her husband
had no personal objections but had asked, "suppose one of our
friends saw you both there together?"

The final irony, in Hoge's eyes, was that a principal activity at
Carnival in Rio has "men dressing like women and mincing
around for four days, winking and swishing."

A man need not be Greek or Latin to be infected with a bad case
of sexual machismo. The navy captain mentioned in Chapter 8
described the sexuality of American male aviators as "fragile"
and "notorious." It is common for an aviator to become impotent
on his wedding night, the captain declared, because he has gotten emotionally close to someone—a frightening prospect. If an
aviator who regularly had sex with his wife once or twice a week

found his "positive maleness feedback" diminishing in work or play, he would not hesitate to suddenly demand intercourse with her twice every night.

Among women, sexual machisma, in the terms outlined so far, would seem to be defensive and learned, assertive rather than aggressive, just as female combat responses were. A true sexual role reversal is hard to accomplish because a woman, in general, does not have the physical strength to overwhelm a man, nor the eons of cultural approval to dominate him as a sexual object. Whatever a woman does—besides a well-placed knee in the groin that is only temporarily effective—must come under headings such as manipulation (emotional, intellectual, physical), counterattack, verbal dominance, or disinhibition. Women do express sexual hostility to men by withdrawing from them into celibacy or by substituting the affections of other women. But neither celibacy nor lesbianism is *necessarily* hostile. According to some psychological theorists, hostility may also show itself by a woman turning to prostitution. None of these choices, however, approaches the violence associated with machismo. The most observable trend in sexual machisma in contemporary United States culture is less an attack and more an adventure, involves fewer role reversals and more role inventions, does not so much adapt masculine sexual attitudes as create satisfying new female attitudes. Sexual machisma, compared to machismo, is less violent and more playful, less a demand for dominance and more of an appeal for equality.

The outstanding difference between men and women on the sensation-seeking scale* appeared in the category "disinhibition," which was described as the appetite for alcohol, drugs, gambling, wild parties and sexual variety. "It could have been called the 'swinger' scale," wrote its leading researcher, Marvin Zuckerman. Women as a group scored significantly lower in "disinhibition" than men, suggesting that for the majority of women free-

* See Chapter 8 for overview.

dom did not include greatly expanded sexual experimentation. Nor did high scores in "disinhibition" correlate with general "sensation-seeking" as did the other main categories—experience-seeking, thrill- and adventure-seeking, and boredom-suscep-tibility.

The minority of women who did show high interest in "disin-hibition" revealed themselves as very sex-conscious and more likely to have more affairs with more partners than women fur-ther down on the scale. "Some women call high male sensation-seekers 'macho,' and some men call high female sensation-seekers 'nympho,'" Professor Zuckerman commented. Leaving such loaded terms aside, a specific look at women high on the general-ized sensation-seeking scale showed them more apt to label themselves sexually responsive, to masturbate, to be permissive parents and to be interested in erotica. They also tended to pre-fer frequent intercourse, to keep up their interest in sex during pregnancy, to experience multiple orgasms often, to show "co-pious vaginal lubrication" during intercourse and to become sex-ually excited with ease.

They also usually slept in the nude. No wonder one enterpris-ing university research assistant used the sensation-seeking scale test results to find himself women to date!

Very little cultural or educational influence turned up in stud-ies of uninhibited women. Sexual appetite, along with other ap-petites, declined with age. And hormones played an important part in the chemical make-up of men high on the "disinhibition" scale. Interestingly, highly disinhibited men had high levels of female as well as male sex hormones. (Females were not meas-ured for sex hormones because their levels change with their menstrual cycles.) Overall, the one fact that astonished Zucker-man was that women continued to have "much higher criteria" for sexual partners than men did.

Taken as a whole, the sensation-seeking data indicated that some women, not necessarily nymphomaniacs or neurotics, were biologically and culturally inclined toward more sexual adven-ture than the norm. Many were the same women who sought physical and intellectual adventures, and many shared a low threshold for boredom that translated into shorter-term romances with a greater variety of men.

Were these the same women I met on venturesome vacations, performing daredevil acts, participating in risky sports, staking claim to business or artistic frontiers? Some were, some were not. Nancy Snell, the Aspen shop owner, mentioned her need for "new people," including men, which led to relationships that didn't last long. The women of the Annapurna expedition, who kept their emotions largely to themselves, still felt strong sexual desires once the climb was over; the couplings on the road back from base camp were their outlets. (One participant did mention masturbating alone in her tent during the climb, to relieve ongoing tension.) After our arduous Sikkim trek, Sarah Larrabee sought out male companionship. Several, but not all, of the athletic, military, business and artistic adventurers profiled earlier volunteered stories of unusual, homosexual or hyperactive sex lives. The key common denominator was emotional or physical closeness, not conquest.

The athlete most identified with sex appeal, both in the gossip columns and by virtue of her own frankness, has been Suzy Chaffee, a self-styled "wholesome exhibitionist." Suzy was never one to hide her personality behind ski goggles. From the age of six, she could be goaded by a coach who told her, "you're a pretty little thing but you're never going to make it" to championship level. She was not an assertive person in every instance, but such remarks fired her up, motivating her to seek victories on skis. In addition, she believed that she (and everyone else) possessed amazing amounts of potent, nonspecific "energy" that could be harnessed in every conceivable way, including sexually. "Living on the edge" in a high-risk sport certainly fueled her. So did the "hey, aren't you Suzy Chapstick?" calls of recognition she got from her commercials.

"I have a Joan of Arc in me, a Lady Godiva, a poet, a philosopher, an actress, a businesswoman," she liked to say. Parlaying

her celebrity, her all-American looks and her verve into a model-
ing career was one logical result of this attitude. Chaffee accepted her attractiveness and put it to use, persuasively arguing
that handsome male athletes from Johnny Weismuller to Bruce
Jenner had capitalized on theirs. At the start of the eighties,
Suzy was thirty-three years old but claimed to have the biological body of a fifteen-year-old. She had already skied, roller-
skated and flirted her way through multiple careers as a professional skier, a lobbyist for amateur sports, a stuntwoman, a
model and a television personality.

Her flirtatiousness was exceedingly visible in places like Washington, where sex and power reinforce one another. Columnists
linked her name with Senator Edward M. Kennedy, among
others, although she contended theirs was strictly a ski-slope
friendship. She did wangle an invitation to the White House
from Zbigniew Brzezinski, President Carter's national security
adviser, a man regarded as no slouch himself in the flirting department. Chaffee, who is part Polish, wrote fellow-ethnic Brzezinski a letter about the impending visit to the United States of
Pope John Paul II, the most famous Pole in the world. To both
of them, she offered pairs of roller skates, her latest enthusiasm.
When Brzezinski told her to skate right over, she spent about
twenty minutes with him on the eve of the Pope's visit. She gave
him a set of elbow and knee pads. "These are to cushion the
arms race," she lettered on them. Chaffee did not meet the Pope,
but was present for his trip to Washington and forwarded pads
to him, too. On a visit to the Soviet Union, she was just as
unabashed, bringing a pair of roller skates as a gift for Leonid
Brezhnev and noting she was also part Russian. When a Moscow
host tried to put her off by saying the Soviet leader already had
skates, Chaffee responded, "well, the CIA told *me* Brezhnev
doesn't and feels terrible about it." She did not get to make her
presentation but had a jolly time anyway.

A vivacious, harmless and very publicity-conscious woman,
Chaffee was quite candid about her relationships with numerous
men. (She did not keep count, she insisted.) But her boasts,

which were toned down as she grew older, did not come close to the cavalier sexist bragging of male athletes like Joe Namath. Furthermore, Suzy's swagger was softened by an engaging vulnerability. "I see in the eighties the birth of a new-boy system instead of the old-boy system," she said in one conversation. "The new-boy system consists of athletic men who are self-confident and intelligent enough to be supportive of women," particularly those with their own self-confidence, athleticism and intelligence. Men, she contended, found these qualities in her a "turn-on." But despite many proposals, Chaffee had never gotten married. She felt ambivalent about sacrificing a portion of her boundless energy to rearing children. Nor had she ever found the perfect mate. "We're still pioneering," she said of herself and her female peers, with a laugh that had a faintly uneasy ring.

Could adventurous, independent women achieve a stable marriage? Neither Chaffee nor anyone else knew until she tried it. Suzy wanted to be sure she had a "great mate" for having children, as well as someone who would be a "synergistic force." Her romances tended to last an average of six months. Sex was not the problem; she had found many "giving" men who were "great humanists in bed." But sooner or later, either Suzy or the humanist would start feeling hemmed in. And for all her blatant flirting, she was not the aggressor in love affairs. "I give them assertive training out of bed and they give me more assertive training in bed," she said, dissolving in a peal of laughter. Suzy Chaffee and the Suzy Chapstick sex symbol, evidently, were not always the same person.

Kate Alexander, the heroine of Gael Greene's picaresque novel, *Blue Skies, No Candy,* was as assertive as they come (no pun intended). Better than any other character in recent popular fiction, she illustrated how willing contemporary women could be to dive into sexual adventure but remain as exposed as ever to finding themselves emotionally over their heads. According to Greene, Kate Alexander, though a creature of the imagination, could be taken as an introduction to real-life adventurers who plunge into uninhibited sexuality.

In the novel, Kate was a fabulously successful screenwriter who loved her husband but who still needed something on the side. A whole lot, in fact. A "late-blooming adulteress," she was devoted both to her work and to her sensual needs, primarily food and sex. Among her casual lovers were a writer of commercial jingles, a restaurateur, and a Waldbaum's grocery boy. Kate at first appeared extraordinarily liberated from bourgeois notions of sex. She was smart, witty, aggressive and terrific in bed. Through much of the book, though, she admitted to private doubts about her self-image. She had attacks of guilt, and wondered what the limits of her libertinism are. Her carefully arranged, sophisticated life in Manhattan (with sensory swings through Europe now and then) was thrown into chaos by a domineering Texas stud.

The second half of *Blue Skies, No Candy* detailed the affair between Kate and the Cowboy, as she called him, from mutual flirtation to gymnastic passion to dangerous encounters with dominance and submission. Their tour de force went miles further than Isadora Wing's European romp in *Fear of Flying*. Kate Alexander obviously won her wings years before. Both she and the Cowboy (who was, in fact, a businessman) were as adept at choosing French country inns as they were at cavorting upon French country inn beds. The book reached its climax when the couple reached the Cannes Film Festival. With Kate making no attempt to cover up, word of their liaison got back to her husband in New York. The husband, enraged, had Kate's *secretary*— how up-to-date!—call her in Cannes to notify her he was moving out of their apartment. The Cowboy, meanwhile, wanted Kate to leave the husband and join him on his Texas spread. She opted for security, her own home and her own world when she realized the Cowboy's road would lead to degradation. At the end, both men were departing from her life.

Kate Alexander was manifestly macha; she was the woman as Conqueror, not just concubine. "I still have a list of the first thirty-three boys I went to bed with, names, dates and how many times," she said early in the novel. Later, following intercourse, a man asked her, "where did you learn to eat cock like that?"

" 'I eat exquisite fudgicle too,' I reply modestly," read the text.

This was a woman who made her sexual demands explicit and who flaunted her "prowess"—her hyperexcitability and her staying power. What made the book fascinating as social comment was that the author stood a few steps removed from her heroine at all times, commenting ironically about how Kate's self-assurance was a mask.

Gael Greene liked her heroine in spite of the mess she left her life in. Yes, Greene agreed, Kate Alexander was a sexual adventurer, however full of rationalizations, because she had "the capacity to enjoy sex without any emotional involvement." She could "step into another world where sex is fun for its own sake." But Greene also viewed Kate as a victim of her desires, not only as a conqueror. "She is a woman who seizes the initiative and says, 'I want you.' She sets out to seduce a man, maybe succeeds or doesn't." On the other hand, humiliation was built into her once-a-month gambit with the jingles man, since he set the timetable for their meetings. That did not quite make Kate a victim, said Greene, but it indicated she was not "totally in charge." With the Cowboy, she grew totally out of control—a feeling the author believed excited her heroine and also placed her in the victim category.

One aspect of sexual adventure can be measured, Greene continued, by distance traveled. She herself, like Kate, had once flown thousands of miles to spend a night with a man whom she did not know well. "It's sort of stepping out of your life for 24 hours into a fantasy that is, maybe, better than fantasy. It's in another city, and you are both so far away from your realities. And you may never see each other again!" Greene made it plain that romance, as opposed to love, was a highly desirable ingredient in such affairs. So was discretion. Broadcasting one's sexual excursions was not Greene's idea of adventuring.

At the core of a female sexual adventurer, according to Greene, was "a willingness to feel anything, and to risk something wonderful for the unknown." The adventure was "more emotional" for a woman than for a man. Greene acknowledged that sex for fun still required more than a purely physical commitment on the woman's side. But female sexual adventuring included plenty of physical activity as well, not excluding sadism, masochism, lesbianism and game-playing: "You can be anything in bed, and it doesn't mean that's what you are. You can be a slave or a queen, or a child or the opposite sex, for that moment. And then you get up and go on and live your life."

The women Greene knew in real life who were sexual adventurers were "very ordinary" women, the kind with families or at least a steady mate. Their complicated sexual lives were kept separate from their home life. Nor were they necessarily beautiful or young. They were sexually special in being totally comfortable with their female selves and in being able to find a route close to the height of sexual response. These were women who got high on sex the way others would on drugs. One imagines them sending tremors through the sensation-seeking laboratory that would register on the Richter scale. Regardless, Greene did not equate a macho man's need for conquest with a woman's need for seduction. A woman's idea of success had to contain an element of love or emotion, not merely "scoring."

The sexual adventurers Greene knew did not have to prove themselves in other high-risk areas. Sensuality was more important to them than physical daring. Even among "gourmands of love" who were also gourmets of the table (Greene is best known as a food critic) the correlation was not always exact. Greene once received a long, sensual letter from a man about her food writing, a letter she interpreted to be 80 percent about food and 20 percent about love. Intrigued, she encouraged further correspondence. He wrote back with longer, more passionate descriptions of meals. Eventually, they planned to meet at Paul Bocuse's famous restaurant in France. Gael assumed that for her pen pal, the date had the sexual excitement she would have

felt in arranging a get-together for herself and Warren Beatty.
Alas, halfway through the Bocuse meal she understood that it
was indeed food the pen pal was interested in, and he did not
have her in mind as dessert. "What a shock!" said the nation's
most sensuous cuisine critic, looking as let down as a fallen
soufflé.

Women talk among themselves about sex far more clinically than
do men, whose "locker room" talk commonly is limited to gener-
alities. To inject a subject like impotence, homosexual stirrings or
any other "taboo" would be regarded as unmanly. In contrast,
women, nonadventurers and adventurers alike, are willing to
confide losses as well as wins to their female friends. Gael
Greene surmised that the absence of the "conquest" mentality
permitted women to be honest with each other.

This was certainly the case for three women I interviewed at
length who judged themselves as sexual risk-takers. All fitted
Greene's description of being outwardly "ordinary"—none was a
statuesque Bo Derek nor a high-powered Mary Wells Lawrence,
although they were attractive and gainfully employed. They
shared many of Suzy Chaffee's attitudes towards sex as an outlet
for healthy energy, but none was an athlete. And a plaintively
reiterated theme was that their "conquistador" style was merely
a shield behind which trembled a romantic postadolescent female yearning for true love.

These women set themselves apart from what one called "the
dopers, waitresses and punkos" who looked for kicks and for
whom "sex is a kind of toy." (The model could have been the Bo
Derek character in the film 10, a male fantasy figure who, upon
closer inspection, was a shallow marijuana-toking bubblehead.)
Two of the three women—all of whom were in their thirties—
kept score. But their scores were well under a hundred men
apiece. Male friends in the same age range had told them of
sleeping with several hundred women apiece, confirming Zuckerman's thesis that women are more choosy about partners.
These three did conceive of themselves as "adventurous," yet not

"predatory," even when they took the initiative in inviting a man
to have sex, which they each did in their individual ways. "Girl-
talk," they argued, no matter how raunchy, was a means of com-
paring notes and making sure others had experimented with the
same "taboos"—oral sex, anal intercourse, threesomes, mechanical devices, kinky underwear, and lesbianism, among other
things. They strongly differentiated this from male "locker-room
talk," believed by women to be pure, often false, boasting.

Only one of the three women, a Midwestern Protestant, did
not mind picking up men in bars or restaurants. "I'm on the road
alone so much of the time that I think like a man," she said. "On
a business trip, I get great pleasure out of walking into the hotel
bar at 5 o'clock and seeing how many men will ask me to dinner.
The best sexual nights I've had have been with somebody I've
met that afternoon. It becomes an all-night, torrid affair, awake
until dawn. But very often I'm not interested in that person
again. Unfortunately, it seems that once I achieve the conquest,
a lot of the glitter is gone from the relationship."

There were other drawbacks to casual affairs. The second woman, a Jewish New Yorker, had a friend who once met a man
on a bus and took him home with her that night. She left her
front door slightly ajar because an elderly neighbor, understanding her proclivities, tacitly kept an ear open for sounds of
distress from the woman's apartment. As it happened, the two
bus passengers were so compatible that by the middle of the
night, the woman was moaning with enjoyment. The trouble
was, she was so vocal that her neighbor ended up banging on
her door, afraid the woman was being raped!

All three had no hesitation about making their sexual needs
known, a quality that either spurred on their partners, or threatened them. "Guys say they want you to be up-front, but when
you say, 'let's use my vibrator' or you ask for a strange position,
they think you're a nymphomaniac," said one. "If they're into a
macho number, they may not like you because you're not as
tough a conquest for *them* as some other girl they really had to
coax into bed," said the magazine woman.

The Midwestern woman saw her situation in a socioeconomic
light. "Weak men are attracted to me because of my strong personality and business success. I'll get involved with a man, and
then I find out I'm carrying *him*. The types *I* enjoy most—
successful, confident men—don't need my attitude. They often
have dealt so well with their own lives they're just looking for a
woman to do the 'female' thing, a nice little girl who can tell
them how great they are. With the weaker man, the sex can be
satisfying. But soon I start realizing that I'm so much stronger
than that person. Sexual satisfaction and respect are very tied together in a long-term relationship. When I lose the respect for
him, I can no longer sexually respond."

The New York woman complained she was left unsatisfied
enough times to become angry. The classic case was a man who
could not get an erection and then refused to pleasure her either
orally or manually. Interestingly, she was not always permanently upset by such a man. If she felt there could be an emotional involvement between them, she would ascribe his problem
to opening-night jitters. Sometimes she was right. One man
whom she did not give up on later became her second husband.

The three women felt freer and more daring in their sexual
odysseys away from their home communities, a carryover, perhaps, from their middle-class upbringing, in which the community standard was, "nice girls don't." One-night stands were
viewed as an ongoing search for acceptable partners, to whom
they could remain faithful for several months. Variety was important too, but the women more often than not had sequentially
monogamous affairs, rather than numerous simultaneous ones.
Only one of the three women, a Roman Catholic by birth, had
had sex with another woman, although she was primarily heterosexual. "It was an experiment, and it was fun," she said simply. A second believed that she was missing out by *not* sleeping
with other women: "Bisexuality seems more well-rounded," the
New Yorker remarked. The Midwesterner thought, intellectually,
that sex with a woman probably would be "terrific." But it was a

taboo she could not get past: "when I'm approached by a woman I absolutely flinch."

Would these women qualify as sexually daring? Yes! they replied, in that they were ready to "try on" any man for the sake of the illusive emotional, mental or physical "perfect fit." But underneath, they all claimed to be as vulnerable as the next woman. As one woman put it, "I'm hurt by rejection, of course! I've had a lot of male attention in my life and I've become reliant on that. I pride myself on doing things well and if I'm rejected I feel I've failed."

What the three each hoped for, at some point, was a stable relationship. This did not have to be a conventional marriage. Two had been married, both to men who did not live in the same city; the eternal lure of romance led each to think their separations and joinings would help keep the marriage fresh. Neither marriage worked, but the three women were as cautiously optimistic as Suzy Chaffee that some day, the perfect fit would be made. To these women, who could get as lonely on a weekend and as entangled in an affair as their less adventurous sisters, "liberation" did not mean forever liberating love from sex.

The biggest sexual risk-takers are women who do consciously divide love and sex. Some, like Kate Alexander, do it for fun. Some, like Susan Stern, do it for a thrill. And some, like Barbara Hetzel, do it for money.

Susan Stern, the Weatherwoman, was an ambiguous sexual adventurer. She was out to prove her rebellion in bed, not just in the Weather underground. Meek, apolitical and sexually repressed as a married woman in college, Stern grew progressively more belligerent, more politically active and more sexually active as a radical. She felt the same thrill foraging for male bedmates, night after night, as she did fighting policemen in the streets of Chicago. She and a friend branded themselves the "Macho Mamas," a sardonic term for their reverse-chauvinist adventures.

In Stern's autobiography, they read like parodies of a *Hustler* subscriber's wet dreams:

> I was in my prime; flashy and vulgar, hard and funny, aggressive and dramatic. I got the Sundance boys hordes of dope, I forged checks. . . . I fucked them all methodically, one by one, whether they wanted me to or not. It was part of my act. . . .

These "Macho Mamas" called men "cuties" or "cocks." They worked at a bar together (their "turf"), where they would guzzle the house booze and single out their partners for the night. But Stern had to swallow downers on top of liquor and smoke marijuana to go through with this ongoing ritual. She would wake up sick and full of self-disgust. It did not take long for her to realize what a farce the "act" was. It was, as well, an act of barely concealed hostility, the opposite emotional pole from intimacy.

How much hostility is there in sexual adventuring? It depends on the adventurer. Women surely are justified in growing hostile toward men who repeatedly fail to satisfy them. When a woman seeks solace elsewhere, what a century ago would have been looked upon as promiscuous today would be a sign of independence. Sensual gambles for their own sake, such as those of Kate Alexander, are often filled with a healthy curiosity, even joy. Sampling men in search of an ideal lover, as the three risk-takers do, sounds worthwhile, not hostile. Repelling unwanted advances can be both sensible and hostile.

In the opinion of psychoanalyst June Singer, the archetypal women who displayed "detachment from men, if not an outright hostility toward them" were the Amazons. Hypsipule, a Hellenic Queen descended from the Amazons, had her followers kill all men including their husbands in order to take over the island of Lemnos. Artemis, the divine huntress of Greek mythology, was pointedly the goddess of virginity. The "Artemis-Amazon type of woman," according to Singer, was a product of a transitional culture, a reactionary figure whose withdrawal from men was a

mark of opposition to patriarchal rule. At the same time, Singer
called her "the prototype of the radical feminist who has little
interest in relating to men," who has adopted "masculine" characteristics and who identifies with male concepts of power. "She
renounces the capacity to relate lovingly," Singer concluded.
Singer never specified which radical feminists she had in mind.
Despite troubles with men, many radical feminists have not lost
interest in relating to them lovingly, and would rightfully quarrel
with this odd comparison.

There is one pervasive heterosexual approach to men that is both
macha and, in the view of some psychologists, often associated
with hostility: prostitution. One research team drew this composite of the typical prostitute's background—haphazard religious
upbringing; no more than a high school education; previous experience with unskilled, frustrating and dead-end jobs; a frag-
mented family; fatherly neglect; and in a few cases "seduction
or rape by a father, stepfather, older brother or uncle."
    The hypothesis is that such severe rejection can lead a prosti-
tute to worship power, to see in a pimp a substitute father, and
to unconsciously seek revenge on the natural father through interminable sex for hire with many men. It does not take much to
uncover the agonizing insecurities of prostitutes. Still, these are
macha women. They brag about how much money they make,
they flaunt their earnings in the form of mink coats and dia-
mond-studded necklaces, and they put a defiantly proud face on
their position as societal outlaws. They may not love their work,
but there is an attractiveness about "the life" that is germane to
the subject of female risk-takers. "To the women who enter it,
prostitution seems, of all the fields open to them, the one most
likely to provide the glamour and excitement they crave," wrote
the researchers, Sam Janus, Barbara Bess and Carol Saltus.
    A former New York prostitute, who was both a streetwalker
and a call girl as well as a go-go dancer, affirmed these generalizations. Indeed, her life graphically illustrated many of them.

Though she was not hostile toward men, her story showed the pitfalls that lurk where sex and adventuring are conjoined.

At twenty-seven, Barbara Hetzel had lived through more adventure than most women experience in a lifetime—and she did not go to the Himalayas, Hurricane Island, Africa or Bulgaria to find it. She had been a truant, a heroin user, a go-go dancer, a prostitute, a failed suicide and a jailbird. Now, as she explained sitting cross-legged on the rug of her small Manhattan flat, she was going "straight"—working as a cook in a theater district pub. She was a pretty, broad-shouldered woman who had put on some pounds since her go-go days, and she chain-smoked Kools. Her brown hair was pulled back in a long pony tail. She could easily have been taken for a bank teller or a secretary. However, there were bits and pieces about Barbara that did not fit together. She had limpid blue eyes, but their softness was hidden by black eye-liner. She wore a tee shirt that proclaimed "Revolution Is Not A Dinner Party—Chairman Mao," but around her neck was a gold cross. She spoke in gruff New Yorkese, yet she grew up in the middle-income suburb of Lindenhurst, Long Island. She was articulate, yet had no high school diploma.

Always a rebel, Barbara had beaten up a girl in the eleventh grade and had been told to either quit high school or be thrown out. She had quit. The cause of the fight? "She was talking about my brother," Barbara said ominously. "Nobody talks about my brother like that."

Barbara was the youngest of four children. Her father, who worked at a Long Island factory, had deserted the family when Barbara was five. The family became poorer as her mother "worked her butt off" selling infants' wear in Sears. The job kept her away from the house in the course of Barbara's formative years. Nevertheless, her mother scraped together money to pay for violin and dance lessons.

The little girl handled herself all right until her teenage years. It was then that Barbara became rebellious with a vengeance. At fourteen, she and a boyfriend started shooting heroin. They weren't totally hooked, at first. Before many months went by, though, Barbara was stealing her grandmother's social security checks to pay for her habit. Finally, she began staying away from home. During one absence, her mother discovered her "works"—syringe and spoon—in her bureau drawer. Mrs. Hetzel went looking for her daughter, whom she found stoned in a bar. With help from Barbara's older sister, the mother dragged the nodding girl outside . . . and took her directly to a police station. "Straighten her out," Mrs. Hetzel begged the police, "I can't deal with this." As Barbara came out of her stupor, she went into a rage, tearing down the flimsy holding-pen partitions and trying to strangle her mother. When she calmed down, she learned that her mother had given her a reprieve; she would not sign papers to have her daughter committed.

Barbara had always gotten a charge out of shocking her mother. Once, Mrs. Hetzel asked her what she wanted to be when she grew up. Barbara answered, "a ballet dancer, but maybe I'll be a prostitute because they make more money." Now, it was Barbara who was shocked, enough to kick the heroin habit and live a more normal life for almost three years.

First, Barbara worked in a thermometer factory, then moved on to waitressing. Soon, she and a girl friend were spending their off-hours at a bar that featured topless dancers. One night a dancer did not show up for work, and everyone began to make book on which of the regular hangers-on would fill her shoes. They egged Barbara on. She said no, no, no, getting drunker and drunker, while the betting money piled up on the bar. At last she said, "what the hell?" She took the money, stripped and danced. She was seventeen years old.

It was not hard to be a go-go dancer in 1970 on Long Island. The pay—$50 a night for five hours' work—was more rewarding than waiting on tables. In her pasties, G-string, stockings and heels, Barbara felt nearly clothed. The patrons of the places she worked were "home-town" men and couples, and she did not have to perform any closer to them than six feet away, on a raised platform. She learned the new trade thoroughly in seven months. Then, seeking the excitement only the "city," Manhattan, could offer, Barbara made her move to The Forty-Niner, a garish bar off Times Square. As the best dancer in the house, she got the most tips, from $50 to $100 a night. And the hours were shorter than on Long Island. "New York City was more glamorous," Barbara said, recalling her naïveté. "You wore all these hand-beaded costumes and stockings and silver shoes and chokers, long chokers. And pasties and wigs and tons of makeup. You worked on a big, glamorous stage." She mulled over the adjective and repeated it. "Glamorous. It really was."

If it wasn't the New York City Ballet, it was a damn sight better than the thermometer factory. That is, until Barbara moved her dancing to the Wagonwheel and got "kidnapped."

The Wagonwheel, also in Times Square, was a gathering spot for pimps. Leaving the bar one evening, Barbara was offered a ride in the sleek Cadillac of one of the regulars, a black man she knew. She shrugged and accepted. He took her to his apartment where he locked her up for almost two weeks in order to convince her to join his stable of hookers. Feeling brainwashed, she agreed. At eighteen, she was in the street.

Within the month, she was arrested on a prostitution charge for the first time. A customer, on his own first outing as a "john," felt so sorry for her that he gave her $75 instead of the usual "$20-and-10"—$20 fee plus $10 for the hotel room. A few days later, he returned with a detective. "You really don't belong in this business," the young man said earnestly. After much talk, Barbara made the detective understand that she would be in trouble with the pimp. The detective drove her all the way home to Lindenhurst instead of booking her. Barbara told her mother, who had known about the go-go jobs, that she was having "man problems." She did not tell her she had been hooking.

Gradually, Barbara drifted back to Manhattan. She settled into hooking for a pimp she liked, turning from eight to fifteen "tricks" a night. Many times, her clients just wanted to talk; Barbara's youthfulness told them she was willing to listen. She got as much as $100 a trick, although her standard price for "straight" intercourse or oral sex was $20. (Prostitutes required the female-superior position in "straight" sex, she noted. They were afraid of getting trapped or bruised otherwise; being on top also enabled them to manipulate men to come more quickly. Their birth control method was the condom, to prevent both pregnancy and venereal disease.)

By the time a year had gone by, Hetzel had a steady clientele. A chauffeur from a limousine company would occasionally pimp for her too. Her regular station, with about a dozen other prostitutes, was Sixth Avenue and Forty-fourth Street. "Most of the women didn't enjoy what they were doing, but they enjoyed the life itself," she recalled. "I always felt it was kind of exciting because I was doing something illegal." The group had a street camaraderie. One woman resembled Barbara; when their "tricks" could not find one, they would take the other. They and their pimps had plenty of spending money. Where did it go? Not into the banks whose doorways served as their posts. "Clothes, over the bar, up my nose, in my stomach—any way I could spend it," said Barbara. She bought expensive clothes for her pimp, diamonds for herself. The women liked to strut among one another, showing off their jewelry and their fur coats. The more money a prostitute made, the higher her status among the others. What counted was not the number of tricks, it was how much cash they could collect in a night without exercising too heavily.

Personally and professionally, the women were tough. Hetzel's definition of "macho women," as she called them, was "dominant over their tricks *and* their personal lives." In truth, they were absolutely controlled by their pimps. But they saw themselves as independent, able to take care of themselves, holding great power over men. A few were lesbians, yet one prostitute who let herself be picked up for hired sex with a *woman* was scorned. It was a peculiar pecking order. Disliking most of their male tricks, the women often stole from the men, sneered at those who wanted "bondage," and generally showed contempt for male desires. At the same time, they made nasty remarks about Ruby, the hooker with a regular female customer who collected Ruby in an impressive Rolls Royce. Ruby ignored the taunts. She got several hundred dollars an evening from the woman. She even claimed to enjoy the client's company. One day, for $300, Barbara went off with the two in the Rolls and had a good time. The rest of the group did not speak to her or Ruby for weeks. Perhaps it was only jealousy. The lady with the Rolls began picking up more and more of the hookers in the group, until there was no one left to taunt.

After more than three years, Barbara began to cut down on her work. The money was good, but she could never save it. She still thought herself daring—there was always the danger of physical injury—but it was wearing thin. She felt nothing in the act of sex with a trick; it was a depersonalized routine. "You're not supposed to enjoy it," she explained. "With a john, I would just shut my mind off." When she was with her boyfriend, sex was personal, enjoyable, emotional. The path that led away from prostitution grew more enticing as Barbara became more deeply attached to Joseph, her lover. Hooking began to alienate her; it was a "no-status, insecure" job. She returned briefly to go-go dancing to fill the gap left by her declining prostitution income.

Barbara Hetzel's precarious world came crashing down on her the day of one of the city's memorable celebrations, July 4, 1976. She had to dance a sixteen-hour shift because everyone else wanted to watch the Tall Ships in New York harbor. To fight exhaustion, she took amphetamines, washed down with glass after glass of champagne bought by her reveling audience. At four in the morning, she finally went home, taking one Seconal to make sure she would sleep. Joseph was furious at seeing her blind drunk and doped up. They fought bitterly, Joseph blaming her condition on her line of work. "I can't stand this any more," he yelled, "I don't want anybody looking at your body!" In her G-string and stockings, Barbara stumbled into the bathroom and slit her wrists.

She didn't really want to kill herself. She just wanted some sympathy. But blood was spouting from her veins like a red geyser and she was so stoned she did not even feel hurt.

Horrified, Joseph telephoned for an ambulance. At the hospital, it took a lot of stitches to sew up her tattered arms. The doctors also asked her to remain there for five days for psychiatric evaluation.

She finally returned home to Joseph. She never returned to hooking or go-go dancing.

The transition occurred in stages. Her next job, after her arms healed, was as a barmaid in a topless bar. Although, for Hetzel, it was a giant step out of the mire, it was not a big enough one for Joseph, and they split up. Barbara later took a second step up to the cook's job in a "normal" bar. The transition was by no means smooth. It took a long while for Hetzel to communicate freely with women from the world outside her subculture, sensing that some of them were disdainful of her. A period in psychoanalysis helped, as did time, and her instinct for survival.

More than two years after she had danced her last go-go number, Barbara was saving her money, studying for a high school equivalency diploma and planning ahead for a nursing career. Counter to the conventional wisdom that to prostitutes, men are merely customers, Hetzel held no hostile attitudes toward the opposite sex, although she knew she had given up seeking a surrogate father in a pimp.

As for her mother, Mrs. Hetzel never told Barbara exactly what she knew about her daughter's adventures. What mattered, thought Barbara, who was no longer a rebel, was that her mother was always there for her when it counted.

13

THE ARENA: POLITICS

It is rare for any woman to truly synchronize her aggressiveness and the gentler, more nurturing side of her personality. To hold onto one's "feminine" qualities while succeeding in a macho field is to invite insult, ostracism and reproach. Nearly every woman who tries, pays at least a minimum price, although the experience may strengthen her "character." Nowhere is this more evident than in politics.

The most successful female American politicians traditionally have been those who, hiding behind their husband's business suits, indirectly (and sometimes directly) wield as much power as they can manage in proportion to his *power*. Eleanor Roosevelt was the ideal model, grasping the slippery reins of the First Lady and harnessing the energy of that "office" to aid humanitarian projects. Those who came after her—women such as Lady Bird Johnson and Rosalynn Carter—were ceded even more power over their favorite "problems" (roadside beautification, the mentally ill, education) because by then it was acceptable

for a First Lady to be involved. But there never was any question that these women acted as did the President's appointees: at
his pleasure and with his approval. Whatever private influence
Rosalynn Carter might have managed, she never disagreed with
Jimmy Carter up-front.

The real female political risk-takers were those who chose to
do it by themselves, either with a husband genuinely in the
background or with no husband at all—women with such differ-
ing philosophical and regional postures as Jane Byrne, Barbara
Jordan, Elizabeth Holtzman and Phyllis Schlafly. Not all of these
were "macha." Elizabeth Holtzman, who beat the pants off
the venerable Brooklyn Democratic organization in her initial
run for Congress, undeniably *lacked* either charisma or machisma. Indeed her insistence upon issues and her determination
to keep her "flair" to a minimum happened to be honest.

Few would argue that the most revolutionary of the new breed
of macha politicians was Bella Abzug. And few contemporary
women in either major party took such heat for leading the
charge up Capitol Hill.

The Abzug dilemma, left unresolved during her years as a
United States Representative and as a candidate for other offices,
was how to win a crusade for peace and minority rights ("feminine" concerns, in the minds of some) with the aggressive political style that got her as far as she had gotten in the first place. In
both career risk-taking and daring to stand up for principles,
no American female politician ever came close to Abzug. The
paradox was that she could not have achieved success without
her pushy, raucous manner, but that very manner stymied her attempts for greater success. To make matters worse, when she
revealed some of her sweetness, the public took no notice.

Male politicians, during Bella's Congressional years, got away
with stealing, lying, subverting the Constitution, using public
office for private profit, philandering, berating reporters and staff
with foul language and similarly outrageous acts. Bella was
called to account for comparative misdemeanors of style. Some

were shared by others—like badgering overworked assistants and, at times, inflating her own importance. She was not guilty of the serious lapses perpetrated by the likes of Lyndon Johnson, Richard Nixon, Herman Talmadge, Wilbur Mills, Wayne Hays and Richard Daley. Nor was she a match for some of these men on the level of being grating, obnoxious personalities. Still, it was Bella who was singled out long before the public caught up to some of her fellow office holders.

She came to elective office late, after a legal career distinguished by her representation of underdogs. She had also been a leader of the Women's Strike for Peace, an early sixties group that counseled against nuclear power years before it became a favorite issue of mass marchers. At the age of fifty, in 1970, Abzug challenged and defeated a Democratic hack thought to be entrenched in his Greenwich Village district. It was not the first of Bella's surprises, nor the last.

In 1950, pregnant and alone, Abzug had traveled to Mississippi to be the lawyer for Willy McGee, a young black man accused of raping a white woman. He had been convicted twice. This was his last appeal. For a "white woman lawyer," as local newspapers referred to her, to take on such a case was remarkably brave. Some papers went so far as to suggest sending the lady to the electric chair with her client. When Abzug arrived on her first visit to Laurel, Mississippi, no hotel would give her a room and an unmarked car tailed her taxi. The driver suggested a hotel way out of town. Instead, she had him leave her at the bus station. "I sat up all night, and in the morning I used the public shower," Abzug later recalled. "I came into court and evryone looked pretty astonished."

McGee was convicted again and executed. Though questions were raised that remained unanswered, principally about McGee's relationship with the victim, Abzug never wavered in her pride at accepting the job. It was, she said, the riskiest thing she had ever done. Her reason? Principle—the right of blacks to be on juries in the South, the idea of justice for an underdog. She did not regret her defense of clients labeled as Communists in the Joseph McCarthy witchhunt, either. "My life has not been motivated by how I can be secure in personal terms," she commented.

As a labor lawyer and an activist, she, more than most lawyers, brought an adversary style to the halls of Congress. Yes, she was tough. A girl didn't work her way up from the Bronx, the daughter of a socialist butcher, without true grit. Many famous stories about her are true, such as the time the House doorkeeper, "Fishbait" Miller, asked her to remove her hat and she responded by telling him to perform a sexual act upon himself. On the other extreme, Bella could project warmth and softness to friends and constituents that made most politicians look like bloodless posturers. There was always time for a quick hug, a pat on the cheek, a chat with elderly people sitting on Greenwich Village stoops. She was hurt repeatedly by remarks about her sex, her girth, her husband and her leftist past. She did not handle them very well, but Harry Truman did not handle slander well. Truman was hailed for giving his enemies hell; Abzug was condemned.

Did she scream at her staff? Certainly! At the top of her lungs. Staff members took it because they respected her. "I love her anger," an assistant once confided. "It's part of her charisma." Was she unyielding on some issues? Undeniably, because she felt she had been elected to speak for women, urbanites, poor people. If she did not hold out for legislation to benefit these groups, who would? Was she contemptuous of colleagues who did not do their homework? Openly, because she spent long hours doing hers.

Abzug paid heavily for her abrasiveness in the mostly male Congress right from the start. According to Susan and Martin Tolchin's *Clout*, a standard book on women in politics, "her fellow legislators sabotaged her at every turn. The House, acting with unusual speed after convening at the stroke of noon, called up a resolution of Rep. Abzug and quickly tabled it" while Bella, not realizing what was happening, made small talk near the door. In later years, she did learn to tone down her voice, to make deals when necessary, to work with subcommittees, thus becoming an effective congresswoman. She was credited with deliberately keeping a low profile on a debate over bombings in Cambodia, for the sake of preserving an endangered mass-transit bill. She also cooperated with others, rather than go it alone, on the resolution to impeach President Nixon. But only a handful of insiders would know about these actions. Newspaper and magazine stories about her could be vicious. Right-wing politicians across the country could count on winning a crowd with a nasty crack about the Bella-of-the-big-hats and the bigger mouth.

The real Bella sometimes cried when she saw an unflattering photo of herself splashed across page three of the New York *Daily News*. She was dismayed by personal attacks on her from fellow Democrats when she made the hard-nosed, realistic decision to campaign for the House seat of her colleague William F. Ryan, who was dying of cancer. Why hadn't the same Democrats been upset with the power play that led to her decision—a redrawing of Congressional district lines that chose her district for dismantling? Ryan died before election day; his embittered widow decided to run against Bella. At one acrimonious newsroom debate, I watched the two square off. Patricia Ryan's eyes smoldered with hatred. Bella's hands trembled under the conference table and she fought to keep her voice steady. Ryan all but accused her rival of kicking aside the cancer-ridden body of her husband, with whom Abzug had agreed on most issues. Abzug responded that the two had been allies and that she would not have run against him, had he been truthful about his illness. After she had won the election, Abzug told friends it had been the most awful victory of her political career.

In fact, she had to force herself to continue being the "battling Bella" everyone expected. "I used to get up in the Congress and say to myself, 'my God, I've got to do it again. I'd better do it or else they'll mow me down.' It took the most enormous amount of pressure on myself to talk about nuclear testing or radiation. I used to talk, and get about 30 votes," she said with a wry shake of her head.

Abzug took another hefty risk four years later. She gave up both her secure seat in the House and her mounting seniority to run for the Senate. Her defeat in the primary by Daniel P. Moynihan, by a margin of less than one percent of the vote, was the most painful blow she suffered in politics. It left a scar, for the Senate seat was the one she had always coveted. The defeat "made my life less satisfactory in some ways," she admitted years later, but that was as much as she would admit. She sat, composed, in her quiet lower Manhattan law office. The walls were decorated in typical political fashion, with framed photos of herself and other famous people, except they showed Shirley MacLaine and Gloria Steinem where her colleagues might have featured John F. Kennedy or Hubert Humphrey. The Senate race, she continued with a shrug, was something she "had to do —a political step that was necessary for the people I represented." After losing another primary in 1977, this one for New York mayor, she threw up her hands in disgust at the question of why she kept pressing for a comeback. "I'm a politician—I run for office! I really don't think it's appropriate to suggest I shouldn't practice my profession!" Men were forever trying political comebacks; yet voters viewed her tries as if it were "a sin to run."

Abzug's organizing skill made the 1977 International Women's Year meeting in Houston a rousing victory for feminists. In return, she was praised by Jimmy Carter—and then dismissed when Abzug persisted in keeping the IWY organization action-oriented. Once more, her aggressive style was the scapegoat. She sat in helpless annoyance in front of her television while Rosalynn Carter told Phil Donahue, "I like Bella very much. She has performed greatly. But this is a quieter time, and we need somebody less loud to pass the ERA and to reach the homemaker." Bella, incredulous, muttered, "would you believe that?"

She was thinking how many hours she had spent keeping her voice modulated, her stance diplomatic. She had become the most recognized female politician in the nation. Few who worked with her or against her would deny the sincerity of her

commitment, her passion, or her legislative know-how. Yet long
after she had outgrown her Calamity Jane image, nearly everyone, supporters included, dwelled on that version of Bella, or the
Woody Allen version, the "Saturday Night Live" version, the
caricature.

The underdogs knew better. Greenwich Village gay militants
and Ninth Avenue scrubwomen had faith in her. People reached
out to touch her the way they did Bobby Kennedy, as if a spark
would jump across the synapse and magically ignite a lamp of
justice. Her notoriety derived from her strengths as much as from
her weaknesses. High profiles make large targets. The Abzug
dilemma was that her willingness to act as a catalyst for change,
her bold adventuring in a male province, made her easy prey for
jackals.

Nevertheless, any political woman who felt it necessary to as-
sure voters "I do things differently than Bella" was, said Abzug,
perpetuating the myth that a powerless group could get its message across better by whispering. Echoing Kanter's corporate
findings, she noted that powerlessness was the problem, not gender. And any woman who followed a Molloy "dress-for-success"
pattern was stepping into her own straitjacket. Bella had been on
a talk show with Molloy and remembered it with a grin that
stretched from one high Slavic cheekbone to the other. "I said
that he's never going to get any women anywhere. I *murdered*
him on the program!"

Nearing sixty, Bella Abzug was not terribly changed from the
Bella Abzug I had met ten years earlier. She was slimmer. She
was bloodied. She was still unbowed.

Margaret Mead was wrong; attractive female achievers *are* forgiven more, at least in politics. Gloria Steinem and Jane Fonda
had their attractiveness as a shield, whether they wanted one or
not. It helped defend them against cheap shots. Abzug, not con-
ventionally beautiful, took those shots. Worse, she made no move
to defuse the ambiguities of machisma. She did not hide her
competitiveness, love of the limelight, aggressiveness, ambition.

They cost her her political life. She was stripped of her power within seven years of taking her first oath of office.

Other powerful female politicians held their ground with difficulty, even those who had the key sponsorship of powerful men. The moment Jane Byrne became mayor of Chicago, she had to wrestle with political misogyny. She was the product of the Daley machine, rather than an outsider like Abzug. Her style, compared to Abzug's, was lace and perfume. Beginning in 1968, her male mentors "wanted me to be a good little girl. I understood that, so I wore a bow in my hair for six months. I played the demure part until I got established," she explained.

A lot of good it did her! Once the power was in her hands and she rid City Hall of some of Daley's cronies, they howled in protest, calling her "some tough broad." Byrne retorted that Chicago government had been "a real bastion of male chauvinism for years, one of the worst places in the country for it. It was filled with this big macho stuff and I had to take it on right from the start."

Rightly or wrongly, Bryne received about as much support for her unconventional attacks on male supremacy as Bella had. Politicians since Roman times have appointed friends who are expert in a certain field to be "dollar-a-year" advisers. In effect, Rosalynn Carter ably filled such a slot (although without even the dollar) for Jimmy Carter, candidate and President. But when Jane Byrne appointed her husband, a former newspaperman, as an unpaid press adviser, the Daley leftovers in Chicago cried "nepotism." The complaint swelled to a roar when she made him a paid member of her staff. In politics, the double standard holds sway, a decade after being discarded in more enlightened American businesses and households.

Jane Byrne was not the female politician from Illinois most people thought of when they spoke of power or charisma. No, the Queen of Illinois politics, of national right-wing politics, was an impeccably groomed, self-styled Alton "housewife" and a Republican to boot. Her name was Phyllis Schlafly, and she was as macha as Bella Abzug. It was only one of the many cunning contradictions of her frighteningly cool personality.

Her story is familiar to friends and enemies alike by now—mother of six children, wife of a supportive lawyer-husband, lawyer at age fifty-one, holder of a Radcliffe master's degree, rousing speaker, fierce debater and a business executive who never practiced what she preached—that a woman's place is in the home. What was less well known, though it was repeated by anti-Schlaflyites from Gail Sheehy to Gloria Steinem, was that Schlafly learned her independence and her Republican rightwing extremism from her parents. Her mother worked to support the family when her father lost his job during the Depression. Phyllis herself began earning her own living at the age of ten—she sold magazine subscriptions to *American Girl*. Even while out of work, her father remained a Republican and young Phyllis kept among her souvenirs of the 1940 Presidential election a button that read, "I Don't Want Eleanor Either." According to Sheehy, "Schlafly's passions for 30 years had nothing to do with matters of family or women's status." Instead, her passion was politics, one of the country's great male bastions. She was the author of a 1964 tract promoting Barry Goldwater's presidential candidacy, and in the seventies she was as knowledgeable about (and as against) the Panama Canal Treaty as she was the Equal Rights Amendment.

Schlafly's macha side was even less well known than her lifelong devotion to the extreme right wing. A recent, generally admiring biography noted that as a "super-student" at the Convent of the Sacred Heart in St. Louis (which also produced writer Jane O'Reilly) the former Phyllis Stewart was "super-competitive," although she was also generous in helping less brilliant classmates. She had friends, but a former classmate remembered her for her self-sufficiency and self-assuredness. Nor was young Phyllis one to duck a dare. She was not a sportswoman, yet took riding lessons because her friends did. When they entered an annual horseshow one year, so did she—and won a ribbon. (Not long afterward, still a nervous rider, Phyllis was

thrown by a horse and chose never to climb back in the saddle
again.)

During World War II, while attending college during the day,
Phyllis performed even more daring feats at night. To pay her
way through college, she was a machine-gunner. She tested am-
munition manufactured for rifles and machine guns at the St.
Louis Ordnance Plant, firing up to five thousand rounds in a single eight-hour shift. "That was a man's job in those days," she
later told her biographer with pride.

In 1949, at the age of twenty-four, Phyllis Stewart married a
lawyer as conservative politically as she was. Fred Schlafly was
fifteen years older, and he told his partners of the engagement
with unwitting irony: "the undersigned is pleased to announce
that . . . a new partnership is being formed to be known as
Schlafly and Schlafly . . . The senior partner—not in years—in
this firm [the forthcoming marriage] is now Research Director
for the St. Louis Union Trust Company and the First National
Bank in St. Louis . . ." The consensus among those who knew the
couple, including several of their children, is that it *was* a partnership. Fred might not be Mr. Phyllis Schlafly, but neither was
Phyllis often referred to as Mrs. Fred.

Fred knew what he was getting himself into. The two had a
habit of writing verse to one another. During their courtship, he
composed these lines:

> Cover girl with executive know how
> You don't desire a home now.
> For Küche, Kirche, and Kinder,
> Will surely a career hinder.

Her career was not hindered, but neither did she opt for the traditional line about "love, honor and obey" in the actual wedding
ceremony. The final word she uttered in that trio was "cherish."
Shades of Amelia Earhart and G. P. Putnam!

Phyllis, a good Catholic, began her brood of six children within
fourteen months of her marriage to Fred. John, her eldest, was

only eighteen months old when she made her first try for Congress in 1952. In 1970, when she ran again, her youngest daughter was five. The only unusual part of Phyllis Schlafly's devotion to both home, ambition and a career was her hypocritical testimony that glorified homemakers over careerists.

Schlafly's eldest daughter, whose birth name was Phyllis but who changed it to Liza, was able to attend Princeton University because, under pressure from equal rights activists, it began allowing women to attend in the seventies. Not surprisingly, Liza, when questioned about her goals, sounded confused: she hoped to go into journalism, law or both. "The women I admire are those who have made a success in a traditionally man's world. I don't admire women who are really only successful in the women's movement and sit around whining," she said. Apparently, the reporter did not bother to contradict her by noting that Liza would not be at Princeton, would not be able to enter journalism or law easily, were it not for the whiners who had come before her. Added Liza: "I most certainly plan to have a career. That's a given . . . a career and a family. I don't consider them mutually exclusive."

Phyllis Schlafly's own macha qualities asserted themselves most forcefully through the years in debates and appearances before the press. Her willingness to face hostile "libbers" and reporters was brave and risky, although like every good risk-taker from Janet Guthrie to Bettina Parker, she reduced her chances of failure by arming herself with arguments before each occasion. I watched her field tough, persistent questions from a roomful of the most informed women's-rights reporters in the country during the IWY Convention in Houston in 1977. She was unflappable and self-assured. Some of the questions were my own. She never answered them to my satisfaction, but I grudgingly admired the way she turned them aside so deftly.

Schlafly never got away with her act in the voting booth. Unlike Abzug and Byrne, she was a loser in elective politics. Her success as the principal opponent of the Equal Rights Amendment might rest on the fact that it was a great deal simpler to

fight against a single issue than to fight *for* several, as Abzug did.
Schlafly's has been an exercise in negative machisma. About the
only thing I like about Phyllis Schlafly is the phrase she used in
describing herself as a high school student; she had, she wrote, a
"fierce determination to always look forward to adventure."

Once they began storming the male fortress of politics, women
from such opposite poles as Abzug and Schlafly demonstrated
that they held as many dissimilar opinions and reached them
from as many divergent backgrounds as male politicians. Jan Peterson, an early women's liberation radical, managed to combine a political career and family, but any similarity between her
passage and that of either Bella or Phyllis ends there.

Jan Peterson kept a cloth scroll depicting the covered bridge in
Cedarburg, Wisconsin hanging in her Brooklyn kitchen to re-
mind her of her hometown. Years ago, she had ridden away from
Cedarburg on a Greyhound bus bound for New York, vowing
never to return. Yet the route from Wisconsin to her white working-class neighborhood across the river from Manhattan could
best be described as a philosophical full circle.

With straight blond bangs and rosy cheeks inherited from
Swedish forebears, Jan could easily pass as a member of her
neighborhood's Polish ethnic majority. The area, Greenpoint,
was full of butcher shops with kielbasa in their cases and photos
of Pope John Paul II in their windows. Her home, like her neighbors', was a two-story attached house with wooden shingles.
Many of her neighbors were born within walking distance of
those same homes.

When Peterson came to Greenpoint in 1969, she was an outsider and a troublemaker. As a radical community organizer, she
anticipated that the residents would be white ethnic racists like
those she had hated in Cedarburg. More than a decade later, at
thirty-eight, her journey from the Midwest to feminist communes
to the White House and then back to Brooklyn brought a half-

smile of amazement to her face as she sipped coffee in her kitchen.

"Women who have a lot of choices don't generally choose children," she said. Jan *had* chosen that option in the late seventies. Moreover, she made it remarkably adventurous by marrying a man who already had custody of his three children, including two teenaged girls, and then adding a baby of their own.

Peterson's father, a blue-collar electrical worker, had been killed on the job in Cedarburg when Jan was ten years old. During an uneventful stint at the University of Wisconsin on a scholarship, Jan became engaged to the boy next door. But she postponed marriage to travel to New York upon graduation in 1963. She checked in at the Manhattan YWCA, took a job with the Welfare Department in order to get involved in civil rights, and hid her diamond engagement ring. She was not about to settle down in Cedarburg.

For the next eleven months, Peterson dated black men, searching for someone who would woo her away from her hometown fiancé. Proving one's liberalism by socializing with black partners was in style then among civil rights workers. What Peterson did not count on was pregnancy.

Abortions were illegal in New York, although she got an illegal one on a table in a tenement in the South Bronx. The experience was so harrowing that the following day, Jan headed straight to Cedarburg to be married. Her first New York experience gave her no clue that she could cope on her own. It was better, she thought, to place her hopes on her new husband, who met the criteria for acceptance in her blue-collar family—he loved her, didn't drink, and was going to be a lawyer.

They remained in Wisconsin for two years as she put him through law school by doing social work. She also collected her master's degree. In 1966, they moved to New York, where he landed a job with the Chase Manhattan Bank and she joined Mobilization for Youth, a ghetto self-help organization. As Jan secretly began seeing her former black boyfriend again, it soon was apparent that she and her husband were moving in different directions. He wore pinstripe suits and carried an attaché case downtown each morning; she wore jeans and went to Harlem.

At last, she bolted. Without telling either her husband or her boyfriend of her whereabouts, she got herself a slum apartment on the Lower East Side. She was growing more plucky with each passing year. She also had discovered the women's liberation movement.

"It was like the old proverbial lightbulb switching on over my head," she recalled. "I found out I was not unique, I was not crazy. I found out why I had to talk louder than anyone."

She plunged into groups, raps, demonstrations. She picketed St. Patrick's Cathedral in favor of legal abortions. She joined Redstockings, a center of radical feminism, left the black man she lived with, helped organize a feminist commune in Brooklyn, became engrossed in Greenpoint's ethnic coalitions. Confronting her class consciousness along with her feminist consciousness, she learned why proud working-class women rejected poverty program handouts and angrily denounced Harlem residents who accepted million-dollar grants. She saw, however, that places like Greenpoint desperately needed more government services. The cross-pollenization of her women's liberation ideas and her neighborhood social work produced a desire to turn loose the energy and talents of local, home-bound women. Like other women, they wanted to control their destiny, but "women's lib" still met with hostility in their homes.

First, Peterson helped them set up the Ethnic Neighborhood Action Center, a storefront office operated by local volunteers. By 1974, with Peterson a guiding force, the women enlarged their center into the National Congress of Neighborhood Women.

Love intervened, in the seventies, to bind Jan even closer to Greenpoint. The man was Daniel Colbert, a telephone installer and lifelong resident of the area. She was very committed to him when, in 1977, an old friend, Midge Costanza, called on her to join President Carter's White House office on minorities as a white ethnic specialist.

Peterson was ready. She was tiring of being "Mother Earth" to the neighborhood, and she was curious about climbing on an upwardly mobile career track. It was time for new risks. With his three children, Daniel, who was divorced, moved to Washington to be with her. Then he and his former wife got into an ugly custody battle. Caught in the middle, knowing the publicity from her personal life could taint Costanza's office, Jan decided to marry Colbert. The two of them strolled into a judge's chambers in Washington one afternoon, he with his telephone tools on his belt, she in her White House executive dress. After the ceremony, Daniel went back to work and Jan returned to the White House for a party.

Washington was an alien environment for Peterson. She soon decided that outside of Costanza, no one on the President's staff had a feeling for ethnic minorities. The fallout from Colbert's custody fight had wounded her standing within the White House and among feminists anyway, so shortly after their marriage, she transferred to a position in Action, the umbrella agency that included the Peace Corps.

In December of the same tumultuous year, Jan found she was pregnant. Ever the adventurer, she wanted the experience of having a child. She was thirty-seven years old, still getting acquainted with her stepchildren (who were having trouble adjusting to Washington themselves), just beginning a new job. Bad timing? Perhaps. But Jan and Daniel went ahead with plans for the new baby regardless. A bold woman (her adventurousness was a major reason Colbert loved her, while she loved his warmth and supportiveness), she saw her pregnancy in terms of wonderful possibilities, not risks. She *did* get nervous as the baby's birth drew near. What if she didn't like it when she finally delivered it?

She did not need to worry. Her newborn son, Robert, turned into a joy, and Jan waded excitedly into the seas of motherhood and family life at once. "Just the holding and hugging," she said softly. "It was all very different. His first word—the wonder! I had never understood before what women were talking about. I had gone through everything as a feminist, and now I was throwing it all up in the air to be a mother. It was fun! And I found I liked him."

She slipped into the bedroom and brought back a baby wrapped in a blanket. His round brown eyes stared out at the pine-paneled kitchen. Robert gurgled. Jan giggled. "We like *each other*," she corrected herself.

Soon after he was born, the family moved back to Brooklyn. It was a compromise for Daniel, who felt he was moving up in the world by going to Washington. But the older children needed the stability of the same school, in the same neighborhood. Jan returned to work with the Congress of Neighborhood Women. This was another risky decision: she would be a full-time mother *and* a full-time organizer.

At the age of three weeks, Robert was sleeping in a drawer of a Boston hotel room while his mother attended a conference. At three months, he clung to her shoulder as she toured a project in Puerto Rico. One bonus was that the other mothers in the Congress were enthralled by the baby. At her Greenpoint office, women who came to see Jan greeted Robert, not her! It bound her more warmly to them. Spending nearly every spare moment among local women with children, Jan got important advice on childrearing from them. The feedback was inspiring. "Someone else might find it threatening," she explained, "but I don't know how to clean the house as well as they do. And the women look at me differently. I'm one of them. They teach me about health and cooking. Turning the situation around, they see that I can be a freer mother, not an anxious one, because I have so much else going for me."

Not without pride, but also with determination, Jan summed up her altered circumstances: "I'm setting up a new role model for these women, and I'm showing some feminists that being a mother is possible."

It was a tricky combination. Jane felt an occasional tug of war among her stepchildren (two teenaged girls and a near-teenaged boy) and husband, felt the struggle to keep her home together while meeting her personal needs. Yet, like other daring women, she enjoyed each new bend in the road. As a single, childless feminist, she had feared that she and her friends would create a nifty life-style for themselves that would have little connection with the "real world" as she knew it among the Brooklyn working class. She refused to be left out of anything, even motherhood.

She interpreted the challenges she posed to herself—whether that meant fighting redlining by Greenpoint banks or dealing with teenage rebellion among her teenaged stepdaughters—as her competitive side. "My idea of 'competitive' is to bring other people along with me. I feel I can motivate people. I'm the greatest for seeing everyone's potential," she said. "I'm all for strong women, as long as they're not stepping on other people's bodies to get where they're going." For this strong woman, the decision to assume the triple role of wife, mother and organizer was as radical as picketing for free abortions, as risky as enlisting in the armed forces. There was machisma involved as well—not only did she do it with a flair, but to prove a point.

The most charismatic black female politician of the seventies took still another route to prominence, perhaps the hardest of all, considering the color of her skin. Barbara Jordan was not as important in legislative matters in Congress as was Bella Abzug, but her moral force was greater and her impact on white America at large more positive. She rode to power on the coattails of Lyndon B. Johnson, yet was never singed by the flames of public wrath that consumed him during the Vietnam war. What power she had was probably due more to her near-religious oratorical skill than her knowledge of the Constitution, and it was a shame she never debated Phyllis Schlafly. (If she ever does I'm convinced Schlafly will be trounced.) Still, at the height of her fame, Barbara Jordan unaccountedly lost her taste for the limelight. Her departure from Washington was as abrupt as her rise there to almost legendary stature. Her choice remains puzzling. But while she represented her Houston district, she was impossible to ignore. There used to be a joke among women: "Have you heard the latest news about God? She's black." Whenever I heard that joke, I thought of Barbara Jordan.

Now, Barbara Jordan could not be God, because God would not have been a character witness for former Texas Governor John Connally; God would not have resisted joining her family church until she reasoned that "believing" meant following a path of extreme "self-sufficiency"; God would not have been baptized only after coming to the conclusion that "power" was the operative word in religion.

However, Jordan's *mother* was a preacher in early life, famous for her passionate oratory, and her father became a preacher when she was a young girl. Barbara herself distinguished herself as an orator while in high school, yet her academic studies and singing also won high marks. She was never a saint, yet she took herself quite seriously and she took risks that few young black women took, regardless of how those risks frightened her. She also grew up to be aware of her electric presence, aware enough to make up her mind, when questioned by President-elect Carter about a possible high-level appointive job, to consider nothing less than Attorney General. (It was not offered.) As she told one interviewer, "I never intended to become a run-of-the-mill person."

Barbara Jordan was never an all-work-no-play person, either. As a child, she rode not one, but three bicycles. She loved games, and by her own acknowledgment "I did play hard." She disliked piano lessons to the point that she refused to continue them, an act of rebellion that earned her spankings from her mother, a strap in her hand. When the spankings did not end soon enough to suit Barbara, she would fall down and kick back. She liked the feeling of being brighter than her classmates. She also got her kicks from doing her own rendition of the song, "Money, Honey" at secret Friday night parties with fellows from a local air force base.

In high school, she discovered she loved the challenge of debating and hated the idea of losing. After an early victory, she wrote, "I was riding on a great big high." Not long thereafter, in college, the competition was supposed to get tougher; she debated against whites as well as blacks. After her first win in a racially mixed contest, she decided haughtily, "Why, you white girls are no competition at all." At Boston University Law School, it was evident that she had gotten ahead previously "by spouting off." Now, she had to learn to reason through a speech before delivering it in that golden voice. Like any human being from a humble background, she was scared stiff on the verge of her first airplane flight and cried when she walked off with her law degree.

She arrived in Congress in 1972, following an apprenticeship as a Texas state senator, the first black of either sex in that legislature since 1883. Just two years later, improvising from a batch of notes, she delivered the speech that capped all the years of oratorical training: her defense of the Constitution during the House Judiciary Committee hearings on the impeachment of President Nixon.

David E. Rosenbaum of the New York *Times* described her effect: "The words had rolled from her lips in that formal speaking voice of hers, like a Shakespearean actor . . . or, as one of those in the audience remarked at the time, 'as if the gates of heaven had opened.'" The effect was not lost on Democratic officials, least of all on Jordan. Chosen a keynote speaker at the 1976 Democratic convention, she brought a restless crowd to hushed silence with an oration that proudly pointed out the uniqueness of a black woman in such a spotlighted role. The reaction was a groundswell of support for her as vice-presidential running mate for Carter. She knew it would not happen and, haughty as always, she told her biographer, "They were all kissing my ass, that's all I can say about that time."

The trouble was, Congressional work began to bore her and there was no place suitable for her to go in politics. At the summit of her career in the House, she retired rather than run for a fourth term. Perhaps she was a more pragmatic politician, in that respect, than Abzug. Several years later, she calmly told an inter-

viewer, "I think I had a spectacular career in Congress. I got to
the point where I'd say, 'now just how much longer am I going
to go through this?'"

Invited to accept an honorary degree and deliver one of her
trademark addresses at the Harvard University commencement
exercises in 1977, Jordan first twitted Harvard's supposed superiority. Twenty years before, Harvard debaters had come to her
alma mater, Texas State University for Negroes, when Barbara
was on the debating team. The contest had been declared a tie.
"If Harvard students were so superior," she reasoned, "they
should have won." Since a tie had been declared, she continued,
"*we* must have won. . . . And if you have any surplus trophies
around anywhere I'll take one home to the team," she announced.

"I had them, didn't I?" she asked friends rhetorically in her
hotel room later. Someone wanted to know, as usual, where she
would go from there. "One thing I know for sure," she replied.
"I'm going to buy myself a jeep."

Bella Abzug, perhaps the finer legislator, recognized an equal in
machisma. To control the Houston women's conference microphones, Bella, the presiding officer, decreed a two-minute limit
for all speakers. Well, not quite all. "Everyone except me, and
Barbara Jordan," she said, grinning. Still, both women came to
the hard realization that macha politicians, black or white, were
not comfortably tolerated by male-dominated political parties.
Kaye Northcott, an astute observer of Texas and of Jordan, recalled Jordan's comment about the spontaneous, short-lived
move to draft her for Vice-President. "It's not my turn. When
it's my turn, you'll know it," Jordan had said. Northcott wrote,
"it's hard to imagine that Barbara Jordan, the pragmatist, could
harbor any hope that a big, black, lame, single woman could
land one of the nation's most important offices."

Nancy Friday might have been partially correct when she called
Billie Jean King and Bella Abzug "still marginal figures in a

world where young women are not taught how to express competitive feelings within approved structures." That might have been somewhat true of King, Abzug and Barbara Jordan yesterday. It will be less true tomorrow, still less the day after that. Such women, whether in sports or politics, in the women's movement (as Gloria Steinem is) or in both politics and the performing arts (as Jane Fonda is) pave the way for the next generation. Friday unaccountably referred to Steinem and Fonda as "anti-male" and "unfeminine." That's ridiculous. Friday spoke only for some of her own generation and those older than she—women raised in or before the fifties—in judging such women "models of assertiveness and independence that do not totally convince us."

These models, along with those such as Jan Peterson and—who knows?—perhaps Phyllis Schlafly, have convinced legions of younger women that independence can be gained—for a price. A handful of the converts are determined to resolve the ambiguities. They are weaving the disparate strands of their own lives and the lessons learned from others into a mosaic fabric for the future.

Is it worth the risk?

14

THE AMBIGUITY
OF MACHISMA

Before Sikkim, I saw myself as a "macha woman," at least occasionally. I was no longer ambivalent about being athletic, a feeling that had plagued me in adolescence. As a newspaper reporter, I enjoyed competing with other reporters to get a story first, to fire questions at press conferences, to dash off on assignment in "dangerous" neighborhoods or hazardous territory. I loved skiing fast with the wind rushing by my goggles and my thigh muscles straining on a barely controlled schuss. "Daring" and "risk" were concepts I tried to embrace in my work and play. To be scared out of my wits gripping the stone face of a rock or tackling a front-page story—those were moments when I felt most alive. I believed that I rarely played it safe, on a tennis court or in a relationship.

Outward Bound taught me that my expectations about myself could be more exaggerated than my performances. I might have excelled in rock climbing among the Lindberghs; on the ropes course and at the morning "dip" I was just as terror-stricken as most of my comrades. I did not bravely volunteer to lead off on the rope course as Toni did, nor did I beat back my fears on those logs as Pat did. My companions, most of whom had greater family stress in their lives, humbled me by rising to our shared stresses on Hurricane Island with spirit and humor. I surprised myself on Hurricane Island by not being superior to my companions. At our reunion four months later, when Franny and I ran the streets of Boston in an organized ten-kilometer race, I surprised myself again by feeling nervous at the outset and *non*-competitive on the run. I was exhilarated by the fact that I finished; whether I had been among the first ten across the finish line or the final ten held little significance.

The question was, did I measure up? To what? Or to whom? In Utah and on the Outward Bound course, the reply was, of course I measured up—in comparison to others. In the Boston race, I definitely measured up—to standards I had set for myself. Was that macha? I strutted with pride after I had caught my breath in Boston—*that* was macha. Still, there was an important lesson in those events.

"Macha" and "competitive" did not necessarily go hand in hand. I could be both, chasing a news story . . . neither, on a camping trip.

Another change in my perspective on machisma occurred when I knew I did not want to fly off a hang-gliding hill, ever, unless an invisible helicopter hovered above me holding me aloft by an invisible cord. Daredevils like Jeannie Epper, Mary Kaknes and Diana Nyad were women from some Krypton planet. They were extraordinary . . . different . . . macha. Trekking in Sikkim was a revelation. I could never hope to measure up to the Himalayan explorers or to the Annapurna climbers. I could barely keep up with my own "friend" and because of that, I hated her. For a long time Sikkim made me feel like an abject failure . . . until it made sense not to compare myself to Sarah Larrabee, however macha she might be, not to Alexandra David-Neel, not to Arlene Blum, not to Dyanna Taylor. I would set what I hoped were realistic goals for myself—physical, intellectual, emotional—and try to live up to them. Comparison with others was useless. The genuine articles, the real macha women like them (and like Nancy Lieberman, Sue Mason, Hazel Jacobs, Katharine Hepburn, Bonnie Raitt and Bella Abzug, to name a few) may compete, officially, against others. Primarily, their deepest competition is their own personal standard.

After trekking so feebly in Sikkim and chickening out of further hang-gliding lessons, I was not sure that I was so "macha," after all. Was I sorry? Yes. Was I wrong? Probably. I prefer to think I retain the "good" macha qualities—ambition, self-reliance, flair, aggressiveness—all those words from the masculine side of the "androgyny" scale.

I am not sure any longer that I like, or fit, the rest of the picture that cannot be blacked out of the total phrase "machisma": the boasting, the one-upsmanship, the need to always come out on top. "Machisma" has been used here as a neutral, far-reaching term. But "machismo," among numerous women, is applied as a pejorative term to men. (Alan Alda, the actor, once referred to machismo in a sarcastic essay as "testosterone poisoning.") There are pools of ambiguity that now surround my overall appreciation of women such as Larrabee, Nyad, Blum, even Barbara Jordan. Just as I adore Clint Eastwood but would not want to be married to him, so I like Bettina Parker but would not want to be her business partner . . . appreciate Sarah Larrabee but would not want to trek with her again . . . enjoy Diana Nyad's company but would not want to train with her . . . admire Arlene Blum but would not climb with her . . . love Bella Abzug but would not be her administrative assistant.

Do I really want "machisma" applied to me in its negative as well as positive connotations? Do I want to be seen as I see a macho man—insecure in his masculinity, strutting down a California boulevard or driving a car in Italy, a fellow who is a slave to his he-man image, who wastes his time hanging out with the boys when he may rather be reading or crocheting, who has to "score" with every woman he desires, who becomes a parody of his ideal self? I do not want to play "sufferer" again as I had in

Sikkim (and as Patty had in Utah, as Harriet had on Hurricane Island). Neither would I want Sarah Larrabee to behave again as she did on our trek, so self-absorbed that she ignored and then damned the difficulties of another person. Do I want to push myself through the tortuous rituals of creativity as Patti Smith does? Do I want to keep a scorecard on lovers?

"Machisma" is indeed ambiguous, equivocal. In Greek mythology, the negative aspects of the Amazons and the Maenads outweighed, on balance the positive ones. The derivation of the name "Amazon" itself is in doubt. It could have come from A-*Mazo* (from *amastos*) meaning "without breast," again, because some tribes seared one breast of young women, and other tribes bound one side to restrict its growth, in the interest of improved archery. Another derivation might have been from *amazosas*—"opposed to man." The major apologist for Amazons, Helen Diner, wrote, "Amazons deny the man, destroy the male progeny, concede no separate existence to the active principle, reabsorb it and develop it themselves in androgynous fashion . . . to unite the two fundamental forms of life in paradisical harmony."

Neither derivation nor apology is very appealing. There may be symbolic harmony in the withering of a breast; it makes no sense in our accepted esthetics of the female form, of beauty, of symmetry. "Opposed to man" may be the case in real life; it is not a goal toward which most women would strive. The bellicose nature of the Amazons is abhorrent to women who understand every human's capacity for violence but would rather see it suppressed or siphoned into other pursuits. At the root of Amazon cultures was the killing or maiming of boy children. To accept that would be to make a virtue of barbarity.

It is still possible to applaud the actual virtues of the Amazons —their matriarchy, which gave them command of their own destiny, their exaltation of sports, their zest for adventure far from their homelands. But the applause must be conditional.

The Maenads, known basically from *The Bacchae* by Euripides, were a sorority of worshippers of the god of wine and partying. They were uninhibited revelers who took delicious pleasure in pastoral frolics. Euripides interpreted them as "natural women" who followed Dionysus in ancient versions of the besotted picnic:

> Possessed, ecstatic, he leads their happy cries;
> The earth flows with milk, flows with wine. . . .
> The celebrant runs entranced, whirling the torch
> That blazes red from the fennel-wand in his grasp,
> And with shouts he rouses the scattered bands,
> Sets their feet dancing. . . .

The Maenads were lovely to look at. They embodied virginal merriment, imbued as they were with a religious spirit celebrated in what was, at first, an innocent romp. Edith Hamilton interpreted their rites as the alternative to the more orderly, citified worship represented by temples and towns. She viewed their wilderness retreats as if they were Greek Girl Scout trips into "the clean purity of the untrodden hills and woodlands" with snoozes "on the soft meadow grass" that left them with "peace and heavenly freshness" under "the open sky."

On that plane, the Maenads could be admired as sensuous adventurers. Unfortunately there was more to their scouting than wilderness jaunts. Their attachment to wine resulted in excess—horrible killings, wanton destruction of their mountain home, savage butchery of animals, and madness. Euripides intended his message about this dual nature of devotees of Dionysus for both sexes, but his play illustrated well the ambiguity for women in uninhibited hedonism.

I am ambivalent about wrestling, boxing, weight-lifting and body-building—to name several individual sports one would associate with macha women. Lady wrestlers were promoted years ago as circuslike freakshow performers. Their successors today wrestle nude in mud at pornographic shows. The latest word in violent female freakshows are boxing matches. Boxing is an honorable male sport centered on controlled mayhem; its existence does not mean a female version inevitably must be devised. Both wrestling and boxing require skill, stamina and guts. They also require brute strength. Essentially, they are ugly contests, although a youthful Muhammad Ali or a Sugar Ray Leonard could fool anyone into watching a fight for its esthetics. Jackie Tonawanda and Cathy "Cat" Davis cannot convince me that boxing is a sport for women, any more than the female wrestlers I saw years ago on television could win my affection. Aside from anatomical disputes about whether the greater amount of body fat in women makes us bruise more easily, I suspect that most women would not want to see two female boxers battle one another. Unarmed combat does not celebrate women's bodies; it abuses them. Macho men think it is "cool" to fight bare-fisted over a woman. Macha women would look just as foolish fighting over a man or over prize money, in an alley or in a ring.

Power-lifting as a competitive sport is about as interesting for spectators as watching cows chew their cud. The participants usually are grotesque. The issue, once again, is brute strength. There is little grace or poetry in power-lifting. Why, then, should women bother? A physical education teacher who had tried nearly every sport said sky diving was the "ultimate thrill" while power-lifting was the "ultimate challenge." It is a challenge that one could meet for one's own sake.

Within limits, with conventional weights or on a Universal or Nautilus machine, weight-lifting and body-building are superb exercises for women. It seems excessive to turn conditioning into a competitive television spectacle. Macho men flex their muscles on the beach to impress girls. Are boys similarly impressed by macha women straining under barbells?

Another freakshow is peculiar to the age of technology: sky diving. As a last resort for a pilot like Sue Mason, it is a survival mechanism. As a thrill sport, for men or women, it has few redeeming qualities. Risking one's life in the execution of an athletic feat is part of the thrill, but can't there be limits? Even a high-wire artist—a Philippe Petit walking a tightrope from one World Trade Center tower to the other—has the chance to grab the wire if he slips. There is no margin for error in sky diving. If that constitutes the thrill, those who practice it for sport should be judged accordingly. They are at best foolhardy, not brave.

A final category of macha freakshow involves those who must be judged mentally ill in carrying out an act of thrill-seeking. Brenda Spencer was an angelic-looking sixteen-year-old with long golden tresses who "just for fun" aimed a loaded .22-caliber rifle she had received as a Christmas gift at the children headed for the elementary school across the street from her home. She was obviously disturbed. In a fifteen-minute spree, Brenda killed two men and wounded eight children and a police officer outside Cleveland Elementary School in San Diego on January 29, 1979.

She was later characterized as a maladjusted tomboy from a broken home, who fantasized about being a sniper. Besides her gender, however, there was nothing to distinguish her from the crazed killers of the past who went on the same kind of binge. Brenda pleaded guilty to counts of first-degree murder and assault, and was incarcerated in a reformatory with psychiatric care. Asked what prompted her attack, she replied, "I just don't like Mondays. I did this because it's a way to cheer up the day."

Brenda Spencer's case was not ambiguous. She was merely a depressing footnote to the development of equal opportunity among the sexes.

The most lingering of ambiguities implied by the word machisma is the concept of competition. It was not so many years ago that feminists, especially, zeroed in on competition as a "bad thing," and their antipathy was understandable. A review of their attitude helped me grasp why women's movement pioneers of the sixties were slow to value sports, and how the larger issue of competition can be integrated into a positive image of machisma.

Women who formed the nucleus of the movement included veterans of civil rights and antiwar campaigns dating back to the lunch counter sit-ins, freedom summers and "ban-the-bomb" marches. They were pacifists with a powerful aversion against combat and, by extension, perhaps unconsciously, against the "moral equivalent of war," sports. They also participated in alternate life-style experiments—the counterculture of be-ins, hippies and communes—that were antithetical to disciplined athletic training. Startlingly adventurous as these life styles were, they fostered no particular identification with touch football or mountaineering.

A historian, Sara Evans, wrote that hippies "glorified gentleness, love, community and cooperation, and spurned competitiveness. . . . Crucial ingredients for the future of women's liberation lay in this counterculture's rejection of middle class standards . . . and its focus on personal issues." The pioneers thus dismissed fitness for fun, and regarded competition as frivolous concerns of the bourgeoisie.

In addition, early feminists had been angered by the macho, competitive style of the men of the radical left. Hungering for self-reliance and a place among the leaders, women were told instead that their only position in civil rights was "prone." When radical women left to fight their own battle, noted Evans, their groups "tended to oscillate between total formlessness . . . or a kind of collective authoritarianism." The result was often a breakthrough, such as the technique of consciousness-raising. But such groups could not relate "team play" to "team sports." Furthermore, they had precious few role models then in organized sports. Billie Jean King was a little-known amateur in 1967. The most heralded young athlete in those years was Joe Namath, a macho male whom no self-respecting feminist could stomach.

Women did recognize quickly that physical weakness and emotional passivity were as dangerous as oppression by male-dominated social systems. They promised not to make the mistakes men made. Several did advocate self-defense as a tool with which to fight *back*. In 1970, Robin Morgan called for "training camps" where radical women could learn "skills" such as the martial arts, use of firearms, Morse code, and cryptology. Morgan's "us-against-them" tone presaged the belligerence that was sweeping aside pacifism in most radical left movements. Eight years later, Morgan ruefully remarked that her "training camps" had the ring of "playing war." They certainly gave no hint of "playing games," not even a volleyball game now and then. Maybe radical women remembered too well the compulsory, ugly old high-school gym suits. In addition, the original chasm between heterosexual and homosexual feminists made some "straights" scorn athletics as "dykey."

Anger as a by-product of feminism, just as surely as natural gas was the by-product of crude oil, continued to be a troubling matter. Women began taking judo, karate and aikido with great industriousness. Could anger be a cleansing agent, provoked or not? What about feeling combative? Violence, Morgan wrote, was an issue only touched on indirectly: "Yet the question runs deep, remains unanswered."

When feminists did think about violence it was violence perpetrated *against* women by men, through rape and domestic fighting. In self-defense workshops, women could use their bodies as weapons without guilt. Secondarily, women were discovering the confidence that athleticism can impart not just to the body but the brain. The next step was to confront the question of competition, a cousin of violence that some felt was nearly as malignant.

Competition in organized sports is fitted into a pattern designed to regulate the violence inherent in physical contact.* At least, that's how men philosophize about sports. But some years ago, feminists who spoke of competition usually had in mind competition *among* women *for* the attention of men. It was precisely this kind of competition they wanted to undo. A 1972 *Ms.* essay called it "every woman's dirty little secret." In reality, wrote Letty Cottin Pogrebin, competition was "the survival tactic of a second-class human being . . . bereft of self-esteem" who

* It should not go unmentioned that there has been an unfortunate tendency lately to circumvent that principle, notably in men's pro hockey.

was playing "the only game in town that seems to offer a
payoff." Pogrebin herself had once memorized basketball statistics to please one boyfriend and learned tennis for another. To
her and to others, there was a confusion between playing a game
to win a man and playing a game to measure oneself against
"standards of excellence."

The confusion did not endear such women to female athletes
and physical adventurers then scrounging for respect. Billie Jean
King once said impatiently, "feminists get hung up on labels."
For Suzy Chaffee, persuading the women's movement of the importance of fitness and competition was a major task.

By the end of the seventies, both women would see a turn-
about, as women from every political faction cheered them on.
Meanwhile, Wilma Scott Heide, former president of the National
Organization for Women, proposed a nice semantic pirouette
over the hurdle of "competition." Since "sport" was "a test
with oneself and/or others," and "contest" a test "*against*
others," she made up a word—"comtest"—defined as "testing
with another, not a power struggle against another to destroy or
defeat."

Physically active women today do not have to be taught
"comtest." Nor, outside sports, do Jane Fonda, Anne Waldman
or Patti Smith. Each has been competing in search of her own
excellence all along.

Could it be that women might appreciate "comtest" at a
deeper level than most men? Male competitors are so inculcated
with winning and losing (the supposed advantage they learned
in boyhood pick-up games) that personal gratification, the joy
gained from improvement, can be an afterthought. Among weekend amateurs, men are apt to react harder to "getting beaten."
Women, raised with a more equivocal attitude toward winning,
sometimes are better losers. It is rare for even the most competitive women to lose sight of the fundamental reasons for playing
aside from winning: the enjoyment and entertainment. As long
as a touch of this ambiguity resides within a macha woman, she
will not become intolerable.

There are more than two sides to the question of ambiguity. Besides adventurers said to be "too brutal" (Amazons, boxers, crazed killers) and "too meek" (those concerned with competition) there are those afraid of being "too male." The issue of aggression, a masculine quality usually pictured in harsh colors of black and white, has gnawed at macha women as atypical as Margaret Mead and Sue Mason. One reason: "aggression," by dictionary definition, encompasses hostility; "assertiveness" does not.

Would it be cataclysmic to relationships between men and women if women unleashed all the aggression they were capable of? Both Mead and Mason were afraid it would. What if Mead was right when she said that women are "much fiercer than men —they kick below the belt?" Throughout her career, the anthropologist grappled with the question of how each sex exhibited aggression.

In a famous study, Mead observed Mundugumor women of New Guinea displaying hostile "male" behavior. The tribe's men and women were "actively masculine, virile and without any of the softening . . . we are accustomed to believe [is] inalienably womanly," she wrote. Mead did not care for Mundugumor society because it was "based upon a theory of a natural hostility that exists between all members of the same sex." Women were each other's enemies, yet they were strong and did much of the heavy labor, including climbing coconut trees. Mothers weaned children fast, taught them to fend for themselves and treated them quite unmaternally. Little girls were raised to be as aggressive as boys; only the most aggressive girls were initiated into adult rituals. The adolescent girl could have premarital affairs, which were quick, violent and dangerous. Mundugumor sexual play involved biting and scratching. Once adults, women became "fully responsible trouble-makers."

By contrast, Mead found a nearby tribe, the Tchambuli, in which women were actually dominant while men were dependent, plus a third tribe in which men and women alike displayed a "feminine" parental side. What was a young anthropologist to make of this? Mead concluded that traits such as aggressiveness were *not* sex-linked, but a function of culture. As long as men and women *knew* their cultural roles, she decided, everyone could get along fine. But in a shifting, complex modern society like the United States, those signals were already becoming blurred. By 1946, in *Male and Female,* Mead revealed herself as confused as anyone about sex stereotypes on her home shores. She spotlighted the plight of the successful woman but offered no alternative to the double message then given to American women about being both achievers and nurturers.

"To the woman who makes a success in a man's field, good behavior is almost impossible, because her whole society has defined it so," Mead wrote, long before Rosabeth Moss Kanter's corporate studies. "A woman who succeeds better than a man . . . has done something hostile and destructive." Mead's dark conclusion: "For the success of a feminine woman there can be no alibis; the more feminine she is, the less she can be forgiven."

Betty Friedan could not forgive Mead for the anthropologist's emphasis on the biological differences between men and women. In Friedan's view, Mead laid the cornerstone for the "feminine mystique" by elevating the role of women as child-bearers above all others. Mead thus became an apologist for the argument that anatomy is destiny, said Friedan.

I suspect Betty Friedan overreacted. Mead *was* fearful of aggression. She *did* concentrate to a great extent on women's "tender" traits. She was not a hypocrite like Phyllis Schlafly, but she *was* confused and did not use her vast influence to lead both sexes in embracing the infinite variety of lives open to them. She was, after all, a scientist, not a revolutionary. But neither was it Mead's fault that reactionaries who purveyed the "woman's-place-is-in-the-home" line justified their opinions by quoting her.

The bottom line was that Margaret Mead waffled. Friedan was right about one thing—women would be better off if Mead and her followers paid less attention to every sentence she wrote, and pay more attention to the revolutionary life she invented for herself. However ambiguous she was about aggression, Margaret

Mead lived as perhaps the most consistently intrepid, fearless, daring female adventurer of her time.

Two generations have passed since Mead talked out of both sides of her mouth in *Male and Female*. Still, successful women in men's fields are as uncomfortable as ever about their aggressiveness and how it affects them as human beings. They do not want to imitate masculine styles indiscriminately. Nevertheless, a woman who accepts a "masculine" job is routinely expected to ape men. She is asked to shuffle personal priorities, slipping the cards marked "home life" and "family" to the bottom of the deck, sacrificing them in favor of career demands. Bold in her occupational choice, she is bound to hear internal voices soon ask questions that men, with their priorities sanctioned by society, do not have to face.

A friend of mine, Susan Edelstein, was brought up short by this ambiguity in risk-taking. A Pittsburgh-born, Illinois-raised graduate of Northwestern University, she began adventuring with a stint on a newspaper in Norway a decade ago. She shifted into high gear when, never having been west of the Mississippi and never having seen an American Indian, she journeyed on a writing assignment to the huge Navajo reservation in Arizona. She planned to stay two days; she wound up staying two and a half years, working for the first Indian-controlled school in the heart of the "wild" West.

From there, it was on to Wyoming to drive a truck, then to Grand Teton National Park, Yosemite National Park and the Denver regional headquarters of the National Park Service. The post of assistant public information chief in Denver was a plum, since it mandated frequent trips throughout the wilderness she had come to love. Her executive talent was recognized when, at the age of twenty-eight, she was chosen one of twenty-five Interior Department managers to spend a year in its Washington, D.C. Manager Development Program.

At the end of her Washington year, Sue, whose sensible, nononsense work manner masked a bubbly, restless personality, faced an interesting choice. She could become superintendent of a tiny national park on a remote island in Alaska, or be a well-placed bureaucrat in the Northeast. "Complacency isn't for me," she said, unflinchingly choosing Alaska, where, if she made a good impression, she could move sprightly up the Parks Service ladder. Some acquaintances saw her decision as a substantial risk, since the park was isolated and its staff almost entirely male. Susan's mother was convinced the Park Service offered her Sitka National Historical Park to exile her! But Sue, the risk-taker, saw it simply as another arena in which to live according to her philosophy: "Take a chance, take a fling—it might have great possibilities."

She installed herself alone in the three-bedroom superintendent's cottage on the Sitka panhandle in Southeast Alaska. Sitka was sprinkled with totem poles from the native culture and was also the site of the Russian capital of Alaska from 1804 until 1867. Sue supervised the restoration of one of the remaining Russian buildings and helped Tlingit Indians develop education and crafts programs.

She adored both Alaska and her job. She had great autonomy at Sitka, yet, as a visible token woman in management, she was invited to numerous Park Service seminars in the "Lower 48." Sitka was spectacularly scenic, with soaring mountains that dropped straight into the sea. Her island was connected to the world not by highways or bridges, but by ferries and one airline. After a day of supervising, she was sometimes content just to watch fish leap out of the bay waters, or leaf through the latest Sears catalog, or watch the single local TV station. But she also aided organizers of a shelter for battered women and sexual assault victims. She became fascinated with Alaska's growing pains and with Sitka's colorful community. She got to know many of the "opinion makers" in the state. She *did* feel isolated, but hardly more so than she had on the Navajo reservation. And she had a front row seat, even a small voice, in the great drama of the last American frontier.

The irony was that she had a mind to leave Sitka, quit the

Park Service, find a new profession, and marry a man in Denver. She had not become less daring. Quite the contrary, she had grown more confident of her ability; Sitka was her biggest "test" and she had passed with flying colors. To me, she stood tall as a friend, hero and a role model.

But Sue had put her personal life on "hold" for a decade. "The part of me that likes to help people, wants close personal relationships, and wants roots, is hurting!" she exclaimed toward the end of her second year. She did not look forward to a Park Service life of moving every two years. Marriage, with its compromise of personal freedom while seeking a stable relationship, frightened her more than any "risk" she had taken before. The fact was, she wanted it all—adventure alongside her man, risk opportunities plus the comfort of a real home with friends to whom she would not always be waving goodbye. Her needs conflicted. No trail in the entire Park Service system led to a common ground where they could be reconciled.

Is there a happy ending for the Susan Edelsteins, the daring young women everywhere who are not content to ape male machismo? Among the weekend and vacation adventurers, the thrill-seekers, the mountaineers, the daredevils, the athletes, the explorers, the military women, the businesswomen, the performers and the sexual innovators portrayed here, each is charting a new course, with men's maps as references, not as guides. The trick is to find inventive rather than imitative patterns, to follow new role models rather than worn-out old (often male) ones, and to set themselves up as role models as well.

The simple adoption of a macho "male mystique," whether that involves "dressing for success," learning to be a gung-ho warrior, or rejecting female values of cooperation within competitive systems, would be a travesty. "What I hope we're doing," Pat Carbine, publisher of *Ms.*, remarked, "is defining our *own* adventure." So many women I interviewed were doing just that, to the point of believing that each was the only person of the female persuasion in the country, from sea to shining sea, who was forging a new path. Some of the oldest women, those over fifty such as the late Joan Firey, the Annapurna climber, and Bella Abzug, the former Congresswoman, were the ones who felt most revitalized by their actions, because they had come so far down an unmarked road. Some of the younger women, like Susan Edelstein and Sue Mason, had serious doubts about their enterprises.

I have met women in their twenties, thirties and forties, who think very little about how "unique" or "macha" their lives are. They don't theorize; they *act*. A twenty-three-year-old geneticist, Jane Danska, who does daring experimental studies on DNA, is also a committed mountain-climber in her spare time. Did she think about cloning genes when she was crawling up a rock chimney, I asked. She pondered the question for a minute. "Not consciously, but, you know, it's all part of the same thing," she replied. Huh? "Well," said Jane, "I figure if I had been born a hundred years ago, I would have been an explorer of the land. Now, I'm involved in exploring an inner universe, in the lab. I guess it's all part of my sense of a oneness with the elements."

Until that afternoon, Jane had not explored her own mental universe. That is, she had never felt the sting of the "feminine mystique," had dismissed as nonsense anyone's suggestion that mountain-climbing was for boys, and, as was the case with most daring women, never regarded what she did as uncommonly bold. If there was a key to "machisma," the unambiguous side, it was the act of living in the present moment, of being so confident of one's exceptional qualities that one was "crazy in control," to use Jeannie Epper's words. I was shocked when I first began interviewing women about "macha" experiences, because they rarely considered themselves on the edge. They were, on the other hand, intrigued by my questions, because they were always so busy doing things they did not bother to think about them.

To the truly macha women, the concept of "risk" dwindles into nothingness, because they are so sure of themselves.

There's no end in sight. These women are multiplying, even as Phyllis Schlafly tells us the women's movement is dead. ERA or no ERA, women like those I have written about here (and my choices are quirky, I'll admit; there is no animal-trainer in the book because I'm not an animal lover; there is a poet because I love her poetry) will continue to follow their own paths. The very ones who see "happy endings" to their stories are, moreover, largely women who are erasing the distinction between physical and intellectual daring, as well as those who are stumbling upon communities of women *and* men in which "sensation-seeking" is a way of life.

At twenty-three, Jane Danska never needed to separate the intellectual and physical pieces of her life. At thirty-three, Kathrine V. Switzer had to find those pieces first, shape them, separate them and *then* put them together. She got her initial notices as the result of a daring physical action. In 1967, she wormed her way into the Boston marathon by signing "K.V. Switzer" on an application and completing the course despite interference by an outraged official. Switzer wrote about women's athletics, crusaded for equal rights, lectured on fitness and maintained a world ranking in the marathon. She also got married, worked for a sporting equipment firm, became a television commentator. Still, she never lost the knowledge that on the asphalt outside Boston in 1967 she *was* the first person, female, to run that race.

By 1980, Switzer was manager of Special Promotions for Avon Products and had maneuvered the cosmetics house into the front row of the ballooning women's sports promotional scene. "Remember how I predicted running would be *the* sport for women, how it was cheap and easy and convenient and noncompetitive?" she reminded me. "I was right!" After a pause, she added, "but who would have believed it would happen so quickly?"

Kathy could still run ten miles at a decent pace, but she no longer has to worry about being the only world-class female in a marathon. And her macha goals were no longer athletic, but managerial. Often her "runs" are through airports to catch planes to places like London and Rio. Her project, when we met, involved setting up an international year-long Avon running circuit, one that would stretch from Europe to New York to Ipanema Beach. She has her eye on a vice-presidency at Avon, but while she's pursuing it, don't send her a *Dress for Success* book. She'll do it *her* way, maybe in sneakers.

Jeannie Ramseier has also been a successful executive—public relations director of Steamboat Springs, the Colorado ski resort. Jeannie can go on a major rock-climb/rappel with Outward Bound *instructors,* get mad at herself for being a teeny bit afraid of kicking off a cliff . . . and then volunteer to go first. To see some other "amateur" rappel, she explained, "would lessen my personal battle to overcome my hesitation, and make my victory an empty one." She went first. "I loved it! Shrieked for joy, and wished to just keep on going—a hundred and fifty feet was far too short. I was just getting started when I came to the bottom. Feeling quite self-satisfied, too. I watched the rest descend and congratulated myself on style points."

Listening to Jeannie is like hearing Anne Waldman chant MACHA! MACHA! MACHA! as if it were an incantation. The catch is that *she* won't accept such plaudits. She thinks she's . . . "average." Why? Because she lives in a town packed with strapping, tanned, successful women and believes that her accomplishments pale by comparison to those of her comrades in Steamboat Springs. "If you spent time in this community year round," she told me sincerely, "you'd have an idea of what the peer group ability level is."

I have seen enough of Jeannie's peer group in action in Steamboat and elsewhere to catch her drift. She is not average. Like residents of those towns, she is "normal-special," as Hazel Jacobs calls herself. Neither one is like any man I've met. These women are in a class by themselves.

I am not naïve about what kind of background breeds most macha women. They are from middle-income and upper-income families, often. They are usually white and college-educated. These women are gamblers. In order to gamble, one must have a few chips. A pair of jogging sneakers costs $40, an Annapurna expedition, thousands. Women's opportunities for these gambles have improved in recent decades, but economics is still on the side of the woman who sets out on her path from a "good" white neighborhood in a large city, a well-to-do suburb, or a comfortable rural household that provides the $40 for the jogging shoes. Ghetto kids rarely have those opportunities.

Government figures throw into sharp relief the numbers that prove how much "machisma" might rest on the balance of economic power shifting toward independent, college-trained, single women. In coming decades, more American women (some blacks, Hispanics and Indians included) will have more time, money and education to devote to "a room of one's own." Among women between the ages of twenty-five and thirty-four (the ages of the majority of women I interviewed or researched), a full 60 percent are now in the labor force. Some entered it because their families needed the money. But once on the job, many women found they *liked* working. They also liked the extra money that would pay for both baby shoes *and* their own jogging shoes.

Married women with children have dominated the female work force in the past; they will not in the future. The proportion of married women in the U.S. population is dropping steadily, as both men and women remain single longer. Single women tend to fare better financially; "never-married singles" as of 1976, were collecting an average of 85 percent of men's average salaries, while women overall were collecting only 60 percent. This income allows single women to buy jogging shoes and an adventurous scuba-diving or Outward Bound vacation, too.

Only 15 percent of women surveyed in 1976 by the American Council of Life Insurance agreed with the feminine-mystique adage, "a woman's place is in the home." Now, this figure— fifteen women out of every one hundred—may elicit nothing more than a yawn from a thirty-year-old investment banker who has just participated in a hang-gliding contest. But consider: how much larger would the percentage be if only the *mothers* of the twenty-five to forty-four-year-old women had been asked, instead of both mothers and their macha daughters!

If polls are a clue, sexual stereotypes are being revamped steadily among both mothers and daughters. A recent Roper poll showed that among women over forty years old, 13 percent (a higher number than I would have guessed) participated "frequently" in active sports. For those under forty the figure was a full 25 percent. A scant five years before, the poll's sponsor, Virginia Slims, had not bothered to pose the question. Roper also found that nearly half the husbands of the women queried helped take care of their children, four out of ten men often did the laundry, and more than two in ten helped to mend clothes. Eight of every ten mothers believed their sons should be as responsible as daughters were for doing the wash, seven out of ten that girls as well as boys should mow lawns, and five out of ten felt the siblings should share the mending equally. That's not liberation or revolution, but it's something. The Roper survey pointed to "a future in which men and women will share tasks more freely. . . . People will tend less to define masculinity and femininity by what kinds of work people do."

Teens have sprinted so far on the issue of sexual stereotyping that they've left their older brothers and sisters practically crouching at the starting blocks. One 1979 poll had 72 percent of teenaged girls agreeing with the statement, "Before I marry, I will make certain my husband supports my career goals." The one thousand teens polled by Gilbert Youth Research were almost unanimous in believing there is nothing wrong with premarital sex or living together outside marriage. Half the female teens said yes to "childless marriage can be satisfying," and those girls were looking for high paying jobs that offered big bucks, "challenge," and "advancement." The one career they turned thumbs down on was the military.

By now, there's no reason to quote the statistics on female sports participation. Suffice it to say that "jocks" among high school girls and college students are not the exception today, they are the rule. Even here, though, even as they cast off stereotypes and absorb notions of competition and machisma, they do not simply accept male models. Their favorite team sport is not football but basketball, where cooperation and team unity are as prized as individual effort, just as they were on the Annapurna expedition.

What about children and preteens, the younger sisters of the scholastic athletes, the daughters of the politicians, performers and joggers, the granddaughters of pioneering mountaineers and business executives? Take a gander at a classic pop barometer of children's attitudes, their comic books.

For years, there was only *Wonder Woman* to satisfy little girls' hunger for female superheroes. And what a wonder she was! As Gloria Steinem pointed out, she appealed to girls growing up in the forties and fifties while she abstained from the gorier exploits of her male counterparts. *Wonder Woman's* creator, said Steinem, understood "secret fears of violence" among the comics' young readers:

No longer did I have to pretend to like the 'Pow!' and 'Crunch!' style of Captain Marvel or the Green Hornet. . . . Here was a heroic person who might conquer with force, but only a force that was tempered by love and justice. She converted her enemies more often than not.

Steinem may have internalized more of "Wonder Woman" than she ever realized, to judge by her tireless trips in search of converts to the women's movement cause.

Her comic heroine's purpose was to change "a world torn by the hatreds of men." "Wonder Woman" tried, until she was toned down to the point of inanity in the late fifties. Gloriously reborn in comics on television (with Jeannie Epper as the actor's double!) in the seventies, "Wonder Woman" had almost no competition until the end of the decade. By the eighties, however, a new wave of superheroes, female variety, hit the comic stalls: *Spider Woman*, *Red Sonja*, *Ms. Marvel*, and the *Savage She-Hulk*.

There was a sound justification for these female heroes—girls comprised almost half the comic-book buyers.

I don't mean to interpret female superheroes as more significant indicators of change than they deserve. Still, when I was a child "Wonder Woman" was my hero, along with "Superman." I did not identify with Lois Lane. She was just a *girl*, planted in the *Daily Planet* newsroom as a foil for Clark Kent. So my jaw goes a bit slack when I pick up (as I do, regularly) a copy of the book devoted to the most successful comic female superhero of the new age.

A cousin of the "Incredible Hulk," she is dubbed the "Savage She-Hulk," and she is no pacifist. In her other identity, she is Jennifer Walters, a tough criminal lawyer ("I live with danger!"). As a gigantic, curvaceous green warrior, she is dedicated "to righting the wrongs that were beyond my abilities as Jennifer Walters, Attorney." She pulverizes people with her mighty green fists, yet she can also cry over the death of a friend.

The lessons youngsters are learning from comics, let alone from the high school and college competition denied or deprioritized among earlier generations, are not likely to be forgotten. Also on the youngsters' side is the expanding range of role models that give them myriad options in careers for tomorrow's autonomous, androgynous women.

In her study of androgyny, Singer approached the new breed of macha woman from a Jungian point of view. Androgyny, a mixture of qualities considered masculine and those considered feminine, already existed within all people, she wrote. What was needed in a woman of today was the recognition that the two sets of characteristics could coexist in an equilibrium, in her own mind. The first step was to become independent, to cast off the bonds of passivity. Next she would feel the anger that spilled out of women when they realized how they had been oppressed by men and by their internal ideas about what femininity consisted of. The anger would lead to hostility and aggression, the kind manifested, as mentioned earlier, in ancient times among the

Amazons. Beyond lay the understanding that aggressiveness did not have to be feared, that it could be integrated into a dynamically whole personality.

One woman who made this mental journey told Singer that one result was, she did not need "always to be the assertive doer." Singer envisioned a woman of the future who could comfortably be "at once tender and firm, flexible and strong, ambiguous and precise, focused in thinking and diffused in awareness, nurturing and guiding, giving and receiving. It would be like listening to a duet skillfully played by a pianist and a violinist, when one does not hear the two separate instruments so much as the harmonious interplay between them."

Does this lovely metaphor translate into the conduct of an actual day-to-day life? Perhaps women such as the ones whose dynamic lives have been briefly outlined here vibrate with that harmonious melody. I like the sounds I've heard as I replay the conversations I've had with these women. I may feel ambivalent about some of them, and I cannot banish the ambiguity that nestles, like a cat with claws, in the lap of the issue of "machisma."

Still, these women present a staggering array of role models, in all sizes, shapes, ages, ethnic origins and marital status. They show that being childless is not incompatible with taking risks, nor is having children . . . that you can break new ground by playing war games in the sky in a jet plane, by running for office in a big hat, by becoming not John Raitt's daughter but Bonnie Raitt, singer. I'd trust my daughter, if I had one, to pick the model she liked best.

There is one element that *is* incompatible with these women's personalities: "playing it safe." They go to the edge of the rim. They go beyond. Some slip and don't recover. Some become wildly successful. They do not shake their heads and step backwards. As Helen Keller wrote, "security is mostly a superstition. . . . Life is either a daring adventure or nothing."

The daring, macha woman is here to stay, in her varied guises. Like her or hate her, she's the woman of the future. At her best, she is also brave, vigorous, fit, inspirational, intrepid, optimistic and "full of beans." She is the newest daughter in a long line of pioneers. Maybe she's your daughter. Maybe she's you.

Whoever she is, all of us are going to have a hell of a time keeping up with her. She is tomorrow's epitome of the all-American girl.

BIBLIOGRAPHY

ABC Television Network Booklet. "Women in Sports: A New Market for the Television Advertiser." New York, 1977.

Adams, Jerome. Project Athena III. Report of the Admission of Women to the United States Military Academy, West Point, New York, June, 1979.

Albertson, Chris. *Bessie*. New York: Stein and Day, 1972.

Alcott, Louisa May. *Little Women*. Middlesex, England: Puffin Books, 1953.

Arenson, Karen W. "Chairman Griffiths: A Limited Leader?" The New York *Times*. New York, July 11, 1980.

Ashley, Elizabeth; Firestone, Ross. *Actress: Postcards from the Road*. New York: Fawcett, Inc., 1979.

Basic Initial Entry Training Test Report (BIET), Fort McClellan, Alabama.

Beauvoir, Simone de. *The Second Sex*. New York: Alfred Knopf, 1953.

Bem, Sandra L. "The Measurement of Psychological Androgyny." *The Journal of Consulting and Clinical Psychology*, Vol. 42, No. 2, 1974.

Bennetts, Leslie. "Bella Abzug: Picking Up The Pieces." The New York *Times*. New York, December 1, 1978.

Binkin, Martin; Bach, Shirley J. *Women and the Military*. Washington, D.C.: Brookings Institution, 1977.

Blum, Arlene. *Annapurna: A Woman's Place*. San Francisco: Sierra Club Books, 1980.

Blum, Arlene. "Triumph and Tragedy on Annapurna." *National Geographic*. March, 1979.

Brownmiller, Susan. *Against Our Will*. New York: Simon and Schuster, 1975.

Broznan, Nadine. "Training Linked to Disruption of Female Reproductive Cycle." The New York *Times*. New York, April 17, 1978.

Burke, John. *Winged Legend: The Story of Amelia Earhart*. New York: Putnam, 1970.

Cannon, Carl M. "Aftermath of A Lonely Day." *The San Diego Union*. California, January 27, 1980.

Castillo, Carlos; Bond, Otto F. University of Chicago Spanish Dictionary, revised edition. New York: Pocket Books, 1975.

Cipolla, Deborah. "New Girls vs. The Old Boys." *California Magazine*. California, May, 1979.

Cookridge, E. H. *Sisters of Delilah*. London: 1959.

Crawford, Tad. "Sky Sports: The Thrill of Flight." *Harper's Bazaar*. May, 1977.

DeFleur, Lois B.; Gillman, David; Marshak, William. "Sex Integration of the United States Air Force Academy: Changing Roles for Women." *Armed Forces and Society*, Vol. 4, No. 4, August, 1978.

——. "The Development of Military Professionalism Among Male and Female Air Force Academy Cadets." Unpublished research paper, 1977.

DeFleur, Lois B.; Mattley, Christine. "Career, Marriage and Family Orientations of Future Air Force Officers." Unpublished research paper (preliminary), May, 1979.

Diner, Helen. *Mothers and Amazons*. Garden City, New York: Anchor Books, 1973.

Douglas, John H.; Miller, Julie Ann. "Record-Breaking Women." *Science News*. September 10, 1977.

Drexler, Rosalyn. "The Most Powerful Women in the World." *New York Magazine*. New York, September 10, 1979.

Dubrow, Marsha. "Competition and Femininity." *Harper's Bazaar*. New York, May, 1977.

Euripides. *The Bacchae and Other Plays*, translated by Philip Vellacott. Middlesex, England: Penguin Books, 1972.

Evans, Sara. *Personal Politics: The Roots of Liberation in the Civil*

Rights Movement and the New Left. New York: Alfred A. Knopf, 1978.

Fabrikant, Geraldine. "Why Nick Nolte Doesn't Wear Neckties." The New York *Times.* New York, July 29, 1979.

Felsenthal, Carol. *The Sweetheart of the Silent Majority: The Biography of Phyllis Schlafly.* Garden City, New York: Doubleday & Co., 1981.

Fong-Torres, Ben. "Ain't Gonna Be Your Sugar Mama No More!" *Rolling Stone.* December 18, 1975.

Foxworth, Jo. *Boss Lady.* New York: Thomas Y. Crowell, Inc., 1978.

Friday, Nancy. *My Mother, My Self.* New York: Delacorte, 1977.

Friedan, Betty. *The Feminine Mystique.* New York: Norton, 1963.

Gaylin, Jody. "What You Want Out of Life?" *Seventeen.* March, 1980.

Gillman, David C.; Harris, Dickie A.; Hampton, Steve. "Anxiety and Stress During Combat Oriented Training: A Comparison." Unpublished research paper (preliminary), May, 1979.

Godfrey, Robert. *Outward Bound.* Garden City, New York: Anchor Press, 1980.

Gordon, Ruth; Kanin, Garson. *Adam's Rib.* New York: Viking Press, 1972.

Greene, Gael. *Blue Skies, No Candy.* New York: Warner Books, 1978.

Guerin, E. J. *Mountain Charley: Or the Adventures of Mrs. E. J. Guerin, Who Was Thirteen Years in Male Attire.* Norman, Oklahoma: University of Oklahoma Press, 1968.

Habeler, Peter. The Lonely Victory: Mount Everest, '78., translated by David Heald. New York: Simon and Schuster, 1979.

Halliwell, Leslie. *The Filmgoer's Book of Quotes.* New York: Signet, 1973.

Hamill, Pete. "Leather and Pearls: The Cult of Amelia Earhart." *Ms.* March, 1976.

Hamilton, Edith. *Mythology.* New York: New American Library, 1971.

Harragan, Betty Lehan. *Games Mother Never Taught You: Corporate Gamesmanship for Women.* New York: Warner Books, 1978.

Harris, Dorothy V.; Jennings, Susan E. "Self-Perceptions of Female Distance Runners." *Annals of New York Academy of Science,* Vol. 301, New York, 1977.

Haskell, Molly. *From Reverence to Rape: The Treatment of Women in the Movies.* New York: Holt, Rinehart, and Winston, 1974.

Hazleton, Lesley. *Israeli Women: The Reality Behind the Myths.* New York: Simon and Schuster, 1978.

Henning, Margaret; Jardim, Anne. *The Managerial Woman.* New York: Pocket Books, 1978.

Herzog, Maurice. *Annapurna.* New York: Popular Library, 1976.

Higham, Charles. *Kate: The Life of Katharine Hepburn.* New York: Norton, 1975.

Hoffman, Greg. "Alias: Suzy Chaffee." *Women's Sports.* December, 1979.

Hoge, Warren. "Machismo 'Absolved' in Notorious Brazilian Trial." *The New York Times.* New York, October 28, 1979.

International Dictionary—Spanish/English—English/Spanish. New York: Simon and Schuster, 1973.

Ivins, Molly. "Five Hundred Eclipse Groupies Follow the Sun to Totality." *The New York Times.* New York, February 28, 1979.

Jacobs, Karen Folger. *GirlSports.* New York: Bantam Books, 1978.

Janus, Sam; Bess, Barbara; Saltus, Carol. *A Sexual Profile of Men in Power.* Englewood Cliffs, New Jersey: Prentice-Hall, 1977.

Jordan, Barbara; Hearon, Shelby. *Barbara Jordan: A Self-Portrait.* Garden City, New York: Doubleday & Co., 1979.

Kanin, Garson. *Tracy and Hepburn.* New York: Viking and Bantam, 1971.

Kanter, Rosabeth Moss. "Some Effects of Proportions on Group Life: Skewed Sex Ratios and Responses to Token Women." *The American Journal of Sociology,* Vol. 82, No. 5, March, 1977.

——. *Men and Women of the Corporation.* New York: Basic Books, 1979.

Keil, Sally Van Wagenen. *Those Wonderful Women in Their Flying Machines: The Unknown Heroines of World War II.* New York: Rawson, Wade, 1979.

Keller, Helen. *Open Door.* Garden City, New York: Doubleday & Co., 1957.

Kennedy, Eugene. "Hard Times in Chicago." *The New York Times Magazine.* New York, March 9, 1980.

Kiev, Ari. " 'Daredevil' Behavior Masks Depression." *Drug Therapy*. February, 1977.

Kinzer, Nora Scott. *Stress and The American Woman*. New York: Ballantine, 1980.

Kirkpatrick, Curry. "The Game Is Her Dominion." *Sports Illustrated*. December 3, 1979.

Klafs, Carl E.; Lyon, M. Joan. *The Woman Athlete: Conditioning, Competition and Culture*. St. Louis: C. V. Mosby Co., 1973.

Klemesrud, Judy. "Female Superheroes Get Star Roles in the Comics." The New York *Times*. New York, January 4, 1980.

Korda, Michael. *Power: How to Get It, How to Use It*. New York: Random House, 1975.

———. *Success!* New York: Random House, 1977.

Krantz, Judith. *Scruples*. New York: Warner Books, 1979.

Kundsin, Ruth B., ed. *Women and Success: The Anatomy of Achievement*. New York: William Morrow, 1974.

Larned-Romano, Deborah; Leavy, Jane. "Athletics and Fertility." *Ms*. October, 1979.

Lear, Peter. *Goldengirl*. New York: Doubleday & Co., 1978.

Leavy, Jane. "Play to Win." *Harper's Bazaar*. May, 1978.

Levine, Susan Braun; Lyons, Harriet, eds. *A Decade of Women*. New York: Paragon Books, 1980.

Lichtenstein, Grace. "How Women Are Faring At the Air Academy." The New York *Times Magazine*. New York, September 11, 1977.

———. "Learning to Escape on The Wind." The New York *Times*. New York, August 5, 1979.

London, Harvey; Exner, John Jr. *Dimensions of Personality*. New York: Wiley Interscience, 1978.

Marill, Alvin H. *Katharine Hepburn*. New York: Harcourt, Brace, Jovanovich, 1973.

Mayo, Anna. "Why Men Fear Bella." *The Village Voice*. New York, July 4, 1977.

Mead, Margaret. *Sex and Temperament in Three Primitive Societies*. New York: William Morrow Co., 1935.

———. *Male and Female*. New York: William Morrow Co., 1949, 1977.

Miller, Luree. *On Top of the World: Five Women Explorers in Tibet*. England: Paddington Press, Ltd., 1976.

Molloy, John T. *The Woman's Dress for Success Book.* New York: Warner Books, 1978.

Morgan, Robin. *Going Too Far: The Personal Chronicle of a Feminist.* New York: Random House, 1977.

Northcott, Kay. "Barbara Jordan." The New York *Times Book Review.* New York, February 18, 1979.

Nyad, Diana. *Other Shores.* New York: Random House, 1978.

Oglesby, Carole A., ed. "Physical Parameters Use for Female Exclusion From Law Enforcement and Athletics." By Jackie Hudson. *Women and Sport: From Myth to Reality.* Philadelphia: Lea & Febiger, 1978.

Ostrovsky, Erika. *Eye of Dawn: The Rise and Fall of Mata Hari.* New York: Macmillan, 1978.

Pogrebin, Letty Cottin. *Getting Yours: How to Make the System Work for the Working Woman.* New York: McKay, 1975.

——. "Competing with Women," *Ms.* May, 1972.

Powers, Thomas. *Diana: The Making of a Terrorist.* Boston: Houghton Mifflin, 1971.

Random House Dictionary. New York: Ballantine Books, 1978.

Reiter, Joan Swallow. *The Women (The Old West Series).* Alexandria, Virginia: Time/Life Books, 1978.

Revell, Joseph E. "If the Army Expects Its Women to Fight, Why Aren't They Trained Like the Men?" *Army Times.* February 9, 1976 and February 23, 1976.

Ridgeway, Rick. *The Boldest Dream: The Story of Twelve Who Climbed Mount Everest.* New York: Harcourt, Brace, Jovanovich, 1979.

Robertson, Wyndham. "The Top Women in Big Business." *Fortune.* July 17, 1978.

——. "Women M.B.A.'s Harvard '73—How They're Doing." *Fortune.* August 28, 1978.

Rockwell, John. "Patti Smith Battles To a Singing Victory." The New York *Times.* New York, December 28, 1975.

Rosen, Marjorie. *Popcorn Venus.* New York: B.J. Publishing Group, 1974.

Rosenbaum, David E. "Black Woman Keynoter." The New York *Times.* New York, July 13, 1976.

Rush, Cathy; Mifflin, Lawrie. *Women's Basketball.* New York: Hawthorn, 1976.

Safire, William. "Machisma." The New York *Times Magazine.* New York, December 9, 1979.

Schmedel, Scott R. "Jane C. Pfeiffer Is to Become Chairman of RCA's NBC Unit, Director of Parent." *The Wall Street Journal.* September 13, 1978.

Schrag, Philip G. "For Two Extremely Short Minutes Everyone Gaped Into the Sky." The New York *Times.* New York, July 30, 1972.

Schuyten, Peter J. "A Sure-Footed Climb to the Top." The New York *Times.* New York, December 10, 1978.

Schwartz, Tony. "NBC Chairman Reported Resigning, as Requested." The New York *Times.* New York, July 8, 1980.

———. "NBC Chairman Relieved of Duty Following Public Refusal to Quit." The New York *Times.* New York, July 9, 1980.

Segal, David R.; Kinzer, Nora Scott; Woelfel, John C. "The Concept of Citizenship and Attitudes Toward Women in Combat." *Sex Roles,* Vol. 3, No. 5, 1977.

Sheehy, Gail. "Women in Passage." *Redbook.* April, 1978.

Singer, June. *Androgyny: Toward a New Theory of Sexuality.* New York: Anchor/Doubleday Co., 1977.

Smith, Patti. *Babel.* New York: Berkeley Publishing, 1974, 1975, 1976, 1977, 1978, 1979.

Stern, Susan. *With the Weathermen.* New York: Doubleday & Co., 1975.

Sullivan, Walter. "Rare Eclipse Sweeps Across Width of Africa." The New York *Times.* New York, July 1, 1973.

Tax, Sol, ed. *The Draft: A Handbook of Facts and Alternatives.* Chicago: University of Chicago Press, 1967.

Tolchin, Martin; Tolchin, Susan. *Clout—Womanpower and Politics.* New York: Coward McCann and Geoghegan, 1973, 1974.

Trahey, Jane. *Jane Trahey on Women and Power.* New York: Rawson Associates Publishers, 1977.

United States Bureau of Commerce, Bureau of the Census. *A Statistical Portrait of Women in the United States.* April, 1976.

United States Department of Labor, Bureau of Labor Statistics, Bulletin 1977. *Working Women: A Databook.* 1977, 1980.

Ullyot, Joan. *Women's Running*. Mountain View, California: World Publications, 1976.

VerMeulen, Michael. "The Corporate Face of Jane Cahill Pfeiffer." *Savvy*. May, 1980.

Vermilye, Jerry. *Bette Davis*. New York: Harcourt, Brace, Jovanovich, 1973.

———. *Barbara Stanwyck*. New York: Harcourt, Brace, Jovanovich, 1975.

Waldman, Anne. *Fast Speaking Woman*. San Francisco: City Lights, 1975.

West, Mae. *Goodness Had Nothing To Do With It*. New York: Manor Books, 1976.

Woolf, Virginia. *A Room of One's Own*. New York and London: Harcourt, Brace and World, 1929, 1957.

Williams, John W. Jr. "The Integration of Women Cadets Into the Air Force Academy (An Update)." Prepared for The American Psychological Association Meeting, September, 1979.

Zuckerman, Marvin. "The Search for High Sensation." *Psychology Today*. February, 1978.

———. "Are Sensation Seekers Crazy? Machismo, Masochism, Mania and Monoamines." Paper presented at The American Psychological Association Meeting, September 3, 1979.

———. "The Sensation Seeking Motive." *Progress in Experimental Personality Research*, Vol. 7, 1974.

INDEX